Managing Electronic Government Information in Libraries

Issues and Practices

Edited by Andrea M. Morrison
for the Government Documents Round Table

American Library Association

Chicago   2008

Andrea M. Morrison is associate librarian at Indiana University, Bloomington, and a current ALA councilor-at-large. She holds an MLS and MA in comparative literature from IU. She is active in service to GODORT, having served as chair of GODORT (2003/4), chair of the GODORT Publications Committee, coordinator of the GODORT International Documents Task Force, and in many other capacities. She is an adjunct professor for the IU School of Library and Information Science and lectures on government information. Morrison is coauthor with Barbara J. Mann of *International Government Information and Country Information: A Subject Guide* (2004) and has published articles on government information in scholarly journals. amorriso@indiana.edu

The paper used in this publication meets the minimum requirements of American National Standard for Information Sciences—Permanence of Paper for Printed Library Materials, ANSI Z39.48-1992. ∞

Library of Congress Cataloging-in-Publication Data
Managing electronic government information in libraries : issues and practices / edited by Andrea M. Morrison for the Government Documents Round Table.
    p. cm.
    Includes bibliographical references and index.
    ISBN-13: 978-0-8389-0954-6 (alk. paper)
    ISBN-10: 0-8389-0954-X (alk. paper)
    1. Libraries—Special collections—Electronic government information. 2. Electronic government information—United States—Management. 3. Depository libraries—United States. 4. Federal Depository Library Program. 5. United States. Government Printing Office. 6. Information policy—United States. I. Morrison, Andrea Marie, 1957– II. American Library Association. Government Documents Round Table.

Z688.G6M37 2008
025.17'4—dc22   2008001058

ISBN-13: 978-0-8389-0954-6
ISBN-10: 0-8389-0954-X

Printed in the United States of America
12 11 10 09 08   5 4 3 2 1

Contents

Preface

The expanding production of digital government information and new electronic government (e-government) strategies and applications presents a host of challenges to twenty-first-century libraries. Library users' demands for e-government information will consistently grow as digital government provides essential services and information to citizens and the public. To meet these demands, libraries and librarians must continually design and implement new methods of managing e-government information and incorporating new technologies in the identification, acquisition, access, and preservation of digital government information. More and more, libraries are exploring collaborative efforts in order to solve the problems posed by digital government information in the areas of reference, information literacy, collection development, cataloging, and archival preservation.

Promoting permanent public access to government information is one of the missions of the American Library Association's Government Documents Round Table (GODORT), but providing access to e-government information is a role all libraries should embrace. This book provides information to libraries and librarians on the benefits of pursuing this goal.

Depository libraries, whether federal, state, or international, have a significant role in preparing for the e-government future. These institutions are legally committed to providing access to government information for their library users and the public. The specific ways depository libraries can improve access and services for digital government information in libraries are covered in each chapter.

This book also serves as a handbook for all types of libraries, whether public, academic, special, or school. Many innovative library projects with practical applications are described. The book provides a current snapshot of the issues and covers the benefits, challenges, and best practices of managing digital government information in libraries for librarians in differing positions: government information librarians, library administrators, scholars, students, researchers, and other information professionals.

DIGITAL GOVERNMENT INFORMATION DEFINED

What is digital government information? Since the mid-1990s, public institutions have adopted new information and communication technologies (ICTs) to increase the efficiency and effectiveness of internal and external organizational processes and of delivery of e-government services. "The term *digital government* has in many respects grown to refer to the development, adoption or use of ICT as a key component of a public organization's internal information and control systems, as well as any use of ICT to facilitate interaction with external stakeholders" (Hinnant and Sawyer 2005, 1012). Federal, regional, state, and local governments use ICT systems, such as the World Wide Web, to provide information to foster democracy, meet legislative requirements, and provide services. Hinnant and Sawyer refer to fostering democratic processes via electronic media as *e-democracy*, which they divide into two subsets of activities: *e-politics* and *e-government*. E-politics are activities surrounding citizen awareness and participation in political processes; e-government is "the use of ICT by government agencies to provide programmatic information and services to citizens and other stakeholders" (2005, 1012). The United Nations Division for Public Economic and Public Administration provides an even more succinct definition: "utilizing the Internet and the World Wide Web for delivering government information and services to citizens" (Schelin 2005, 11).

DIGITAL GOVERNMENT INFORMATION ENVIRONMENT

According to a 2007 Pew Internet and American Life Project reporting on a national survey, American Internet users relied on online government information to help them address common problems. Seventy percent of Americans expect government information to be available online, and 78 percent of Internet users have visited government websites (Estabrook et al. 2007, 7). Nearly two-thirds of Americans (64 percent) have Internet broadband access at home or work, 13 percent have dial-up access, and 23 percent no access (Estabrook et al. 2007, 3). The survey found that users reported good results finding and using information especially when they consulted government agencies, librarians, and the Internet; that government documents should be created and delivered in many ways, with most respondents preferring online access; that e-government is a necessity; and that those users who turn to libraries have success and appreciate all the library resources available, especially access to computers and the Internet (Estabrook et al. 2007, iii–vi). This access may be via personal computers or computers at public and private institutions such as libraries or via mobile phones and emerging technologies. ICT has become increasingly affordable, even in developing countries; in particular, in the past few years mobile telephone access to the Internet has allowed for unprecedented accessibility for the average user (United Nations 2008, 23). In this environment, government-to-citizen activities have changed. It is common for citizens to pay taxes, license fees, and request information or other services from public organizations via ICT.[1]

Libraries have an increasingly significant role responding to this environment of high user expectations and need to plan for rising demands for Internet government information.[2] Government agencies in the United States and worldwide will continue to produce online information, authenticate official information and transactions, digitally preserve existing information, and improve services and access at accelerated rates. In this context, this book will be useful for many years.[3] Individual chapters describe and analyze government information policy, especially for U.S. federal, state, and local agencies but also for international government agencies. The efforts of the leading federal and international agencies in information dissemination products and development (e.g., U.S. Government Printing Office, National Archives, and Library of Congress; and the United Nations) are highlighted. Also described are library collaborations and partnerships that illustrate how libraries currently manage e-government information challenges and prepare for the future.

ORGANIZATION

Part 1 of this book (chapters 1–6) explores the background issues for managing e-government information in libraries. Part 2 (chapters 7–16) covers the practical ways that libraries and librarians can handle e-government information, addressing the special needs and questions of public, academic, school, special, and government libraries.

The chapters in the first part take a broad perspective on the issues, touching on government policies, historical and current trends, library strategies and best practices, user needs, practical library resources, and future challenges. Topics include U.S. federal government information policy and the future of the electronic federal depository library; the impact of technological developments on managing access to e-government information in libraries; a philosophical and historical perspective on preservation of e-government information in libraries; how libraries may best provide access and services for e-government information to diverse populations and those with special needs; library outreach to youth with e-government information; and the challenges of handling digital spatial data in libraries.

Chapters in the second part cover practical areas of management, including both traditional library management areas and specialized government information areas. Each chapter analyzes the current library environment and challenges for its subject, discusses opportunities, and provides practical information for implementing and improving services. Detailed case studies illustrate best practices in libraries, with philosophical issues and historical trends included as background. Traditional library activities concerning e-government information are discussed in the chapters on collection development, cataloging, bibliographic control and processing, reference service for online government information resources, information literacy, and current digital preservation projects. Chapters 13–16 cover specialized areas of digital government information (local, state, international, and foreign country), discuss library management for the area, and provide practical library advice for collection development, cataloging, technical services, reference, management of web guides, archiving and preservation projects, instruction, and out-reach. Every chapter also includes information on best online resources for its topic.

The future role of libraries in managing digital government information is a major theme of this publication. As new technologies develop, faster and more sophisticated means of creating and delivering e-government information will be available. Governments will progress in transforming e-government to connected government, using knowledge management (United Nations 2008, 14). Librar-ies must meet the challenges of providing user access to expanding and increasingly sophisticated online government information. Libraries must also prepare for expand-ing user expectations. Each chapter of this book discusses specific ways libraries can prepare for the challenges posed by digital government information.

NOTES

1. For more background information about the Internet in public administration worldwide, see Anttiroiko and Mälkiä (2007).

2. The discussions in Kumar (2006) support the significance of the library's role in providing access. This volume covers specific topics of providing access to government information, particularly for preservation, reference, and depository library issues.

3. Changing URLs are one of the challenges of digital government information. If broken links occur for references in this book, the editor recommends searching the Internet with the following tools: an organization's internal search engine, a government search engine such as USA.gov, or a general search engine. For example, the Federal Depository Library Program (FDLP) updated its home address to www.fdlp.gov, but the editor suspects the redirects for the FDLP URLs referenced here will be active for some years, and if not, a search of the FDLP website will likely be successful.

REFERENCES

Anttiroiko, Ari-Veikko, and Matti Mälkiä, eds. 2007. *Encyclopedia of Digital Government*. Hershey, PA: Idea Group Reference.

Estabrook, Leigh, Evans Witt, and Lee Rainie. 2007. *Information Searches That Solve Problems*. Pew Internet and American Life Project and Graduate School of Library Information and Science, University of Illinois at Urbana-Champaign. www.pew internet.org/PPF/r/231/report_display.asp.

Hinnant, Charles C., and Steve Sawyer. 2005. "Electronic Government Strategies and Research in the U.S." In *Encyclopedia of Information Science and Technology*, vol. 2, ed. Mehdi Khosrow-Pour, 1012–1017. Hershey, PA: Idea Group Reference.

Kumar, Suhasini L., ed. 2006. *The Changing Face of Government Information: Providing Access in the Twenty-first Century*. New York: Haworth Information Press.

Schelin, Shannon Howle. 2005. "A Primer on e-Government." In *Encyclopedia of Information Science and Technology*, vol. 1, ed. Mehdi Khosrow-Pour, 11–15. Hershey, PA: Idea Group Reference.

United Nations. 2008. *UN e-Government Survey 2008: From e-Government to Connected Governance* (ST/ESA/PAD/SER.E/112). http://unpan1.un.org/intradoc/groups/public/documents/UN/UNPAN028607.pdf.

Acknowledgments

Many people have contributed to the production of this volume. In particular, I wish to acknowledge the GODORT Steering and Publications Committees for believing in and approving the project. Their support resulted in many GODORT members responding to the call for authors and volunteer chapter editors. Their willingness to share their expertise is greatly appreciated. I also thank all authors for their dedication, patience, and diligence in working through the process and the many questions that arose.

The volunteer chapter editors' contributions were timely and invaluable. Not only did they give another perspective on the content and language of the chapters, but they also shared their expertise on the content of the chapters. The volunteer editors are Chelsea Dinsmore, James R. Jacobs, Mary Martin, Aimée C. Quinn, Victoria Packard, Deborah Smith, John Stevenson, Amy West, and Elaine Winske.

I also extend special thanks to Barbara J. Mann, the GODORT Publications Committee liaison on this project and coauthor of the chapter on information literacy. As chair-elect and chair of the GODORT Publications Committee for consecutive terms 2004–2008, she worked with me throughout the process. Her efficiency, prompt responses, constructive criticism, and most of all encouragement contributed to the success of this project.

I hope these efforts inspire GODORT members to share their expertise in future publishing projects that support GODORT's educational and professional mission to advocate permanent public access to government information.

Abbreviations

AACR2	*Anglo-American Cataloguing Rules*, 2nd ed., rev.
ACRL	Association of College and Research Libraries, American Library Association
ALA	American Library Association
ARL	Association of Research Libraries
CDL	California Digital Library
CGP	Government Printing Office's *Catalog of U.S. Government Publications*
CIC	Committee on Institutional Cooperation
CRS	U.S. Congressional Research Service
DDM2	Documents Data Miner 2
DHL	Dag Hammarskjöld Library (United Nations)
DLC	Depository Library Council
DLG	digital line graph
DOQ	digital orthophotoquadrangle
DRG	digital raster graphics
EPA	U.S. Environmental Protection Agency
EU	European Union
FDLP	U.S. Government Printing Office's Federal Depository Library Program
FDsys	U.S. Government Printing Office's Federal Digital System
FEMA	U.S. Federal Emergency Management Agency
FIU	Florida International University
FRAD	Functional Requirements for Authority Data
FRBR	Functional Requirements for Bibliographic Records
GIS	geographic information systems
GODORT	Government Documents Round Table, American Library Association
GPO	U.S. Government Printing Office
IDTF	International Documents Task Force, Government Documents Round Table, American Library Association
IFLA	International Federation of Library Associations and Institutions

IGO	international government organization
ILS	integrated library system
IMF	International Monetary Fund
IRS	U.S. Internal Revenue Service
ISBD	International Standard Bibliographic Description
JCP	Joint Committee on Printing (U.S. Congress)
LC	Library of Congress
LCSH	Library of Congress Subject Headings
LOCKSS	Lots of Copies Keep Stuff Safe
MARC	machine-readable cataloging
OCLC	Online Computer Library Center
OMB	Office of Management and Budget (U.S.)
NARA	National Archives and Records Administration (U.S.)
NASA	National Aeronautics and Space Administration (U.S.)
NCLIS	National Commission on Libraries and Information Science (U.S.)
NTIS	National Technical Information Service (U.S.)
ODS	Official Document System (United Nations)
OECD	Organisation for Economic Co-operation and Development
PCC	Program for Cooperative Cataloging
PRC	People's Republic of China
PURL	persistent uniform resource locator
RDA	Resource Description and Access
RSS	really simple syndication
RUSA	Reference and User Services Association, American Library Association
SuDocs	Superintendent of Documents Classification System
UNBISnet	United Nations Bibliographic Information System
UNT	University of North Texas
USGS	U.S. Geological Survey
WAW	Web Archives Workbench (OCLC)
WTO	World Trade Organization

Part I

Issues

Chapter 1   Federal Government Information Policy and the Electronic Federal Depository Library

William Sudduth

The U.S. federal government produces, manages, and distributes more information than any entity in the world. Despite this, it does not have a comprehensive information policy. Instead, it has a group of policies related either to specific issues or to the general information needs of our society.

The lack of a comprehensive information policy can be explained in at least three ways. First, federal information policy in the broadest context has never been of high priority among the legislative or executive branches in the federal government. Second, although information is an important commodity inside the Beltway, government information for mass consumption has a short shelf life. There is always new information, which is distributed and handled by government employees as needed to perform their duties. Finally, aside from policies, regulations, and laws, there is no significant public demand for much of the information produced and distributed within Washington, DC. The general public shares the DC policymakers' interests in information: individuals tend to want only the personally relevant information they can ingest from their daily newspaper, local and national news programs, and Internet alerts. In fact, most people ignore the vast amount of information available to them every day.

The purpose of the information programs of most government entities is management of internal information; public information is left for their public affairs staff to manage. Only a few entities are charged by the federal government to produce, gather, and distribute government information to the public. That the

William Sudduth is head of the government information, microforms, newspapers and maps departments at the University of South Carolina's Thomas Cooper Library. He holds a BA in history from Randolph-Macon College and an MS in library science from UNC-Chapel Hill. He has served as technical services/ reference librarian at Williams College and as reference librarian/coordinator of government information at the University of Richmond. He was 2002/2003 GODORT chair and on the Depository Library Council to the Public Printer from 2004 to 2007.

vast amount of government information exists on the edges of the daily lives of most of the nation, including policymakers, should be put into context with the estimated FY 2007 budgets of those few entities. The Library of Congress, the U.S. Government Printing Office (GPO), the National Archives and Records Administration, the National Library Programs (Agriculture, Education, Medicine, and Transportation), and the Institute of Museum and Library Services combined were projected to spend just over $1.5 billion on producing, gathering, and preserving government information—0.056 percent of an estimated $2.7 trillion federal budget—according to the Office of Management and Budget (OMB).[1]

HISTORY AND BACKGROUND

Technological advances such as the Internet continue to have a vast and profound effect on the production and dissemination of federal government information. The rules and processes under which these efforts operate, however, were developed in the nineteenth and twentieth centuries, shaped by government policies designed to provide guidance for production and dissemination via print, telecom, and television technologies.

The history of U.S. federal government information policy begins with the Constitution in 1789 and continues today by the minor actions and inactions of federal agency officials who determine whether information is for public consumption in print or on the Web, and how long the information should remain available. This varied and odd collection of constitutional, statutory, and regulatory actions constitutes one of the world's most complex and decentralized information policies. Librarians, and in particular government information librarians, often focus on the actions associated with the creation and evolution of the Federal Depository Library Program (FDLP). But federal government information policy also encompasses statutory authority in the creation of many of the executive agencies, the printing and distribution of statutes and treaties (1789), creation of the Library of Congress (1800), creation of the Army Surgeon General Library (1846), creation of the National Agriculture Library (1862), the Espionage Act of 1917 and the creation of the Committee on Public Information (1917), the first security classification executive order (1940), and the Freedom of Information Act (1966) (McClure et al. 1989, 26–29). Most recent acts also include the Paperwork Reduction Act (1995), USA PATRIOT Act (2001), and E-Government Act of 2002.

Understanding the complexities of the federal government information environment requires looking first at the five broad categories of issues that affect government information policy, as identified by Hernon and McClure (1987, 1):

- the structure of interagency information policies
- the relationship between the federal government and other stakeholders in the information sector
- information technology

- the economics of government information
- public access and availability of government information

The Structure of Interagency Information Policies

The amount of information available from the federal government has always been too voluminous to account for properly. It is simplest to divide government information into three categories: nonpublic (administrative), public, and a third, gray area of information that falls between the first two. Most individuals understand that personnel records, information generated for internal consumption, and information classified to protect sensitive and ongoing operations of the government should, until no longer useful, remain nonpublic. Over the past several decades, however, tensions evolving around the Freedom of Information Act and increasing desires by the executive branch to reclassify materials out of the public domain have heightened policy conflicts along the public/nonpublic information line.

Another tension along this line happened as a result of the *INS v. Chada* decision, 462 US 919 (1983), which reiterated a need to maintain a strict constitutional separation of powers between the legislative and executive branches, and in turn validated more than two hundred federal statutes. It eliminated the concept of congressional veto of executive decisions as unconstitutional under Article 1, Section 7, of the Constitution. Though not directly related to government information policy, this decision has profoundly influenced the stalemate of government information policy development over the past twenty years and weakened GPO and congressional Joint Committee on Printing (JCP) authority over executive branch information policy. The erosion in GPO supervisory authority and the constitutional challenge to JCP control over executive branch printing (Relyea 1998, 472–473) created an opportunity for the OMB to issue OMB Circular A-130 in 1989 (see OMB 2000).

Since the *Chada* decision in 1983, the federal government information environment has moved from a legislature-dominant environment to an executive-dominant environment (Hernon et al. 1996, 265–267). Any change in the near future seems unlikely.

Relationship between the Federal Government and Other Information Sector Stakeholders

Who owns the information produced by and for the federal government? The "peoples' view" is that government information produced by and for the government should be available to those who are governed—the people. The "market view" holds that government information is a resource and an economic good that must be managed. Title 44, Sections 501 (establishment of in-house printing plants), 504 (direct purchase of printing by an agency), and 1903 (sale of cooperative publications that must be sold to be self-sustaining) provide agencies an opportunity to waive printing and distribution through the GPO (Hernon et al. 1996, 271–272).

Electronic government (e-government) information provides the opportunity for an agency to deliver its information directly to the user. As long as the government entity can maintain the authenticity of the information, there are few questions. What does come into question is whether practices from the pre-electronic era must be maintained. These include bibliographic control (indexing/metadata), authenticity, and archiving (maintaining information beyond the anticipated public need).

Information Technology

The impact of information technology on federal government information has been well documented. Since the first distribution of a CD-ROM via the FDLP in 1987 to the public's current explosive use and daily access to the Web, information technology has dramatically affected and blurred the issues. From the 1986 House committee report on electronic access to government information through the 1998 Office of Technology Assessment report "Informing the Nation" and the passage of the 1993 GPO Electronic Information Access Enhancement Act, the federal government has yet to establish a clear structure to manage and preserve electronic information (Relyea 1998, 471–472).

Economics of Government Information

Issues arising out of the privatization of government operations in the 1980s created tension around whether government information is a public good or an economic resource that must be managed. Who bears the cost of producing, disseminating, and providing access to government information? The public-good argument holds that all costs should be borne by the producer and done with sufficient appropriated funds. The economic-resource view argues that users need to pay incremental costs of information access. This issue came to a head with the January 1989 revision of OMB A-130, according to which agencies should

- avoid offering dissemination services that were available in the marketplace
- sell electronic information at "no more than the full cost of dissemination"
- "concentrate dissemination activities on supplying basic information" and avoid offering "value-added" products to end users
- avoid monopolistic practices with their information resources and resources produced and provided by their contractors (McIntosh 1990, 19–20).

Another economic factor affecting the management of government information has been the shrinking federal discretionary budget. During the 1990s, federal agency information resource management looked to electronic information to downsize internal printing and distribution programs. The GPO bore the brunt of this scrutiny because of the view within the federal government that it had a monopoly on the printing and distribution process. Agencies freed from GPO regulations could produce information resources in-house and manage distribution in what they thought to be more economical ways.

Public Access and Availability of Government Information

The economics of government information distribution has changed drastically over the past twenty years. The GPO currently distributes more than 95 percent of its information via the FDLP in electronic format. Federal depository libraries have gone from worrying about space implications in the 1980s, when they agreed to receive information on microfiche, to worrying about what titles should remain "essential" or remain available in paper. Much of the Depository Library Council's "'Knowledge Will Forever Govern': A Vision Statement for Federal Depository Libraries in the 21st Century" (DLC 2006) addresses these issues, but they have never been adequately resolved. One of the main questions this document asks is, does a federal depository program designed for the nineteenth- and twentieth-century paper environment provide adequate access in a twenty-first-century electronic environment?

INFORMATION POLICY AND THE INFORMATION STAKEHOLDERS

Congress

Of the three branches of government, only Congress has structural entities to artic-ulate and shape information policy (Hernon et al., 1996, 46). The House and Sen-ate share both the Joint Committee on the Library (JCL, oversight of the Library of Congress) and the JCP (oversight of the GPO). Both committees share members from the Senate Rules and Administration Committee and the House Committee on Administration. The chairs of the JCL and JCP rotate each Congress between the Senate and House. For much of the 1970s through the mid-1990s, the JCP pro-fessional staff communicated regularly with the GPO, making it an important player in GPO success or failure (Abbott-Hoduski 2003). In 1995, Congress defunded the JCP, which now can provide only cursory oversight, relying heavily on the advice of the GPO's constituents (FDLP libraries, library associations' legislative representa-tives, and the general public) to respond to the GPO's transformation of services to a more electronic environment.

Since 1995 much of the GPO's fate has been at the whim of the appropria-tions process, and in 2005 this process was further complicated when the House disbanded its legislative branch subcommittee. The GPO lacks a strong oversight committee to lobby and explain its needs to Congress and must annually propose its budget to the House Committee on Appropriations and the Senate Committee on Appropriations, Senate Subcommittee on Legislative Branch.[2] The GPO outlays by fiscal year (millions) have been greatly reduced, increasing only 3.5 percent in total outlays since 1995, and the Superintendent of Documents outlays have not changed since 1995.[3]

Executive Branch

The OMB's Office of Information and Regulatory Affairs monitors information policy in the executive branch and loosely coordinates information policy among agencies. In addition, each agency has its own office of public information and information dissemination programs. To a large extent, information dissemination at the agency level is focused on administrative communication and public relations/affairs. OMB Circular A-130 requires agencies to publish with or provide publications to the GPO for the FDLP (OMB 2000). For many years the problem has been enforcement. Since 2002, the GPO has attempted to reduce the "fugitive document" problem by initiating several pilot programs, the first of which was a project with the Bureau of Labor Statistics that reduced that agency's overhead if it provided the GPO with camera-ready documents electronically. During late 2006, the GPO announced an agreement with FedEx Kinko's that would allow agencies to use a smart card to print small jobs, again with the understanding that they would provide an electronic copy to the GPO. The second program focuses on capturing the thousands of small print publications produced outside Washington, DC. Since both programs are in the pilot stage, their current success cannot be determined.

The executive branch also has extensive print and information distribution programs not under the auspices of the GPO or the legislative branch. Among the largest are within the Department of Defense and the Environmental Protection Agency. Several agencies, including the Census Bureau and the Department of Energy's Office of Scientific and Technical Information, have significant information collection and dissemination programs and maintain a strong working partnership with the GPO.

In addition to agency-level policymaking, there are many formal and informal task forces and working groups that affect information policy in DC, such as the Federal Publishers' Committee and the Federal Webmasters Committee. Each organization discusses standards and agency policy regarding information dissemination, and the GPO has been active in both organizations since their beginning.

Information Industry

This industry group is broad and difficult to define. Two significant associations from the publishing and software industries, the Software and Information Industry Association and the Association of American Publishers, participate in legislative matters to protect their industries' livelihoods. These organizations have faced many challenges during the recent decades of technological growth, such as the increased amount of information and intellectual piracy.

U.S. information policy is also affected by the telecommunications industry. Early twenty-first-century information policy is being driven by the telecoms (e.g., Verizon, Time-Warner, Comcast, Viacom, and satellite television). Government information policy can no longer be considered a print-only issue but must also focus on the systems and technology that deliver this vital information to the public. Emerging technology is shattering the already fragile rules of the 1934 Telecommunications Act and the Telecommunications Act of 1996.

Library Associations

For many years, library associations have participated in the development of government information policy. The American Library Association (ALA) has the largest membership and an office in Washington, DC, that focuses on legislative issues. Most effort is put toward maintaining and increasing funds for library and education programs and first amendment issues. ALA's focus on government information varies yearly with membership interest and resources. Prior to the mid-1990s, much of ALA government information policy originated from its Social Responsibilities Round Table (SRRT) and Government Documents Round Table (GODORT). Since the mid-1990s, ALA has formalized the importance of government information policy through the establishment of the Government Information Subcommittee (GIS) of the ALA Committee on Legislation (ALA-COL). Today, ALA's Washington office staff is devoted mostly to informing and working for issues identified specifically by ALA-COL and GIS. ALA divisions including the American Association of School Librarians and the Association of College and Research Libraries have also become more active in legislative affairs.

Another important library association that participates on information issues is the Association of Research Libraries (www.arl.org), which represents 120 research libraries in North America and focuses on issues that affect this smaller, specialized membership. Other active library associations include the American Association of Law Libraries (www.aall.org), the Medical Library Association (www.mlanet.org), and the Special Libraries Association (www.sla.org). On many government information issues these associations organize their members and may sign joint letters, but each organization represents a specialized constituency and may be divided on their strategic approach to an issue.

DIRECTIONS FOR FEDERAL INFORMATION POLICY

The federal information policy environment is complex, involving disparate entities and constituents that affect individuals and corporations. Whatever the information issue, the value of an immediate solution must be weighed against possible unintended long-term effects. For this reason most change in government information policy will continue to be incremental, although major changes are needed and must happen in the FDLP.

What is the future of the FDLP in the electronic environment? Although there is no clear-cut answer, the most current and complete response can be found in the Depository Library Council's 2006 vision paper, "'Knowledge Will Forever Govern': A Vision Statement for Federal Depository Libraries in the 21st Century" (DLC 2006). This document provides a comprehensive report on the state of the

FDLP and current needs, challenges, practices, success, and developments. Drafted with input from the library community, the report identifies eleven issues and seven goals that must be met to transition the program from "America's Information Provider" into a twenty-first-century information service. Information on the DLC's activities related to the future of the FDLP and the federal government electronic information environment is continually updated on its website (www.access.gpo .gov/su_docs/fdlp/council/).

> The mission of the Federal Depository Library Program is to ensure the American public access to U.S. government information. Since 1813, depository libraries have safeguarded the public's right to know by collecting, organizing, maintaining, preserving, and assisting users with information from the federal government. Stated another way the mission of the FDLP is "to provide . . . for nationwide community facilities for the perpetual, free and ready public access to the printed and electronic documents, and other government information products, of the Federal government." (DLC 2006, 1)

The report analyzes the goals of the library community and the GPO for the future of federal government information and identifies specific challenges in the delivery and preservation of this information. Although under the current FDLP, the GPO is legally required to print and distribute federal information, and depository libraries to provide public access to it, the report states that "no organizational framework or technological consistency exists to help the public find, use, and understand the government networks, databases, web sites, and data sets proliferating throughout the government. Council [Depository Library Council], the GPO, and the library community are concerned about the lack of infrastructure and standardized methods to handle electronic information" (DLC 2006, 4). The creation of infrastructure and standards will require capital investment to support the following needs of depository libraries and users of government information, which are stated and explained more fully in the report (DLC 2006, 3–4):

1. Document and metadata standards must be developed for information interchange and delivery between government agencies and the public. Currently, government and public institutions are inventing many different systems that do not communicate or interchange this information efficiently, thereby creating many "islands" of information.

2. A centralized coordinating agency (such as the GPO) is needed to aggregate information from various federal agencies for effective searching, thus avoiding the inefficiencies of navigating different websites, databases, and data sets to "fish around" for digital government information.

3. Public tools must be developed to access the information in a common form. This includes electronic interfaces to exchange metadata and document content, as well as a common, easy-to-use technology for the public to access the information. Full-text searching would be required.

4. Electronic deposit of information at institutions (libraries and other public entities) housing government documents and metadata must be developed. It is important that custodians protect the public trust by providing an independent means to ensure information is not altered. Redundancy will protect against catastrophic content loss.

5. Version control of government documents and information must be maintained to provide historical perspective and preserve a record of how the documents evolved, and to create a transparent view of government for the people.

6. Authenticity must be verified and protected to guarantee, with reasonable assurance, that the electronic documents are both authentic and official. This requires development of technologies to ensure the physical content has not been tampered with or altered.

7. Supportive legislation and regulations supporting delivery of digital government information in an electronic environment are required. This includes authorizing courts and other agencies to use electronic documents from an authenticated and official source as official documents in their proceedings. This depends upon a secure and redundant technological framework that will protect the information against vandalism, tampering, and "hacking."

8. Public education on accessing government information in new electronic systems must be further improved.

9. Education for library administrators on the transition from tangible to electronic formats and its effect on library budgets, processes, and personnel must be provided.

10. Excellent public service is required to provide a free and open place for the public, including the physically challenged and economically marginalized, to obtain government information.

11. Preservation of print and tangible collections must be maintained while adapting and investing in new electronic technologies.

The DLC proposes the following goals as a starting point for the library community and government information providers, such as the GPO, to transition effectively to the electronic world. The full report expands and explains these goals in detail (DLC 2006, 5–11):

1. Respond to or anticipate U.S. citizens' need for government information when and where it is needed by providing multiple access points to a network of experts.

2. Provide access to information in appropriate formats.

3. Ensure continuing access to digitally available government information

4. Provide excellent training to deepen and expand knowledge of government information resources.

5. Provide high quality descriptive tools for access to all FDLP publications, portals, and information products.

6. Enhance collaboration or coordination of effort among federal depository libraries, nondepository libraries, the GPO, agencies, and cultural memory organizations that deal with Internet resources.

7. Expand awareness of both the Federal Depository Library Program and government information generally via excellent public relations and marketing.

The report concludes by clarifying future roles for the GPO and libraries, along with a call for specific action:

> GPO, in partnership with federal depository libraries, must meet the need of the public for no-fee access to official, authentic government information in digital and tangible formats. . . . To ensure the continued relevance and viability of the Federal Depository Library Program, libraries must meet the needs and habits of their 21st century clientele, whose information-seeking behavior increasingly bypasses libraries, library services, and depository library collections and services. Federal depository libraries must seek new ways to help users access and understand government information, and to be innovative at the local level. Their challenge is to move forward with a collaborative vision and a set of goals to make that vision a reality. (DLC 2006, 11)

NOTES

1. This according to *Budget of the United States Government, Appendix* FY 2007, Washington, DC: Office of Management and Budget.
2. Congressional Research Service, *Legislative Branch: 2006 FY Appropriations*, updated Aug. 30, 2005. http://digital.library.unt.edu/govdocs/crs/permalink/meta-crs-7812:1.
3. This according to *Budget of the United States Government, Appendix* FY 1987, 1992, 1997, 2002, and 2005, Washington, DC: Office of Management and Budget.

REFERENCES

Abbott-Hoduski, Bernadine E. 2003. *Lobbying for Libraries and the Public's Access to Government Information: An Insider's View.* Lanham, MD: Scarecrow Press.

DLC Depository Library Council. 2006. "'Knowledge Will Forever Govern': A Vision Statement for Federal Depository Libraries in the 21st Century." Washington, DC: U.S. GPO. www.access.gpo.gov/su_docs/fdlp/council/dlcvision092906.pdf.

Hernon, Peter, and Charles R. McClure. 1987. *Federal Information Policies in the 1980's: Conflicts and Issues.* Norwood, NJ: Ablex.

Hernon, Peter, Charles R. McClure, and Harold C. Relyea, editors. 1996. *Federal Information Policies in the 1990s: Views and Perspectives.* Norwood, NJ: Ablex.

McClure, Charles R., Peter Hernon, and Harold C. Relyea, eds. *United States Government Information Policies: Views and Perspectives.* Norwood, NJ: Ablex, 1989.

McIntosh, Toby. *Federal Information in the Electronic Age: Policy Issues for the 1990s.* Washington, DC: Bureau of National Affairs, 1990.

OMB U.S. Office of Management and Budget. 2000. Circular A-130. Rev. "Transmittal Memorandum #4: Management of Federal Information Resources." www.whitehouse.gov/omb/circulars/a130/a130trans4.pdf.

Relyea, Harold C. 1998. "Public Printing Reform: The Wendall H. Ford Government Publications Reform Act Proposal." *Journal of Academic Librarianship* 24 (6): 470–477.

Chapter 2 The Impact of Technology on Managing Access to Electronic Government Information in Libraries

Amy West

Technological change has transformed the manner in which libraries manage access to government information and their role in the information life cycle. From microforms to web-based information, government information collections now contain one of the most heterogeneous sets of formats in library collections. Such diversity of format challenges all aspects of librarianship: acquisition, cataloging, reference, and instruction. Yet there are also new opportunities for government information specialists and other librarians to use their expertise to transform existing government information into innovative and more useful forms.

There has been a clear shift in libraries to consult and acquire information from both information producers and distributors to ensure meeting their users' needs, departing from the previous linear relationship from producer to distributor to library as information collector. Now, both the relationships and the identities of each group, producers and distributors, are changeable. Libraries work with producers to distribute content and alert distributors to new materials; producers and distributors may also maintain archives of content of their own and others. Most of this activity now takes place via the Web, and access is woven into every point in the production/distribution/collection cycle.

In this chapter we discuss pre-web technologies in government information collections to provide context for managing e-government information in the current environment. Our main focus is on web-based government information and its effects on all forms of government information. Although U.S. federal depository libraries feel the effects of these changes most profoundly, they affect all libraries that collect government information or provide services for government information.

Amy West is data services librarian at the University of Minnesota. She received her MLS from the University of Washington and BA in philosophy from Smith College. West cochaired the ALA/GODORT Government Information Technology Committee from 2003 to 2004 and actively serves in GODORT, including coediting the TechWatch column for DttP: Documents to the People. *westx045@umn.edu*

PRE-WEB TECHNOLOGIES

Microforms

The first major new technology introduced into government information collections was the microform, including microfiche, microfilm, and microcards. Microfiche began to be used heavily in the 1960s for FDLP materials and now forms a significant proportion of federal collections. According to the Documents Data Miner 2 (DDM2; http://govdoc.wichita.edu/ddm2/), a depository collection tool and statistical database, as of 2007 about 14 percent of the items available for selection by depository libraries are on microfiche, including up to about 1,400 individual titles, many of which are serial publications. The vendor Readex once sold microcard versions of all government publications, depository and nondepository, resulting in large collections in that particular format. The University of Minnesota's Wilson Library, for example, estimates the size of its incomplete collection to be almost 500,000 microcards for about twenty-five years' government publications. Libraries participating in the United Nations Depository Program purchased Readex microcard and microform sets to supplement the depository program materials. Some state depository programs distributed materials only in microform. Other important microfiche collections of government information include ERIC educational collections, also originally available only on microfiche; the many sets of materials available from LexisNexis; materials distributed through subject- or agency-based depository programs such as the Atomic Energy Commission's depository program or the National Technical Information Service; and nondepository statistical information. Important microfilm sets of government information available from private publishers were also collected by libraries.

Since the 1960s, libraries have had to invest resources into now obsolete technology to maintain access to microformats. Microfilm, microfiche, and microcards each require separate, special readers. In addition, microforms require special cabinets for storage, and often library floors must be reinforced to support the weight of the collection. Although systems exist to print or scan from each microform type (with some systems able to handle all types), they are expensive for libraries and, consequently, for users. Although libraries seek to replace some microform collections with digital collections, cost and intellectual property rights are an issue. Libraries own the microform collections outright but may pay high costs to subscribe, not purchase, a digital collection with the same content. In addition, many of the relevant microforms were purchased from private companies, so libraries may be restricted from migrating that material to another format. Vendors often offer discounts on new, digital formats for libraries that purchased materials from them in microforms, but in the end libraries may pay many times for the same content in different formats.

Microforms, while a true innovation, did not disrupt the traditional linear relationship between the producer, distributor, and collector. Microforms were archival, less expensive to purchase and maintain, and saved the libraries physical space. Similar to books, microforms must be housed with the appropriate equipment and storage facilities in libraries and users must come to them. They also conform to the traditional definition of a publication, since they are but smaller versions of what would have otherwise been in a book. As indicated, the main effect on libraries from microform technology is financial, with space savings offset by costs for dedicated storage, library services, and viewing/printing/scanning equipment.

Disks

In the late 1980s, the U.S. government began to ship publications on 5.25-inch floppy disks and shortly afterward switched to 3.5-inch disks. Luckily for libraries and users, these were short-lived formats. Because different generations of disks were different sizes, one needed a computer with the correct size floppy drive to use them. They were also often formatted for a specific operating system (e.g., an Apple-formatted disk might not run in a Windows-based computer, and vice versa). Although a disk of either size stored more information than a book, this was still a limited format. Governments are one of the primary producers of data (numeric, geospatial, and scientific), and computers are clearly the best tool for working with data. However, it quickly became clear that floppy disks did not hold enough data to be practical, and CD-ROMs, followed by DVD-ROMs, became the new standard. Like microforms, floppies and CD/DVDs do not disrupt the traditional linear relationship between the producer, distributor, and collector, at least in their initial release.

Today, the contents of many floppy disks have been copied to online storage. One good example of large-scale content migration of this type is the CIC (Committee on Institutional Cooperation) Floppy Disk Project, a cooperative project of the GPO, the Libraries at Indiana University, Bloomington, and the CIC (http:// bl-libg-doghill.ads.iu.edu/gpd-web/floppy/floppy.html). By moving the contents of the disks and archiving them on a freely available website, the CIC and Indiana University have become part of the distribution chain and made it possible for non-depository libraries to collect these items by downloading them or linking to them from their catalogs. Traditional collectors of this information, depository libraries, no longer have to retain the physical disks.

CD/DVD-ROMs are like books in that they arrive in libraries as finished products to be marked, shelved, and circulated (or not) as the library sees fit. However, the format itself alters the traditional concept of a publication in that the user may create tables or excerpts of text from these tangible electronic products that might never have been printed at all or printed in that particular way. Disk-based publications do this, broadly, by joining together a database and search and retrieval software. So, whereas books arrive not only as finished products but as static products, CD/DVD-ROMs are finished products but their contents are not completely static.

Unfortunately, publications on disk often use software and proprietary or obscure file formats that rapidly become obsolete. In some cases, depository CD/ DVDs no longer run in current generations of Windows, and many were never compatible with other operating systems at all. Therefore, any library continuing to provide access to CD/DVDs or floppy disks must retain older hardware and software or emulation software that will run in current operating systems. For help with deciding which titles to retain on disk, librarians may search titles via the GITCO CD-ROM Documentation Service at www.lib.uiowa.edu/govpubs/gitco_docs/gitco.html. This cooperative project by the ALA/Government Documents Round Table Government Information and Technology Committee and the CIC is a good example of web technology used to improve library management of e-government information. After the title listed, if the field "Rely on web?" has a "Y" for yes in it, the tangible electronic title need not be retained. The GPO may also be contacted and asked if the online content is equivalent. One can also search the archives of GOVDOC-L (http://govdoc-l.org) or post a question about the title to the list.

WORLD WIDE WEB

Web technology has had a greater effect on the management of government information than any preceding technology because it is a mechanism for change in all roles in the information life cycle: it is a means for producing, distributing, and collecting content, and any person or institution may take on any of these roles. The Web is also an effective tool for repurposing existing library collections and developing new kinds of collections. Libraries now have the opportunity to produce new versions of content that better serve their users' needs, and also the responsibility to help users navigate the complicated online information environment.

Although web publications are widely accessible, they are also easily modified or deleted, thus contributing to a wildly volatile information landscape (California Digital Library 2003). Web publishing breaks down the concept of a publication as an "individual document." A user may generate a report from an online database that contains the same information as a book on a shelf, but if the report is dynamically generated in a continuously updating database it may be impossible to later generate an identical report. Yet the online database may share a title and authoring agency with the book on the shelf. Is the database a continuation of the book? Do the reports generated from it contain the same information and are they the only valid continuations of the book? Which one is a "publication" in a traditional sense, or are they both? If the report has no permanent existence, can it really be considered a document independent of the database in which its parts reside? These remain unanswered and increasingly important questions.

Such questions aside, libraries are also positively affected by web technology in many ways. For example, libraries should see a reduction in the processing of physical items bought or distributed through the depository program, because over half of all GPO item numbers are for online-only titles, and only a fraction of the remaining item numbers have actually had tangible materials shipped, according to the statistics available via the Documents Data Miner 2 (DDM2). Some libraries by choice or contract with the FDLP continue to maintain comprehensive print collections, yet even they have improved user access to online documents. Libraries never in the FDLP now have unparalleled access to historical and current documents of interest to users.

Stakeholders, including libraries and government agencies, now have a role in the production and transformation of government information via the Web. For example, an online search of the title phrase "Foreign Relations of the United States" returns the following within the first ten results: the current volumes of *Foreign Relations of the United States* (FRUS) at the Department of State website, the digitized historical FRUS collection from the University of Wisconsin, digitized related papers from Yale Law School, an article on foreign relations in Wikipedia, two archived Department of State web pages on FRUS, and a press release from the National Security Archive about delays in printing FRUS with full-text links to the controversial pages. The rate and radical nature of change this represents can be best described by noting that FRUS began with the Lincoln administration in 1861. The University of Wisconsin began digitizing it in 2000 and is nearly done. For 139 years users needed to consult a research library to use this title, but, with the completion of this digitization project, it will be available in full, along with related content such as the papers hosted by Yale, via the University of Wisconsin's website, to anyone online.[1]

Distribution can no longer be defined solely as the transfer of a physical item from one location to another, the downloading of electronic files to local servers from central servers, or the copying of a physical file from one hard drive to another. Distribution can be stretched to include the mere existence of an online item. One of the most important features of web publishing is that, once available, it may be reused infinitely. Because online materials are often more useful and convenient than physical materials for libraries and their users, many depository libraries are declining distribution of physical items in favor of online-only access. This is particularly true of the United Nations Depository Program. Member libraries have the option of receiving a partial deposit of print documents at a lower cost. Those wishing to continue to receive printed documents pay a higher print plus deposit fee. Because the UN has aggressively pursued the digitization of their materials, and UN documents are now available free online via the ODS (Official Document System) from 1993, some depository libraries accepted the UN's offer to limit print depository receipts. A related effect of the UN's digitization activities may be the reduction in subscriptions to commercial products such as Readex's UN microfiche collection.

Some collections may be too large for libraries or institutions to digitize, which can contribute to increased library spending on commercial products. Two examples are the Readex *U.S. Congressional Serial Set* Digital Edition and the LexisNexis Congressional Hearings Digital Collection. Another approach to large-scale digitization is to work with companies such as Google and Microsoft. Their profit comes from the advertising revenue generated whenever their sites are used. Therefore, the more content they index and search, the more potential profit. A recent example is the Google Patent Search, which is freely available, has more robust search capability than the U.S. Patent and Trademark Office's search, but uses Google's proprietary image reader to display results.

Other freely available collections and resources made possible by the Web include the searchable online database for World Bank Documents and Reports, archived state publications such as those produced with the Archive-It product by North Carolina, and the OpenCRS network, a metasearch engine covering all sources of freely available Congressional Research Service reports online.[2] Many projects are transforming existing government information and distributing it online. Some outstanding examples include the Stanford University–WTO collaboration on the GATT Digital Library, the IPUMs project from the Minnesota Population Center, and the American Presidency Project at the University of California–Santa Barbara.[3]

Agencies and libraries are also using new technologies such as web feeds to help users find information more easily (West 2008a, 2008b). A particularly interesting example is Research Reports, a link available via a library RSS feeds web guide (http://actlibrary.tc.faa.gov/rss.html) to the Federal Aviation Administration's (FAA) Technical Center Research Reports. These reports were once distributed only through the National Technical Information Service. Most libraries did not collect these publications, so older ones can be hard to get. But now that the FAA posts the full text online and alerts users to the locations of the reports, users can locate them without mediation from libraries.

The Web also extends the types of government information collections possible. The University of North Texas CyberCemetery (http://govinfo.library.unt.edu) preserves the websites and publications of defunct U.S. government agencies—a collection that exists only because of the Web. Web technologies have also stimulated innovative government information resources that have no analog in a print/microform environment, such as climate data at www.weather.gov. This development has implications for commercial information providers. In 2005, Senator Santorum of Pennsylvania proposed the National Weather Services Duties Act of 2005, which aimed to ensure commercial access to data collected by the Weather Service before public access. The argument was that, if everyone accessed www.weather.gov, then companies like Accuweather that run their own web services would go out of business. This has not happened and the bill died, but it illustrates the relationship between the needs of the public and researchers for government information and those of commercial interests.

CONCLUSION

In this era of web technology, traditional publishing relationships and roles have expanded as agencies, libraries, and private companies all engage in production, distribution, and collection of information materials. The traditional concept of a publication has also been fundamentally transformed. The result has been a host of inventive tools that improve access to digital online government information and ease the use of tangible materials.

But the characteristics that make the Web a valuable medium for producing, distributing, and collecting information also make it an unstable medium. Information can be removed or modified with great ease, which carries some risks. If research is founded on reproducibility of tests but researchers are citing transient information, how can one rely on this information to reproduce experiments? Another issue is the authoritative nature of official government information. How may web documents serve as reliable legal resources or influence how law is interpreted when online information may not be relied upon? Government information is also the record of the history of the United States. How may historical research be accomplished if the information is not comprehensively managed and preserved? Is the decision about what information to make available affected more by political considerations in the present than in the past? Is it the responsibility of libraries to act as preservation organizations for all online government information? If not, how may this information be preserved? Could we do it collectively? In the future, could the government negatively impact digitized government information produced by libraries?

Libraries, primarily depository libraries, are struggling to come to consensus on these questions. Librarians must come to terms with the inherent instability of web-based publishing. Is stability always a primary good? Or is there another way to think about government information that embraces the changeable nature of the Web and finds new and different benefits?

NOTES

1. University of Wisconsin Digital Collections. *Foreign Relations of the United States.* http://digital.library.wisc.edu/1711.dl/FRUS/.

2. World Bank Documents and Reports, www-wds.worldbank.org; North Carolina Archive-It, www.archive-it.org/collections/194; OpenCRS, www.opencrs.com.

3. Stanford–World Trade Organization/GATT Digital Library, http://gatt.stanford.edu/page/home/; Minnesota Population Center IPUMs project, http://usa.ipums.org/usa/; University of California–Santa Barbara American Presidency Project, www.presidency.ucsb.edu.

REFERENCES

California Digital Library. 2003. *Web-Based Government Information: Evaluating Solutions for Capture, Curation, and Preservation.* www.cdlib.org/programs/Web-based_archiving_mellon_Final.pdf.

West, Amy. 2008a. Government Podcast and RSS Libraries. www.firstgov.gov/Topics/Reference_Shelf/Libraries/Podcast_RSS.shtml.

West, Amy. 2008b. U.S. Federal Government RSS Feeds. http://govpubs.lib.umn.edu/xml/rssfeeds.phtml.

Chapter 3 Digital Preservation of Electronic Government Information

Grace-Ellen McCrann

The GPO estimated in 2004 that 50 percent of all U.S. federal documents were "born digital," that is, created digitally with no print version (GPO 2004). Two years later the Pew Internet and American Life Project reported that 73 percent of American adults were Internet users (Madden 2006). If one wants to copyright a book, get an extension form for filing a tax return, track satellites with NASA, get a small business loan, or find out how a senator voted on a particular bill, the information may be found on a government website. Clearly the use of online resources is increasing. Online government resources have changed the way students and professors do research and also the way citizens and the public interact with their local, state, and federal governments. How and why should this information be preserved for future access?

In the early years of the U.S. republic, public distribution of government documents was haphazard. Individual bills were passed to authorize the supply of various House and Senate journals, reports and legislation to state executives, territorial legislatures, and sometimes colleges. December 1812 marked the beginning of the formalization of public distribution of federal information when the 13th Congress passed a resolution to not only publicly distribute their own documents but also provide for similar distribution by subsequent congresses. Distribution is laudable, but permanent access to public information also requires the preservation of that public information. In 1859, the 35th Congress instructed the secretary of the interior that he was responsible not only for distributing public information but also for preserving of it.

Grace-Ellen McCrann is assistant professor and chief of the government documents division at The City College of New York, where she manages a collection of nearly half a million documents. Her online government documents bibliography "Government Views of Iraq" is in the permanent electronic collections of both the Library of Congress and the National Archives. gemscot@yahoo.com

Currently public printing and documents in the United States are legally under the aegis of Title 44 of the U.S. Code. In 1993 the government recognized the importance of preserving federal electronic information with the passage of Public Law 103-40, the Government Printing Office Electronic Information Access Enhancement Act. P.L. 103-40 added a new chapter (Chapter 41) to Title 44: "Access to Federal Electronic Information." The new chapter included language that directed the Superintendent of Documents to operate an electronic storage facility for federal electronic information to which online access was available.

Barring physical disaster or theft, print documents should be on a library's shelf when needed, but today's electronic formats introduce new levels of access and preservation concern. Online resources disappear or update rapidly, and the effects may be disastrous for a user. And although there is no one current central source, nor a single format, for accessing preserved digital government information, there are several government agencies, organizations, and libraries involved in preserving digital government information, many through collaborative projects.

In this chapter we examine the historical context of and current trends in digital government information preservation initiatives, which address the problem of "disappearing" e-government information. Chapter 12 extends this discussion to practical advice and examples.

LIBRARY OF CONGRESS

In 1990 the Library of Congress began to digitize some of its historical collections. This pilot project put digitized information on CD-ROMs and some videodiscs, which were then distributed to forty-four schools and libraries nationwide. A survey of the participating schools and libraries as well as visitors to the Library elicited an enthusiastic response. Survey respondents wanted the initial materials as well as additional digitized materials. Today new technologies, the cost of production and shipping, and the awkwardness of using CD-ROMs in public service settings have made them a fading format for libraries, but even by 1994 it had become obvious that CD-ROMs were not a permanent format solution to digital preservation. One of the most frequent requests from the original pilot was for primary source materials. To the Library's surprise, requests for primary sources came not only from academic, public, and state libraries but also from K–12 libraries representing an age group then and now only rarely admitted to the Library's research facilities.

Encouraged by the positive response to the pilot project, the Library of Congress in October 1994 announced its National Digital Library Program, which was to concentrate on digitizing primary source materials. The centerpiece of the program would be the online American Memory collections (http://lcweb2.loc.gov/ammem/index.html), which currently contain more than 9 million online items and have been a phenomenal success. Although many of the online American Memory holdings are not government documents (e.g., 1,500 pieces of 1870–1920 African American sheet music from the Brown University collection), much of the collection did originate as such. Some examples are eighteenth-century documents from the Continental Congress and the Constitutional Convention, presidential papers from the Coolidge administration including several previously unpublished speeches by President Coolidge, and administrative records from the Works Progress Administration's Federal Theatre Project during the Franklin Roosevelt administration.

Digital preservation is, however, still a developing science, with emerging industry standards. Some of the American Memory project's earliest digital preservation efforts used different technical standards than are available today. The Library of Congress currently uses general standards of SGML (Standard Generalized Markup Language) for text documents, which permits searching within the text, and TIFF (Tagged Image File Format) for images. The age and variations of type fonts in older documents are not suited to OCR (optical character recognition) digital scanning, and therefore most of the older documents that have been digitized for this project have been keyed by hand. The bulk of the digitization has been done by contractors, and the Library's agreements require these contractors to maintain a 99.95 percent accuracy level between the original document and the digitized version. The project is enormously complicated and encompasses practically every original format one can imagine.[1]

Much of the Library of Congress's concentration for the American Memory project has been on collections and on the technical side. Librarians naturally want the technical side to work, but so far there seems to have been only modest attention paid to cataloging and providing metadata for online resources. In library MARC cataloging records, there are numerous fields available to connect similar titles and expand patron access, such as alternate title fields and a variety of subject fields. At present, however, it often can be difficult to identify a specific photograph or piece of text within American Memory, and providing ways to achieve this access should be prioritized.

Technology formats are still changing continually. In December 2006, for example, a high-definition version of the DVD format was released commercially. To date, the Library of Congress has not been specific about plans to migrate to new formats as they become available, suggesting uncertainty in the future access and preservation of American Memory collections.

NATIONAL COMMISSION ON LIBRARIES AND INFORMATION SCIENCE

In 2001, the National Commission on Libraries and Information Science issued the report "Comprehensive Assessment of Public Information Dissemination," in which it recommended broad partnerships within the government to assure the preservation and access of publicly available government information (NCLIS 2000–2001). The report was prompted by the proposed closing of NTIS (National Technical Information Service). Much of the income for NTIS had been generated from the sale of government technical reports, but as more and more agencies made their reports available online for free, NTIS found itself with a sharply reduced income. NTIS saw online government information as a threat to its business model rather than as an expansion of access to government information. NCLIS took the broader view that increased electronic access to government information was a positive development. Included in the report were recommendations to both retain NTIS and update its business model; NTIS has since been restructured and still exists.

This 2001 report defended the value of public information in general, stating that "public ownership of information created by the federal government is an essential right." NCLIS also included several recommendations directed at e-government information, such as "evaluate pre-electronic government information for digital conversion" and "identify the federal government's most critical requirement for technologies to manage public information resources." Of particular interest here is the report's general recommendation that the government be encouraged to "partner broadly, in and outside government, to ensure permanent public availability of public information resources."

From its role as supporting player in the 2001 report, e-government information took center stage in the May 2006 NCLIS report "Mass Digitization: Implications for Information Policy." The NCLIS commissioners identified nine issues that could affect national information policy. Since the entire report is about digitization and e-government information, all nine issues touch, at least tangentially, on the preservation of e-government information, but one issue addresses preservation directly:

> Who will assume long-term ownership of books and journals and other media? Who will take responsibility for long-term preservation of books and journals and other media, and preserving the public record? Libraries have the commitment and are the only trusted agents for long-term preservation of digitized materials. Books are best "insured" by digitizing. The Federal government has a critical role in preserving government documents in perpetuity. (NCLIS 2006)

Three U.S. government agencies recognized by NCLIS to have a major role in the preservation of digital government information are the Library of Congress, the GPO, and the National Archives and Records Administration (NARA). One instance of such intergovernment cooperation encouraged by NCLIS was the August 2003 agreement between the GPO and NARA in regards to GPO Access, the GPO's online searchable database of digital documents. The GPO was recognized as an affiliate archive of NARA and the two agencies agreed to cooperate in providing permanent public access to digital government documents. The GPO agreed to maintain physical custody, and NARA assumed legal custody of the more than a quarter million documents on the GPO Access website (National Archives 2003).

U.S. GOVERNMENT PRINTING OFFICE

The GPO is the federal agency most directly concerned with government documents in all formats and has been leading the change to a primarily electronic federal depository system. In FY 2003, 65 percent of the titles in the FDLP were available online, with an expectation that 95 percent availability would be reached by 2005 (GPO 2003)—and it was. Since its 2003 "Information Dissemination Annual Report," the GPO has been working on both sides of the electronic preservation problem—both physically preserving documents in electronic formats and providing access to these preserved documents through its online *Catalog of Government Documents.* The GPO's Electronic Collection encompasses several categories of documents. GPO servers host both legislative and regulatory documents as well as titles managed by the GPO for other federal agencies, and it links and points patrons to additional documents that remain under jurisdiction of the issuing agency.

One integral part of the linking to other agency-hosted online documents is the GPO's PURL program. A URL is a web page's unique electronic address, but URLs can change in a blink of an eye. For those documents whose electronic copies are on an agency website and whose permanent access is not under the direct control of the GPO, GPO catalogers assign a PURL (persistent uniform resource locator), which looks like a regular URL but functions like a switching service that links the end user to the desired web page, wherever it currently resides. The technical name for such a process is a "permanent HTTP redirect." The practical result for end users is fewer dead links and failed searches. PURL providers are responsible for both assigning a unique PURL to a website and maintaining a working link between the PURL and a website's own URL. If a URL changes, it is the PURL provider's responsibility to correct the link. The PURL program is administered by OCLC, and though any organization can become a PURL provider the GPO is one of the major users of the system. All current online government documents are assigned PURLs by GPO catalogers, and the PURL appears as a live link in GPO catalog records. Although occasionally even PURLs go dead, the GPO's PURL program and its commitment to maintaining it means users are much more likely to be able to find online government documents in the future, no matter on which server they actually reside at the time of the search.

Another ambitious GPO preservation project is the digitization of a complete legacy collection of documents that originally were part of the FDLP in printed format (www.gpoaccess.gov/legacy/index.html). The legacy collection is one of the GPO's strategic goals, and the project's intent is to ensure permanent electronic public access to historic and current government information. To meet this goal, the GPO has developed digitization specifications in partnership and consultation with NARA, the Digital Library Federation (DLF), and digital preservation and metadata industry experts. The project's pilot phase concentrates on public and private laws, U.S. Reports, and the U.S. Code. A complementary project is the GPO's National Bibliography program (www.access.gpo.gov/su_docs/fdlp/cip/), which is developing a "comprehensive index of public documents, [including] every document issued or published . . . not confidential in character."

In addition to government agencies, nongovernment organizations and universities have been active in preserving e-government documents, and some of these projects are joint partnerships with the GPO. The GPO also maintains a list of digitized government documents projects on the GPO Access website (www.gpo access.gov/index.html). Individual members of the ARL have collaborated with the GPO in the digitization of the legacy collection. Examples include the Papers of the Presidents series, which is being digitized by the University of Michigan (http://quod.lib.umich.edu/p/ppotpus/) and the University of Wisconsin's digitization of close to three hundred volumes of the *Foreign Relations of the United States* (FRUS; http://digicoll.library.wisc.edu/FRUS/). The FRUS project originated with GODORT, which is also home to GITCO (Government and Information Technology Committee), whose website (www.ala.org/ala/godort/godortcommittees/gitco/index.htm) is a good resource to keep up with current developments in e-government document preservation. Another critical component of the GPO's response to digital preservation is the development of FDsys, discussed in chapter 12.

FLOPPY DISK PROJECT: PRESERVING DISAPPEARING DIGITAL FORMATS

Electronic government documents that were originally issued via the FDLP only on floppy disks are now often inaccessible because most current computers no longer support those formats. One solution to this particular problem is the CIC (Committee on Institutional Cooperation) Floppy Disk Project, a cooperative project of the GPO, the Libraries at Indiana University, Bloomington, and the CIC. The CIC is a twelve-member academic consortium that includes the University of Chicago and the Big Ten universities (Illinois, Indiana, Iowa, Michigan, Michigan State, Minnesota, Northwestern, Ohio State, Penn State, Purdue, and the University of Wisconsin at Madison). Indiana University Libraries hosts this online depository (www.indiana.edu/~libgpd/mforms/floppy/floppy.html), from which government documents originally issued on floppies can be accessed and used free of charge. The depository also houses information on disks originally issued with accompanying print documents. Available documents range from a U.S. Navy *Disaster Preparedness Workbook* to the USDA's *Forest Service Planning Guides* and *President Clinton's Economic Plan*.

CYBERCEMETERY: PRESERVING DISAPPEARING DOCUMENTS

Sometimes online government information disappears not because the federal agency deletes the pages or changes URLs but because the agency has ceased to exist or merged into another government entity and no longer maintains a separate website. One cooperative program that addresses the problem of disappearing agency pages is the University of North Texas's partnership with the GPO, called the CyberCemetery (http://govinfo.library.unt.edu/default.htm). Examples of information collected here are websites of the Coalition Provisional Authority of Iraq (CPA), an authority that was partially authorized and maintained by the U.S. government. When a sovereign interim government was established in Iraq in June 2004, the CPA was dissolved. But from May 2003 through its dissolution, the CPA was the government of Iraq and exercised full authority for functions including the armed forces, banking regulations, courts, government salaries, human rights, trade regulations, copyright law, and the like. Once the CPA was dissolved, it no longer maintained a website, but all of its regulations, memoranda, public notices, orders, and reports are freely available online courtesy of the CyberCemetery.

Other digital information preserved by the CyberCemetery includes that from government entities dissolved by mandate of Congress, such as the National Educational Goals Panel (1990–2002), and temporary government entities such as independent counsels. The CyberCemetery is also a particularly good resource for locating documents of closed federal commissions, which are often constituted for a specific task or time period and then dissolved. Some of the varied commissions the CyberCemetery has archived are the President's Commission on Moon, Mars and Beyond (2004), the National Gambling Impact Study Commission (1997–1999), the National Bioethics Advisory Commission (1996–1999), and the Child Online Protection Act Commission (2000). The CyberCemetery can be searched by keywords and by agency by name, date of expiration, or branch of government. In addition to the CyberCemetery, the University of North Texas has digitized several other document collections (http://digital.library.unt.edu/govdocs/), including three specific to Texas: H. P. N. Gammel's *The Laws of Texas* (1822–1897), an archive of *Texas Laws and Resolutions*, and an archive of the *Texas Register*.

U.S. NATIONAL ARCHIVES

In addition to its collaboration with the GPO, NARA was also involved in a major harvest of government information and websites in late 2004. One predictable federal government change is the transition every four years from one presidential administration or term to another. NARA harvested many existing federal websites in October and November 2004 before the beginning of President Bush's second term. The process produced a public copy that is freely available on the Web and a record copy for NARA's files. Not all federal websites were captured; only those that were first- and second-level sites with URLs ending in .gov and unclassified military websites whose URLs ended in .mil were included in the project. This was a fairly comprehensive project and includes websites from government entities ranging from the American Battle Monuments Commission and Department of Housing and Urban Development to the National Transportation Safety Board and Tennessee Valley Authority.

The National Archives also manages the U.S. presidential libraries. Several of these institutions have been quite active in either digitizing documents or capturing websites and making them available for public access. The William J. Clinton Presidential Library and Museum is a case in point. The first White House website was put online during the Clinton administration in 1994, and the Clinton Library website has preserved five different versions of the White House website ranging in time from November 1995 through early January 2001, the last days of President

Clinton's second administration. The Clinton Library website also makes available a virtual library of searchable online White House documents dating from 1993 to 2001 that includes radio addresses, press briefings, and executive orders (www .clintonlibrary.gov/archivesearch.html).

The Dwight D. Eisenhower Library website has a Digital Documents Project (www.eisenhower.archives.gov/dl/digital_documents.html) that not only covers the high points of Eisenhower's White House years but also includes documents from World War II when he was supreme commander of the Allied Forces and even army reports from 1919 when he was a lieutenant colonel. The documents from Eisenhower's White House tenure are particularly interesting because of the memoranda of presidential meetings, texts of telegrams, and diary entries—the sort of presidential documents researchers find so hard to locate.

The National Archives' Teaching with Documents program (www.archives .gov/education/lessons/) provides secondary school teachers with primary and secondary resources, a significant model for the promotion of e-government information for a K–12 audience by a U.S. agency. NARA has divided U.S. history into eight periods, from the American Revolution to the present, and each period has lesson plans that link to online government information. The lesson plans reflect the National History Standards and the National Standards for Civics and Government and feature digitized primary government documents.

A basic strength of the National Archives is its core mission of preserving government information in general, and preserving e-government information is a logical extension. Since 1968, NARA has had an electronic records custodial program (www.archives.gov/era/) under the aegis of the Electronic and Special Media Records Services Division of NARA's Modern Records Program. Another key player in NARA's electronic information efforts is its Electronic Records Archives Program Management Office (ERA-PMO). Although ERA-PMO does not use the specific term "permanent" in regards to its activities, one of its primary goals is that "all records will be preserved in an appropriate environment for use as long as needed." Another positive NARA electronic preservation initiative is its Electronic Records Archives project "to create a system that will authentically preserve and provide access to any kind of electronic record, free from dependency on any specific hardware or software."

For the most part, neither NARA nor the Library of Congress dates individual web pages on the public screen or in the source code. Failing to specify the currency of the information provided is a major problem for users. These two online sites also expose a need for improved service to users with a wide variety of background subject knowledge and technical skills.

OTHER FEDERAL ELECTRONIC PRESERVATION PROJECTS

NARA, the Library of Congress, and the GPO have missions that directly concern them in the preservation of digital government information, but other federal agencies vary in their development of online resources and commitment to the preservation of such digital resources. Just as there is no one central source for digitized government information, there is also no one central source that creates the U.S. government's information policy. Agencies comply to a greater or lesser degree with information policies. Three of the best agencies in this regard are the U.S. Geological Survey (USGS), National Aeronautics and Space Administration (NASA), and Environmental Protection Agency's (EPA) National Environmental Publications Information System (NEPIS).

The USGS maintains a Publications Warehouse Search Page (http://infotrek .er.usgs.gov/pubs/) through which users can locate more than 66,000 online USGS publications. The database can be searched by author, product type, title, or year. Recent publications can be identified by month of publication and are often available in a variety of digital formats.

The EPA has more than 20,000 current and archival documents online and searchable through its NEPIS system (www.epa.gov/ncepihom/onlinepubs.htm). The agency also provides links to office-specific documents, such as the Office of Inspector General's Homeland Security Reports, Air Reports, Land Reports (including Superfund Reports), and Hurricane Katrina Reports. In autumn 2006, the EPA announced plans to close some of its nationwide libraries in order to concentrate on electronic delivery of resources. News releases promised digitization of currently undigitized resources within two years, but information about specific technical standards for the digitization, provisions for authenticity, migration to new formats, and permanent public access are, as of this writing, somewhat sketchy.

NASA is digitizing not only its current documents but older documents as well. Its Technical Reports search site (http://ntrs.nasa.gov/search.jsp) contains more than half a million online NASA documents going back to the 1930s. Users can search by individual NASA center, publication year, type of publication, subject, or report number.

NONGOVERNMENT INITIATIVES

One early nongovernment initiative aimed at general Internet sites but including government websites is the Wayback Machine at the Internet Archive (www .archive.org/web/web.php), which has been crawling the Web and collecting copies of web pages since 1996. Created by a 501(c)(3) nonprofit corporation, this is an extremely ambitious project with audio, live music, and moving images archives in addition to text—and the site is free. The Wayback Machine has captured large numbers of both U.S. federal and state government websites (more than 55 billion websites overall), but because it crawls international web pages as well this is also a source for foreign government websites and information.

Another well-known document preservation effort undertaken by a nongovernment entity is the online Avalon Project from Yale Law School (www.yale.edu/lawweb/ avalon/avalon.htm). Subtitled "Documents in Law, History and Diplomacy," this is a freely accessible digital collection, but the documents themselves are not true digitized versions of the originals. In many cases Yale has added value to the original textual content of the documents by linking to online copies of supporting documents referred to in the original document. The Avalon Project concentrates on documents in the fields of law, politics, diplomacy, government, history, and economics and the documents range from the seventeenth century (e.g., Articles of Confederation of the United Colonies of New England) to the present.

GOOGLE BOOK SEARCH: A COLLABORATIVE EFFORT WITH ACCESS AND PRESERVATION ISSUES

Google is well known as one of the primary Internet search engines. In 2004, Google launched a massive digitization project in conjunction with Harvard University, Stanford University, the University of Michigan, Oxford University, and the New York Public Library. Contrary to the buzz at the time, these partnerships do not entail digitizing the entire collections of these libraries, but, even so, the sheer number of projected digitized titles is amazing. Assuming similar scanning costs, Google will spend $750 million to scan the 30 million volumes contained in the collections of the five participating libraries (Band 2006, 16). Since the original announcement, other libraries have joined the project with varying degrees of commitment, including the Library of Congress, the University of California System, Madrid's Complutense University, the Libraries of the University of Wisconsin at Madison, and the Wisconsin Historical Society Library.

Many of the titles to be digitized in the Google plan are government documents, and questions have been raised in the government documents preservation community concerning the authenticity and authority of these digital copies—an important point when dealing with documents that may at some point become exhibits in court cases or other legal proceedings. The idea of preserving these documents and other titles is a good one, but Google has not made a commitment to provide long-term access to these digitized copies or to migrate to new electronic formats as they appear in the marketplace. Copyright issues remain a concern and would prevent free public access to some documents. The jury is still out on the ultimate value to future researchers of Google's digitization project.

CASE STUDY: PRESERVING NORTH CAROLINA STATE DIGITAL DOCUMENTS

State governments are also addressing the preservation of official digital government documents. One of the more active states in this regard is North Carolina. In 1999/2000 the Documents Branch staff at the State Library of North Carolina began to notice an increase in the use of digital state documents. The North Carolina Legislature had mandated that several state agencies produce documents only in digital formats; there had been state budget cuts and some officials saw digital documents as a cost-saving measure. But there was no central authority that by law could mandate acceptable formats for digital documents, nor were there any state regulations or official policies concerning the production of digital versus print documents. At first State Library catalogers began to add URLs for documents to their catalog records. State agencies were also required to continue producing enough print documents for the State Library and the libraries in the state government depository program.

These were, however, just stopgap measures, and in 2001 North Carolina applied for a federal Library Services and Technology Act Grant to fund a three-year project called the Access to State Government Information Initiative. Part of the grant included a survey of state agencies. Results published in 2003 showed that 93 percent of North Carolina's state agencies produced documents available only digitally for which there had never been print editions. Another startling statistic was that 51 percent of all North Carolina State information was available only in digital formats. In phase 2 of the project (2002–2003), a work group representing all stakeholders—librarians, technical people, agency records managers, archivists, and State Library staff—investigated issues involved in the production and preservation of digital government information. Phase 3 (2004–2005) was devoted to testing solutions and techniques that had emerged from the work group sessions, including such things as metadata schema, web harvesting techniques and software, workflow issues, and resource needs.

Under North Carolina law, the State Department of Cultural Resources has the legal custody of state government archival records and is the permanent repository for state publications. Both the State Library and State Archives are part of the department, and in 2004 representatives from both agencies formed a task force to address the collection and preservation problems inherent with digital documents. In 2005 a digital preservation policy was drafted, and in 2006 the draft policy was accepted as the basis for North Carolina's Digital Preservation Program (State Library of North Carolina 2006).

It is still early days for this project, but the State Library recently hosted a workshop on best practices for digital preservation in state government. One of the first tangible results of the project was launched with the establishment of the online North Carolina State Government Web Site Archives (www.ah.dcr.state.nc.us/archives/webarchives/index.html), which offers free access to archived North Carolina state government web pages from fall 2005 onward.

PRESERVING DIGITAL GOVERNMENT INFORMATION OUTSIDE THE UNITED STATES

The problem of disappearing digital documents is not limited to the United States. Although a full discussion of international efforts to preserve digital government information is beyond the scope of this chapter, it is interesting to take note of a few projects. The government of Australia has Pandora, "Australia's Web Archive" (http://pandora.nla.gov.au/index.html), which digitally archives both government and nongovernment Australian websites. The project was originally spearheaded by the National Library of Australia but has grown to include ten major Australian libraries and archives as partners. In Britain, the Public Record Office has been archiving the No. 10 website (10 Downing Street is the prime minister's office) since the June 2001 election. French law has been changed to include a legal requirement for digital deposit. There is also a major intergovernmental project in Europe under the aegis of the EU called Digital Preservation Europe (www.digitalpreservation europe.eu). Additional information is available in the chapters on international and foreign government information.

CONCLUSION

Government documents cover the whole range of human interests, and this knowledge must be preserved. The public's right to be informed and research are supported by preserving access to e-government resources in multiple formats encompassing the past, present, and future. The multiplicity of approaches currently being employed, and questions of authenticity, reliability, and commitment to permanent access will underlie continuing discussions as digital preservation techniques and best practices evolve.

NOTE

1. Additional technical specifics for multiple formats can be found at http://memory.loc.gov/ammem/dli2/html/document.html.

REFERENCES

Band, Jonathan. 2006. "The Google Library Project: The Copyright Debate." American Library Association, Office for Information Technology, policy brief, January, 16. www.policybandwidth.com/doc/googlepaper.pdf.

GPO U.S. Government Printing Office. 2003. "Information Dissemination Annual Report, Fiscal Year 2003." *Administrative Notes* 24 (12): 3–9. www.access.gpo.gov/su_docs/fdlp/pubs/adnotes/ad101503.html.

———. 2004. "A Strategic Vision for the 21st Century." www.gpo.gov/congressional/pdfs/04strategicplan.pdf.

Madden, Mary. 2006. "Internet Penetration and Impact." Pew Internet and American Life Project. www.pewinternet.org/pdfs/PIP_Internet_Impact.pdf.

National Archives. 2003. "The GPO and National Archives Unite in Support of Permanent Online Public Access." www.archives.gov/press/press-releases/2003/nr03-60.html.

NCLIS National Commission on Libraries and Information Science. 2000–2001. "Comprehensive Assessment of Public Information Dissemination." http://purl .access.gpo.gov/GPO/LPS9062.

————. 2006. "Mass Digitization: Implications for Information Policy." www.nclis .gov/digitization/MassDigitizationSymposium-Report.pdf.

State Library of North Carolina. 2006. "Digital Preservation in State Government." www.nclaonline.org/grs/NCLA%20Presentation.ppt.

Chapter 4   Electronic Government Spatial Information

Issues, Challenges, and Opportunities

Linda Zellmer

S patial information, in the form of maps, has been an integral part of U.S. government information since the 1st Congress. The first map to appear in a U.S. government publication, "A map by Tassel and some other of the head-men of the Cherokees, to describe their territorial claims," was published in volume 7 of the *American State Papers* (Washington 1789). Since 1984, the U.S. government has been planning and taking steps to deliver more government information electronically (United States Congress 1984, 22–28). This migration toward electronic delivery includes spatial information such as maps and geographically referenced data that can be used with geographic information systems (GIS). The U.S. Geological Survey (USGS) has recently announced that it is working to move toward maps on demand (McDermott 2006), which means that topographic maps would no longer be received through the FDLP; the digital spatial data would be made available to depository libraries. These changes have and will continue to have a profound impact on the services provided in depository libraries.

The first major collection of digital spatial data to arrive in depository libraries was the 1990 U.S. Census TIGER line files and associated numerical census data, which, when joined to the TIGER geographic boundary files, can be used to create maps on a wide variety of topics. The USGS also began distributing digital spatial data about this time, in the form of digital line graphs (DLG), digital raster graphics (DRG), and digital orthophotoquadrangles (DOQ), although the DRG and DOQ lifespans in the depository program were brief.

Linda Zellmer is government information and data services librarian at Western Illinois University. She has a BS in geology and biology from the University of Wisconsin-Oshkosh, an MA in marine science from the College of William and Mary, and an MLIS from the University of Wisconsin-Milwaukee. She has been active in the Western Association of Map Libraries, Geoscience Information Society (GSIS) and is a member of the Special Libraries Association Environment and Resources Management Division and ALA-MAGERT. Zellmer represents GSIS on the Cartographic Users Advisory Council. LR-Zellmer@wiu.edu

Although most government information librarians are able to deal with traditional documents in electronic form, and access to it offers users advantages not available previously, spatial information poses a unique set of challenges. These include keeping up with the technology needed to use and store digital maps and geospatial data, expanding the services that must be offered by libraries, and maintaining access to spatial data. It also includes addressing disappearing government data sets and websites.

TECHNOLOGY REQUIREMENTS

The GPO has issued technical guidelines for computers in depository libraries since 1991. Beginning in 1997, these guidelines included requirements for computers used for accessing cartographic data (GPO 1997). The guidelines for cartographic data computers require a large monitor (currently 21-inch); specialized software such as Landview, ArcView, or MapInfo; and access to a 36-inch printer. Over the years, the technical requirements have evolved through time as the formats for electronic publications have changed. The specifications have required various storage media since they were implemented in 1991: 5.25-inch floppy disk drives (1991–1996), 3.5-inch floppy disk drives (1991–present), Zip drives (1998–2002), CD-ROM drives (1991–present), and DVD drives (1999–present). As new storage media become available, data on older media have to be migrated to other formats or archived elsewhere. One example of a data archive, the CIC Floppy Disk Project (see chapter 3), has archived data received through the FDLP on 5.25-inch floppy disks. Over the years, depository libraries have received spatial information on a variety of storage media, including floppy disks, Zip disks, CD-ROMs, and DVDs. Spatial information is presently being distributed as maps in PDF format or as geospatial data on CD-ROM, DVD, or from government websites; sometimes publications contain both geospatial data and maps in PDF format.

Traditional government publications are fairly easy to use in electronic format; they can be accessed, viewed, and read on a computer screen from almost any location and printed on standard printers. This is not typically true of digital maps. For example, when library users look at a printed 30 x 60 minute geological map (which measures about 40 x 56 inches [105 x 144 cm]), they can see the geology of their area of interest as well as the geology of the surrounding region. This is not possible on a standard computer monitor, or even on the larger monitors required by the minimum technical requirements. To view a PDF version of the same map, the user is forced to examine small portions of the map. To see the regional picture, users must use an extremely large monitor (at least 36 inches wide), print the full map on a plotter, or print it in sections and then tape it together. The user usually has to pay for printing, because most libraries do not fund printing or plotting for their users. Thus, a fee for use of government information has been imposed on people who need these nontraditional forms of information.

SERVICE REQUIREMENTS

Recently, the USGS announced that it will no longer provide topographic maps through the FDLP. Instead, it will distribute the geospatial data for processing on-site (McDermott 2006). Although some depository CD-ROM products come with an executable file that loads the preformatted data so the user can view and manipulate it, most geospatial data must be loaded and manipulated by the user or an intermediary to produce a map. Many improvements have been made by U.S. agencies since the first U.S. Census data CD-ROM was issued via the FDLP. A considerable amount of geospatial data can be downloaded from websites, rather than loaded from a CD-ROM, although population data must be imported before it can be used with some GIS software (this step may be eliminated when ArcGIS 9.2 is released). However, using geospatial data is considerably more challenging than opening a PDF file. To make a map with census data, for example, the user must, at least, open the boundary file of interest, join statistical data to the boundary data, and then determine the best way to depict the data. This example assumes that the library offering GIS services has processed the data in advance to make it more user friendly by downloading boundary and statistical data files and ensuring that there is a common field (such as FIPS codes) on which to join the statistical data to the geographic boundary data.

Library users who are unfamiliar with GIS software require staff assistance to produce a thematic map from most geospatial data. A recent report from the National Academy of Sciences identified several software design issues as barriers to incorporating GIS in K–12 education. The report states that interfaces need to be redesigned to be "more intuitive and . . . provide help and guidance" (National Research Council 2006, 234). It is apparent that working with geospatial data is technologically more complicated than working with other types of e-government publications. Beard (2003) identified five reference service levels for GIS services in libraries: providing access to GIS workstations; delivering data; instruction (teaching class sessions about GIS data and how to use GIS); custom GIS services; and web-based services. Librarians can also contribute data and metadata to outside organizations that provide data and web-based mapping services. GIS services in libraries can take a variety of forms. The most basic is to provide one or more GIS workstations for use with data received through the FDLP. Many libraries also deliver data by making people aware of CD-ROMs and DVDs received through the FDLP, building websites directing users to GIS data, developing a collection of data on a central data server, or contributing data and metadata to central GIS data sites and web mapping services maintained by outside organizations. Because they are familiar with describing and organizing information, librarians can also provide an invaluable service by developing metadata for GIS data sets. By contributing data to local and state data sites and web mapping services, the library can serve a wider group of users. Libraries can also reach a wider audience by creating PDF maps on specific topics or developing web-based mapping systems that allow people to create maps.

Custom GIS services, working with individual library users to create maps on a specific topic, are also offered by some libraries. This can often be one of the most time-consuming aspects of GIS service in libraries, because individual users may be interested in data for widely different areas. While one user may want to work with local data, another may want to work with data for another state, country, or the world. Users' subject interests may also vary widely. One user may want to map U.S. Census data; another may want to map information on the age and location of meteorite impacts in the world. Some of this information may have to be formatted before it can be mapped. Thus, librarians will have to teach library users how to format data for use with GIS. Because GIS can be used by people in different subject areas, including geography, geology, anthropology, archaeology, history, political science, health care, social work, planning, recreation, and education, to name a few, librarians providing GIS services must have a basic knowledge about a broad array of subjects and the data available in those subject areas.

ACCESS CHALLENGES

There are a host of issues to be considered when discussing access to spatial information. At least thirty-two federal government agencies produce some sort of spatial information, either data or maps. Unfortunately, very little of the digital geospatial data available from these agencies can be found using GPO Access. Ideally, the GPO should treat geospatial data as it does other electronic publications: it should be indexed in the *Catalog of U.S. Government Publications* and included in the plans for digital preservation in the Federal Digital System (FDsys; www.gpo.gov/projects/fdsys.htm). In practice, librarians and geospatial data users must search a variety of sources, including a central federal GIS data clearinghouse, individual federal agency clearinghouses, and commercial sites (e.g., www.geographynetwork.com) to determine whether data is available for a specific area on a particular topic. Sites like www.geodata.gov may or may not include information on data available from individual agencies. In addition, the results may be somewhat questionable; a person looking for data on the geology of a small area in the United States, such as Yellowstone National Park, may end up retrieving information about data sets that deal with the entire United States, because metadata creators have not been given any rules for assigning geographic descriptors. Sites that might point users to data on a specific topic, like the USGS National Geologic Map Database, which contains references to maps and geology-related geospatial data available on USGS sites, may not find references to geology-related data from other federal agencies such as the National Park Service or to GIS data stored on state agency websites. Nonfederal data search sites may also produce questionable results; a Geography Network (www.geographynetwork.com) search for geospatial data on Yellowstone National Park retrieved data produced by the government of Canada, including a data set on Canadian electoral districts. Finally, many sites do not rank data by relevance; as a result, the user may have to browse through descriptions of a large number of data sets before finding data at an adequate scale for the area of interest.

When GIS data are distributed through the FDLP, the cataloging is sometimes less than complete. For example, Landview 6 (U.S. Environmental Protection Agency et al. 2003) contains a mapping application for a wide variety of census demographic data, EPA Envirofacts data (seventeen different thematic data sets), and the USGS Geographic Names Information System, an index to place names appearing on 1:24,000 topographic maps. However, the Landview DVD has been cataloged as a single entity; the record for this item in GPO Access does not list the individual data sets included. Thus, a person interested in data on a specific topic might find the desired information on the Landview DVD only if directed there by a knowledgeable librarian. Many other data sets also include more than one set of data, such as the GAP analysis DVDs published by the USGS National Gap Analysis Program (GAP; see http://nbii.gov/portal/server.pt), which contain information on the habitats and ranges of native species. Finally, GIS data sites for individual federal agencies are also not cataloged, so finding these sites may depend on whether a librarian or data user knows that a relevant website exists.

Although this discussion focuses on data distributed through the FDLP, there are other problems as well. Some agencies produce data but distribute them only on request. An example is the EPA's BASINS (Better Assessment Science Integrating Point and Nonpoint Sources), an environmental analysis system that contains data about watersheds and computer programs that can be used for environmental assessment and modeling. The early BASINS CD-ROMs, which were available free on request from the EPA, contained a wide variety of geospatial data, including data on land use, land cover, urbanized area boundaries, populated place locations, soils, dam sites, ecological regions, and data used for environmental monitoring. The new BASINS CD-ROMs contain only the modeling software. The data can be downloaded from the Environmental Protection Agency's BASINS website (www .epa.gov/waterscience/basins/).

In addition to distributing data through the FDLP and on request, some agencies also deliver data in the form of web mapping systems. Examples of federal web mapping sites are the National Atlas of the United States (www.nationalatlas .gov) from the USGS, Web Soil Survey (http://websoilsurvey.nrcs.usda.gov/app/) from the National Resources Conservation Service, American Factfinder (http:// factfinder.census.gov/home/saff/main.html) from the U.S. Census Bureau, and the FEMA Mapping Information Platform (https://hazards.fema.gov/femaportal/wps/ portal/). These sites allow users to map data that have been selected and prepared for use within the web mapping service. As a result, these sites limit users' ability to create maps on specific topic, area, or geographic subdivision of their choice. For example, the National Atlas allows users to map data for counties, but not for census county subdivisions, townships, or smaller geographic areas. In addition, a person who wants to see a map that shows a single U.S. state may have to contend with viewing the state at an angle, because the data are projected so that the user can view the entire United States. American Factfinder also limits user choices. A person who wants to map data for an entire state at a particular geographic level (township, census tract, etc.) will have to use a geographic information system rather than the mapping applications in American Factfinder.

There is also a problem of disappearing data and websites. U.S. government agencies have removed a lot of data from the FDLP through the years, including DRGs and DOQs, which were supposed to be sent to state and regional libraries based on their individual selection. In reality, depository libraries received only 128 DRGs and 275 DOQs before they were removed from the FDLP. Instead, the data were given to Microsoft through a cooperative research and development agreement. Microsoft then made the DRG and DOQ data available through their Terraserver system, but there is a fee for downloading the data. Agencies are not required to notify the GPO or solicit public comments before they establish agreements with commercial organizations.

Since the DRG and DOQ data were removed from the FDLP, several other websites that deliver online topographic maps and imagery have been established. The USGS has even developed a website directing people to these sites (http://nationalmap.gov/gio/viewonline.html); again, downloading data from these sites requires a fee. Since the USGS began selling DOQ and DRG data, many states have developed their own data clearinghouses that allow users to download digital topographic maps, aerial photography, and imagery for free, but the USGS does not maintain a website to direct users to these sites.

Other data have been lost through cooperative agreements. The *Global GIS Database*, a set of user-friendly CD-ROMs for various parts of the world that allowed users to map a wide variety of data, was initially issued through the FDLP. Depository libraries received CD-ROMs for Central and South America, Africa, South Asia, and the South Pacific before they were removed from the program. The remaining CD-ROMs, covering North Eurasia, Europe, and North America, are being sold by the American Geological Institute (see Hearn 2002). The most important data set to U.S. teachers and libraries, the one for North America, could have been copied for the cost of a CD-ROM by teachers who wanted to incorporate GIS in their classrooms if it had remained in the FDLP.

Another agreement has recently been announced between Microsoft and the National Geospatial Intelligence Agency; Microsoft's Virtual Earth platform will be used to "provide geospatial support for humanitarian, peacekeeping and national security efforts" (Federal Laboratory Consortium for Technology Transfer 2006, 1, 4).

Several mapping sites have also disappeared, for a variety of reasons. The U.S. Department of Transportation removed the National Pipeline Mapping System from their website after September 11, 2001, for security concerns (Matthews 2002). Other spatial information disappeared around the same time, including the location of nuclear facilities (Carroll 2001) and EPA risk management plans. Security concerns are not, however, the only threat to spatial information access. The U.S. Department of Transportation recently removed their web mapping service application for viewing and data downloading, mapping center, and transportation GIS links from their website because of budgetary constraints. Some of these data are still available through the *National Transportation Atlas Database*, which is sent to libraries through the FDLP and is available free on request.

ARCHIVAL ACCESS

One question that has yet to be addressed is how data will be archived for future users. Many librarians are familiar with the myth of the 1960 census, according to which 1960 census data could be read only on computers in a museum in Japan and at the Smithsonian. Many of the data from that census were eventually migrated and preserved by the National Archives (Adams and Brown 2000), but not the data showing the boundaries of the census subdivisions, which are needed to map the statistical data with a GIS. The University of Minnesota's Population Center has re-created historical census boundary data with funding from the National Science Foundation; these data are available for free from the National Historical Geographic Information System website (www.nhgis.org). Still, many librarians who have worked with geospatial data can cite examples of "lost data." Data can be lost when equipment is discarded or replaced, so that tapes can no longer be read, or when new versions of data are introduced on commonly used data sites, such as the National Atlas of the United States. Some government agencies do provide access to the older data on request, but if the metadata about the older data cannot be found, users may not be aware of their existence.

In 1998, the Federal Geographic Data Committee's Historical Data Working Group developed a set of questions and guidelines for choosing spatial data sets to be saved (Federal Geographic Data Committee 1998). Zellmer (2003) summarizes the conclusions: data should be saved if it concerns legal issues, can be used by other agencies, would be expensive to re-create, or can be used by researchers to study change over time.

When these guidelines were first developed, the National Archives recommended that data be saved in spatial data transfer standard (SDTS) format, a software-neutral format developed by the USGS. Unfortunately, few software vendors developed SDTS export functions. Several other problems were also encountered with SDTS (Arctur 1998), so it is no longer being supported. The Historical Data Working Group is now evaluating other options, including geography mark-up language (GML), for archiving data (Historical Data Working Group 2006). The Library of Congress has funded two digital preservation studies for spatial information (LC 2004), including one that deals specifically with GIS data. The results of these studies have not yet been released.

Data archiving is an important role that could be assumed by libraries, especially libraries with access to large amounts of storage space. Parry (2003) concluded that the types of data that should be saved are boundary data, data that relate to a geographic entity (attribute data that provide information about a place), and data collected for a specific purpose. Libraries can and should be helping to preserve data about their local area for the future. They can ensure long-term access to data by developing and maintaining contacts with local, state, and federal agencies.

CONCLUSION

Electronic spatial information has advantages and disadvantages. It requires specialized hardware and software and knowledgeable librarians or staff to provide services. Access can be difficult, and archiving standards are not yet in place. But geospatial data processed through GIS can answer a wide range of questions on topics as diverse as crop production, population density, ethnicity, and ancestry. Custom geospatial data analysis can determine, for example, whether there is a relationship between a parent's income and education level and school test scores, whether a hospital should provide maternity care or services to the elderly (based on birth rates and the age of the population near the hospital), whether a library should provide large-print or foreign language books (which can be found using census statistics about the age of the population and language spoken at home), or whether the soil in an area has swelling clays, which requires that buildings have special foundations. Specific analyses such as these are not available in the familiar print government statistical or research reports.

But are libraries able to offer these advantages to their users? In 2005, the ARL surveyed 123 member libraries about spatial data collections and services. About 98 percent of the seventy-two responding libraries were assisting with locating geospatial data; 90 percent of those libraries offered consultations in which a librarian or staff member assisted with data use and manipulation or developing maps (Salem 2005). A similar survey was conducted on GIS services in libraries at small colleges (Kinikin and Hench 2005a). Of the 138 libraries responding to the survey, only twenty-two (13 percent) were offering GIS service and twenty-seven others were planning to introduce it. In a follow-up to this survey, only half of the smaller academic libraries that were offering GIS services responded, and two of them had discontinued their service (Kinikin and Hench 2005b). The follow-up study did not address GIS activity at the twenty-seven institutions that were planning to introduce GIS service. No information is available on GIS services in depository libraries, or why libraries choose not to offer GIS services.

Spatial information has been and will continue to be an important government information resource. As federal agencies continue to develop spatial information in the digital environment, libraries will see a reduction in the number of printed maps they receive through the FDLP. As a result, they should plan and develop services to address present and future user needs for access to electronic spatial information. Librarians can serve a wider community by working with local, state, and commercial data creators to archive data, provide access to geospatial data, and develop web mapping services, either independently or in cooperation with other GIS agencies.

REFERENCES

Adams, Margaret O., and Thomas E. Brown. 2000. "Myths and Realities about the 1960 Census." *Prologue* 32 (4). www.archives.gov/publications/prologue/2000/winter/1960-census.html?template=print#nt7.

Arctur, David, and others. 1998. "Issues and Prospects for the Next Generation of the Spatial Data Transfer Standard (SDTS)." *International Journal of Geographical Information Science* 12 (4): 403–425.

Beard, Colleen. 2003. "Reference Service Levels for Spatial Data Delivery and GIS Activity in Libraries: A Local Assessment." *Bulletin* (Association of Canadian Map Libraries and Archives) 118 (Fall): 4–8.

Carroll, Jill. 2001. "Aftermath of Terror: Government Agencies Shut Some Websites, Fearing Information Could Aid Terrorists." *Wall Street Journal* (Eastern ed.), October 5, 2001, A10.

Federal Geographic Data Committee, Historical Data Working Group. 1998. *Should the Geospatial Data Set Be Saved?* Reston, VA: The Group. www.fgdc.gov/nara/hdwgsave.html.

Federal Laboratory Consortium for Technology Transfer. 2006. "Microsoft, NGA Announce Alliance." *FLC NewsLink*, July 2006, 1, 4.

GPO U.S. Government Printing Office. 1997. "Recommended Specifications for Public Access Work Stations in Federal Depository Libraries." *Administrative Notes* 18 (9). www.access.gpo.gov/su_docs/fdlp/pubs/adnotes/ad061597.html.

Hearn, Paul. 2002. "USGS and the American Geological Institute Combine to Offer a World of Information." USGS News Release. www.usgs.gov/newsroom/article.asp?ID=351.

Historical Data Working Group. 2006. "Historical Data Working Group Work Plan." www.fgdc.gov/participation/working-groups-subcommittees/hdwg/workplan.

Kinikin, JaNae, and Hench, Keith. 2005a. "Survey of GIS Implementation and Use within Smaller Academic Libraries." *Issues in Science and Technology Librarianship*, no. 42 (Spring). www.istl.org/05-spring/refereed-1.html.

———. 2005b. "Follow-up Survey of GIS at Smaller Academic Libraries." *Issues in Science and Technology Librarianship*, no. 43 (Summer). www.istl.org/05-summer/article1.html.

LC Library of Congress. 2004. "Library of Congress Announces Awards of $13.9 Million to Begin Building a Network of Partners for Digital Preservation." Library of Congress Press Release 04-171. www.loc.gov/today/pr/2004/04-171.html.

Matthews, William. 2002. "Walking a Fine Line on Web Access." *Federal Computer Week*, February 4. www.fcw.com/fcw/articles/2002/0204/pol-access-02-04-02.asp.

McDermott, Michael. 2006. Response to July 19, 2006, e-Mail sent to Linda Zellmer (forwarded to Maps-L, Geonet, and GOVDOC-L as "Future of the 7.5´ Topographic Maps").

National Research Council, Committee on Support for Thinking Spatially: The Incorporation of Geographic Information Science across the K–12 Curriculum. 2006. *Learning to Think Spatially: GIS as a Support System in the K-12 Curriculum.* Washington, DC: National Academies Press.

Parry, Robert B. 2003. "Who's Saving the Files? Towards a New Role for Local Map Collections?" *LIBER Quarterly* 13 (1): 39–47.

Salem, Joseph A. 2005. *Spatial Data Collections and Services.* Washington, DC: Association of Research Libraries.

United States Congress, Joint Committee on Printing, Ad Hoc Committee on Depository Library Access to Federal Automated Data Bases. 1984. *Provision of Federal Government Publications in Electronic Format to Depository Libraries: Report of the Ad Hoc Committee on Depository Library Access to Federal Automated Data Bases, to the Joint Committee on Printing, United States Congress.* 98th Cong., 2nd sess. Committee Print, S. Prt. 98-260. Washington, DC: U.S. GPO.

U.S. Environmental Protection Agency, U.S. Census Bureau, and U.S. Geological Survey. 2003. Landview 6: A Viewer for EPA, Census Bureau, USGS Data and Maps. Washington, DC: U.S. Census Bureau.

Washington, George, and others. 1789. "A Map by Tassel and Some Other of the Head Men of the Cherokees, to Describe Their Territorial Claims in: Wabash, Creeks, Cherokees, Chickasaws, and Choctaws: Speeches and Negotiations on Land Boundaries." *American State Papers: Indian Affairs,* 1st Cong., 1st sess., v. 7, no. 2.

Zellmer, Linda R. 2003. "Chasing Mayflies: Archiving Spatial Data." *Western Association of Map Libraries Information Bulletin* 34 (2): 71–75.

Chapter 5   Providing Access to Electronic Government Information to Diverse Populations

Marianne Mason

Fostering the delivery of e-government information, including providing value-added access, promoting resources through outreach initiatives, and enabling a level of self-sufficiency for customers, is a universal responsibility for libraries. In this chapter we address the differences and commonalities faced by library professionals in delivering online U.S. federal, state, and local government information to distinct user groups. Various library types, specific examples of web resources, and best library practices are discussed.

The Web has become a conduit for almost every service sector. With Internet connectivity consumers can shop, pay bills, rent videos, send e-mail or instant messages, and read or listen to the news 24/7. With an Internet connection there is no need to leave home or even leave one's chair to utilize these services. Because of consumer experiences such as these, expectations are high for retrieving and receiving information from government agencies, whether on the local, regional, state, or federal level. Darrell West argues that, until a greater percentage of government websites provide higher-quality content and more interactive services, support multilingual customers, and have an active outreach component, e-government will not have reached its full potential or attained general public acceptance (West 2004). The goal of e-government is to respond favorably to the public's demands, and it is the responsibility of libraries to provide service for and access to this information for diverse and distinct user groups.

Marianne Mason received her MLS from Indiana University–Bloomington. She is the federal documents coordinator at the University of Iowa Libraries and teaches "Government Information Resources" through the School of Library and Information Science. She has also team-taught "Legal Bibliography and Law Library Administration" in the School of Library and Information Science at Indiana University. She was a contributor to Local and Regional Government Information: Where to Find It, How to Use It *(2005) and is active in government information organizations at both state and national levels.*

Unfortunately, obstacles abound. Lack of awareness, on the part of the end users and the information professionals, is a major hindrance to creating a more informed citizenry. For example, the Economic Divide, a major component of the Digital Divide, limits large numbers of households' financial ability to own a computer, let alone their ability to find beneficial e-government information. Success in retrieving needed information, or even the degree of comfort with a computer keyboard, may vary depending on an information seeker's age, language proficiency, education level, or physical ability. In spite of these barriers to access, government programs are created to benefit the entire U.S. public, to improve their quality of life, and to fulfill the right of every citizen in an open society to be aware of government activities. To fulfill their role in ensuring the success of government information providers' efforts, libraries must work to overcome these obstacles.

Government information needs and library services provided vary depending on the characteristics of the library community's primary customer base and the library's size and collection focus. The "library community" itself has become hard to pin down, as web-based catalogs, online databases, and virtual reference services become the norm and leap beyond the boundaries of traditional geographic communities. Just as bookmobiles in the past provided services to those who were unable to travel to the library, online library services offered through web-based public access catalogs now provide remote user populations with interactive forms, research guides, links to community resources, and recreational materials. The tremendous growth of e-government information represents access far greater than was ever possible in the print-only environment. Federal, state, and local government agencies have created an abundance of online information available to the public at no charge. Government information is everywhere. The media is filled with news of government initiatives, programs, and statistics. A disparity exists, however, between the abundance of government information available and the lack of broad-based citizen use of that information.

RETHINKING LIBRARY SERVICES FOR ONLINE GOVERNMENT INFORMATION

The significance of library outreach services for e-government information is best understood within the context of significant developments over the past few decades in accessing this information. Government information collections within libraries have traditionally been "hidden collections" requiring unique promotion and kept out of the research mainstream. Academic libraries in particular relied mainly on the scholarly community to utilize these specialized resources. Separate housing, separate catalogs, separate classification schemes, and separate staffing for often noncirculating collections provided an environment of personalized service to a special, physically separate collection. This environment resulted in a strong dependence on librarian intervention to help users access the materials. It also promoted the belief among users and nondocuments librarians that government information was difficult to find and complicated to use.

With the introduction of the GPO electronic cataloging records for depository publications in 1976, made available via bibliographic utilities such as OCLC and online library catalogs, the hidden aspect of government publications began to fade and the principle of "comparable treatment" of government information started to become a reality. Bibliographic services for GPO records customized to the particular library's profile became available from vendors in the 1980s. On the state and local levels, however, no such transforming events occurred. Although state depository programs existed for the dissemination of documents to libraries, there was no bibliographic standardization from one state to the next. On the local level, few structured programs requiring distribution of local government publications existed. Indexes to state documents (e.g., the Library of Congress's *Monthly Checklist of State Publications*) and to "urban" documents (e.g., Greenwood Press's *Index to Current Urban Documents*) existed, but they were neither comprehensive nor a source of cataloging information. Some utilities like OCLC included bibliographic records for state and local publications, but they were scattered. Also, state agencies did not routinely filter their publications through their state's depository program, making shared comprehensive indexing and bibliographic control impossible. Little has changed in the web environment to strengthen state or local depository programs, although direct access to state and local e-government information is much improved.

An astute observer watching developments in government documents departments could have predicted the expanding base of full-text electronic resources and changing user patterns as early as the late 1980s. Floppy disks were the first electronic disks sent via the FDLP, and by the early 1990s CD-ROMs began filtering into the collections of FDLP libraries with regularity. By the early twenty-first century, CD-ROM collections in regional federal depository libraries numbered several thousand. Over time, maturing technology made CDs, including DVDs, more usable, but disks are still an awkward format and generally require in-library use, with the possible exception of a few titles accessible through local area networks. It is often quite difficult for depository libraries to provide and maintain the infrastructure and equipment needed to provide access to these physical nonprint media. Because of this issue, the FDLP distributes specific technology and equipment guidelines to depository libraries (GPO 2005).

The acceleration of electronic depository distribution of federal government information was instigated by the congressional mandate for the GPO to transition to a more electronic FDLP (GPO 2000). GPO Access (www.gpoaccess.gov), a collection of online searchable databases of government information, had already been created in 1993, but its viability was being tested and challenged to perform more effectively. State and local governments were also beginning to view electronic resources as a way to reduce printing costs and to deliver and promote access to government information. They embraced Internet delivery of information that facilitated customer-based government services. In practice, individual government agencies were more concerned about providing current information online than archiving and preserving information.

While this revolutionary change in format and accessibility was occurring in documents collections and libraries, the Internet (and ultimately, Google) became the research tool of choice for library customers. Declining user statistics such as low gate count, fewer reference questions, and reduced reshelving reported by academic libraries were also noted in government publications departments. As users accepted the Internet as a favored research tool, accessing web resources and online databases from remote workstations became preferable to making a trip to the library. Although many large academic libraries use tangible collection size for collection development measurement, library comparisons, and ranking, the importance of "volume count" in the library's annual report is becoming less important than counting visits to library web pages, the number of PURL hits in the online catalog, and the assessment of services to library users.

Today, in the FDLP, providing access to remote electronic resources via the Web and distributing cataloging records have largely replaced the distribution of tangible electronic formats to libraries. Bibliographic control activities that incorporate PURLs through cataloging records for electronic resources further the integration of government information into research activities, allowing remote desktop access to thousands of publications. Library staff responsibilities have shifted away from processing tangible publications to database maintenance activities that enhance access to Internet-based resources. Tangible serials received through the FDLP are being replaced by remotely accessed electronic format serials, requiring a shift of access methods and changes in record management protocols as libraries provide access via web guides and the online catalog. E-journal collections, including some government periodicals, have become accessible in full text through library catalogs. The vendor Marcive has developed enhanced access to the federal electronic collection through MarciveWeb DOCS database index and "Documents without Shelves," a web-based collection of full-text born-digital publications. Through these and other subscriptions, nondepository libraries have access to the electronic collection of government publications in the FDLP. The former separateness of the government publications collection is giving way to more standardized and integrated services for circulation, cataloging, database management, instruction, and reference services that accommodate user preferences. Government information is no longer in the sole custody of designated depository libraries. Every library with an Internet connection has access to online full-text depository resources, as well as e-government services through agency websites.

Still, much work remains to be accomplished before government publications are no longer considered a "hidden collection." There are several GPO projects in progress that may provide greater user access to the full range of government publications—for one, the GPO-sponsored National Bibliography project. The project's goal is "to develop a comprehensive and authoritative bibliography of U.S. government publications to increase the visibility and use of Government information products, and to develop a premier destination for information searchers." This online National Bibliography will provide searchable cataloging records and, eventually, access to the full-text documents. Another GPO project is to "digitize a complete legacy collection of tangible government publications to make sure that these materials are available, in the public domain, for permanent public access." This legacy collection, when complete, will include all publications that have been distributed through the FDLP since its inception. This ambitious project will take many years to complete even if it remains a priority as GPO leadership changes. A third GPO project, unveiled to the public in March 2006, is the updated *Catalog of U.S. Government Publications* (http://catalog.gpo.gov/F), an enhanced index to federal publications from 1976 with PURL links to many full-text publications. This public component to the GPO's integrated library system will reflect the future developments of both the National Bibliography and the legacy digitization projects.[1]

Until these projects are complete, however, the challenge to libraries is to provide assistance to and expand awareness of tangible historical government resources housed within the library. This may be accomplished through developing value-added library services while enhancing the value of web-based resources beyond the confines of library collections. Packaging resources on the local level and delivering them to targeted audiences through outreach initiatives has become the necessity in the e-government environment.

LIBRARY OUTREACH INITIATIVES WITH GOVERNMENT INFORMATION TO UNDERSERVED POPULATIONS

There is no formula that satisfies the meaning of "outreach"; rather, it is an ever-changing combination of activities and interpretations depending on individual library missions. The common goal of all library outreach initiatives, however, is to create an awareness of the value of resources and to deliver that information to those who may benefit. Outreach and promotion activities valid in the predigital environment, such as classes for interested groups, signage, tours, articles in newsletters and newspapers, exhibits, programs, and word-of-mouth advertising, are still valid today. However, digital government information has created both barriers and opportunities for specific audiences that require specific and active outreach initiatives. Distance education and digital information are natural partners in improving library services to rural communities and underserved populations that previously lacked reliable connectivity. Less traditional activities such as staffing information booths at state and country fairs or establishing a presence at any community and cultural event where gatherings occur provide avenues for libraries to promote government information.

Economic success, educational progress, and personal growth increasingly depend on one's ability to use information sources on the Web. Underserved populations, including minorities, low-income earners, those with low levels of educational attainment, and people over 65, are the least likely to possess those skills. Geography is also a determining factor in the ability to access the Internet. Some rural communities may not have the infrastructure in place to provide in-home

Internet connectivity. Community access centers offer a means for those without home computers to take online classes, find additional training opportunities, or search for jobs, and these centers may be the only points apart from the agency office where information about government programs designed for these under-served groups can be obtained. A library may lack funding to meet the high public demand for computer terminals and Internet access completely, although it is a requirement of the FDLP that depository libraries provide this service to the public.

Communicating with local government agencies to share information in the development of programs, neighborhood workshops, and web guides for relevant social services like housing, health, social security, employment information, and government contact information could complement the work of both libraries and government institutions. But partnerships are not always possible. Government agencies may not provide print copies of web-based forms to their customers but rather refer inquiries to the local library. In the aftermath of the hurricanes of 2005, libraries served survivors of the disaster by providing Internet access to FEMA forms and printed copies that were not immediately available from FEMA. Immigration and Naturalization web forms and citizenship study materials are other examples of many e-government resources accessible through libraries. The Newark Public Library has created a fine example of a pathfinder for immigration resources that incorporates both government and nongovernment resources.[2]

Low income and low-level literacy skills are the key elements driving the disparity of computer use; however, limited English-language skill is also a key factor. In 2001, Executive Order 13166, "Improving Access to Services for Persons with Limited English Proficiency," required that all federal agencies design their websites with a component that serves people with limited English proficiency. Some particularly good examples of U.S. federal agency websites providing multilanguage access to diverse populations are GobiernoUSA.gov (www.usa.gov/gobiernousa/), U.S. Government Multilanguage Gateway (http://pueblo.gsa.gov/multilanguage/multilang.htm), Social Security Multilingual Gateway (www.ssa.gov/multilanguage/index.htm), MedlinePlus in Spanish (http://medlineplus.gov/spanish/), SBA in Spanish (www.sba.gov/espanol/), and HUD in Spanish (http://espanol.hud.gov/index.html).

Acknowledging that the Hispanic population is the fastest-growing minority in the United States, virtually every federal agency publishes electronic Spanish-language information. Many official state websites have some Spanish-language information, but multilingual coverage is inconsistent from state to state. Although Spanish-language information is widely available, the Hispanic population is one of the least likely minorities to own a computer to gain access to this information (U.S. Department of Commerce 2000, 13). Working with Hispanic community leaders to develop effective strategies to promote access at the point of need is an imperative for successful outreach activities.

School libraries and public libraries alike can bring the rich source of e-government information for and about children to their users by tapping into electronic resources that are widely available from both state and federal government agencies.

Virtually every state and every federal agency website devotes space to educational resources for children, teachers, and parents. Although the design features of agency websites vary, content that promotes the availability of free reliable information to educators can be a boon to classroom resources. Creating subject-based web guides with links to curriculum guides available on agency web pages can easily be incorporated in train-the-trainer workshops for media specialists and school librarians. This type of outreach establishes an information cycle that broadens the uses of online government resources for future generations of teachers, parents, and students. Two good examples of government websites about and for children are Medline Plus: Children's Health (www.nlm.nih.gov/medlineplus/childrenshealth .html) and Smithsonian Learn and Explore: Science and Technology (www.si.edu/ science_and_technology/).[3]

Online government information is also widely available for populations age 65 and older. This demographic group is, however, the least likely to own a computer (U.S. Department of Commerce 2000, 41), so establishing library outreach initiatives is particularly important. Senior centers, retirement communities, and community college continuing education programs offer ideal venues to present programs promoting government information on topics such as health and health insurance, housing, estate planning, consumer protection, leisure, finances, travel, and taxes. Two examples of library web guides that have been created for people over 65 are the Tulsa City-County Public Library's Government Sites for Seniors (www .tulsalibrary.org/govdocs/seniors.htm) and Hollins University, Wyndham Robertson Library's Links for Seniors (www.hollins.edu/academics/library/information/ gov_senior.htm).

Through the Americans with Disabilities Act of 1990 and the Rehabilitation Act of 1998, federal agencies are mandated to utilize technology to provide accessible information to individuals with disabilities. Federal depository libraries are directed by the GPO to abide by the recommended standards for access by individuals with disabilities (GPO 2008, chap. 4, 32). The FDLP Desktop also provides links to other important resources that support depository libraries' obligation to provide accessible information, including links to the ADA home page and the United States Access Board website, which describes access standards for electronic and information technology covered by Section 508 of the Rehabilitation Act.

Requirements for providing access to current digital e-government information are addressed in these directives; however, until the digital historical record is also accessible, individuals with vision impairments will be excluded from access to the cultural resources of the legacy FDLP collection. Assistive technology that enables access to digital information has made equal access possible for those with vision impairment, blindness, limited mobility, hearing impairment, deafness, and learning disabilities. Although personal computer costs are declining, assistive technology is expensive and beyond the budgets of many individuals who look to public environments such as libraries for their Internet connection and access to online information. Libraries can remove many barriers that prevent equal access and support independence for library users, but providing special assistive technology services may not be financially supported by all libraries. Those most likely to provide support services and technology for assistive technology are state libraries and large academic and special libraries. In some cases, special grants make it possible for libraries to provide these services.

Barbara Mates (2000) provides a full description of the issues surrounding assistive technology, from web design standards and hardware selection to funding and staff training. Assistive technology includes closed captioning devices for the hearing impaired; visual enhancers, which enlarge print on monitors; screen enlargement software that magnifies a computer display; voice recognition software; speech output; trackballs for those with mobility impairments or repetitive stress injury; and scanners to digitize tangible legacy publications. Several examples of specific assistive technology software include Zoomtext (screen magnifier and reader), Jaws (screen reader), Dragon Naturally Speaking Preferred (voice recognition software), Openbook (scan and read software for vision impairment), and Wynn (scan and read software for learning and cognitive disabilities).

Federal government resources for and about individuals with disabilities are available from the Department of Health and Human Services, Department of Labor, Library of Congress, and U.S. National Library of Medicine and the National Institutes of Health.[4]

LIBRARY INTERNAL CHANGES RELATED TO PROVIDING GOVERNMENT INFORMATION SERVICES

Understanding the technology and equipment needs of special populations is one aspect of providing excellent service for online government information. Also important are the internal library issues and challenges related to services, including organizational, staff, training, and space issues. The organizational structure of some libraries has changed to accommodate new technology, improved access to online information, and changing user behaviors in finding and using online information. Some libraries have abandoned the stand-alone department model by merging government publications and reference units to provide a single service point with the goal of improved and more convenient service to customers. Integration of staff, services, policies, and collections is seen to incorporate government resources more seamlessly into research activities that support the mission of certain libraries. For libraries with a combined service point, cross-training for documents specialists and reference specialists presents unique challenges and an ongoing commitment to a training program to ensure success. Conversely, libraries that support a distinct government publications unit argue that true expertise will be lost in a merged organization. In either model, staff expertise using government resources requires continual nurturing through continuing education and professional development pursuits. High-quality web library guides to online government information support these ongoing training efforts as well as providing important services to library communities.

Generating enthusiasm for online government information among nongovernment information staff within the library can be challenging. It is imperative, though, for providers of general reference services to have a broad understanding of the range of government resources available in order to make appropriate referrals or to incorporate government information in reference transactions and information literacy activities. Staying informed of both depository and nondepository resources—including the look, feel, and navigational conventions of government agency web pages—serves a current awareness function for both the subject specialist and the generalist. All members of the library staff benefit from a better understanding of the range of government resources, how they may be used, and the value of providing electronic access to customers. Creating mechanisms to let all staff know of new and unique government resources through activities such as mini-training sessions, e-mail announcements, or tours of collections can build support for government resources by all levels of library staff. Internal training and communication should also include information elements for and about serving diverse populations. The ultimate goal of increasing the staff comfort level using government information is to pass that information on to library patrons through reference transactions and information literacy programs.

Libraries' arrangement of physical space has also been impacted by digital resources and may require new methods to maximize services for diverse populations. The reference desk itself is often seen as a barrier rather than a service point for reluctant users or those who need assistance from other locations within the library. Some libraries are moving away from the physical reference desk by increasing staff presence in the library stacks. Providing roving assistance to government information seekers at the point of need is convenient for library customers, provides an opportunity for one-on-one instruction, and focuses on the customer's need rather than the librarian's convenience. Mobile phones and in-house phones further facilitate communication for customers and librarians needing to stay in touch with the reference desk or to seek backup reference assistance.

Other issues surrounding new uses of physical space within the library have developed with the electronic environment. Computer clusters and wireless network zones have become well established in new and reconfigured library floor plans. This includes reconfiguration of staff workspace and ergonomically suitable workstations as online processing and database maintenance replace handling tangible library materials. Spaces within libraries such as lobbies, large meeting rooms, and auditoriums are natural venues for alternative uses that complement government information resources. Speaker's forums, guest lectures, History Day or Black History Month presentations, high school debate topics, special celebrations, exhibits, displays, and civic events offer opportunities for government information-rich programming. It is wise for libraries to review their use of space and services regularly so that all possible provision is made for accommodating new information sources and the user community, including those with special needs.

Customer reliance on the Internet makes a compelling argument for library development and improvement of web guides for expanded delivery of online government content. Web pages may provide contact information, links to library instant messaging and virtual reference services, descriptions of local resources and collection strengths, links to local expertise and to services, topical research guides, and instruction-based resources. Each of these web-based services promotes e-government resources and increases visibility of library and government services to a dispersed audience. For two examples of "ask-a-librarian" pages that focus on interactive assistance, see www.library.uiuc.edu/askus/ and www.phoenixpublic library.org/asklib.jsp.

When designing web pages, consider both technological specifications and design standards. At the core of thoughtful web design is an understanding and accommodation of the library's complete patron community. Important issues to be addressed include primary language spoken in the home, socioeconomic diversity, and special needs of individuals such as physical changes that accompany the natural aging process or physical disabilities. Web page usability is impacted by many factors including font style and size, page layout, colors, and image tagging if users have vision, cognition, or dexterity limitations (Hanson 2004).[5]

EXTRA-LIBRARY OUTREACH TO DIVERSE POPULATIONS

Developing creative methods of collaboration among organizations complements services for all those involved. Identifying subject expertise and collection strengths in the region among other libraries allows for informed patron referral and develops an outreach mechanism that enhances the services of each institution. Communication between libraries within the state, drawing on the existing system of FDLP libraries, is an important method of providing mutual support. A requirement of the FDLP is that each state create a "State Plan" to affirm common goals, objectives, and responsibilities of all federal depository libraries within the state, which may include a union list of experts and collection strengths. Partnerships can also be established with other libraries, local governments, and civic organizations to promote the value of the government information, both tangible and virtual, depository and nondepository resources. Two libraries that deliver this range of resources are the New Mexico State Library (www.stlib.state.nm.us/index.html) and the Hollins University Library Government Documents Department (www .hollins.edu/academics/library/information/govdocs.htm).

With the declining number of tangible local government resources, it is particularly important to create positive working relationships with local agencies to establish a collection of tangible resources and to promote digital preservation and permanent public access. Many local and state governments fail to recognize the need to retain revised and amended versions of documents that reflect the complete historical record. Technological obsolescence and lack of a centralized method to ensure permanent public access have resulted in the loss of huge amounts of born-digital government information. The American Association of Law Libraries (2003) has issued a significant report addressing the need to preserve the entire life cycle of e-government information. The report is a state-by-state survey of legislation ensuring public access to government information. It finds that no state comprehensively addresses public access and preservation of e-government information. The goal of this report is to encourage state governments to work with the library community and public access communities to enact legislation that ensures permanent public access to e-government information.

Government information literacy is no longer the sole responsibility of the documents librarian; all public service librarians should promote effective use of online government resources. Integrating nongovernment resources and government sources in all instructional and library outreach programs is a further means of folding government resources into the research mainstream. Government information can be incorporated in almost all teaching opportunities in venues such as residence hall common rooms, remote computer clusters, distance training tele-classrooms, on-site workshops for distinct user groups including school libraries, community centers, retirement communities, continuing education workshops through community colleges, and train-the-trainer workshops both in and outside the home library setting.

E-mail and virtual and chat reference services have become common in libraries, but a unique pilot program specializing in government information called Government Information Online: Ask a Librarian (GIO; http://govtinfo .org) draws on the expertise of many FDLP libraries. All levels of government information are addressed through GIO including local, regional, state, federal, and international sources. This service draws on the expertise of documents specialists nationwide to provide real-time reference assistance, e-mail follow-up, a global knowledge base, and referral service. Established in 2005, this is the only service of its kind.

Local digitization projects offer unique outreach opportunities to promote collections and resources. Such projects are natural avenues to create interdepartmental or interinstitutional partnerships. Shared expertise, shared costs, and increased visibility of enhanced government resources are a few of the benefits. The Iowa Heritage Digital Library (http://cdm.lib.uiowa.edu) is an example of a project that draws on specialized library collections from historical societies, Iowa public libraries, colleges, museums, and archives to document Iowa's history and cultural heritage. One notable component of this digital collection is the Mujeres Latinas Digital Collection, an oral history project established to collect and preserve materials including photographs, letters, and oral histories to document the lives and contributions of Latinas and their families to Iowa history.

SPECIAL CONSIDERATION FOR TYPES OF LIBRARIES

The variety of library outreach activities previously described may be applied in principle to any library setting and in service to many diverse populations served by libraries. Following is a discussion of the differing missions of public, academic, and special libraries, their user needs, and how e-government information delivery may occur depending on library type and population served.

Public Libraries

In general, the mission of public libraries is to support civic communities and to serve as a resource for citizens within a distinct geographic area (Schull 2004), and providing online government information is reasonably considered part of that civic responsibility. The community of users may include all income levels, education levels, ages, social groups, ethnic groups, language skills, and disability status with diverse research and personal interests. It also includes users who need access to e-government services of many kinds. By providing access and information about these services, public libraries fill a current, growing, and even critical need in the population.

Library outreach and the delivery of e-government information begin by incorporating bibliographic records in the library's online catalog that include PURL links directly to web resources. Locally created web pages linking to local, state, federal, and foreign government web resources are methods of delivering thousands of full-text government information resources to library constituents. Links to no-cost locator tools provided by the GPO such as the *Catalog of U.S. Government Publications* provide library users with an even wider range of materials to meet their needs. Digital government information requested by e-mail or virtual reference services can be delivered as full-text documents to a user's desktop. Public libraries and local government are natural partners in providing access to both historic and current local government information by creating value-added indexing and digital archiving. Developing working relationships with historical societies, nearby colleges, and community service organizations also expands the base of government information awareness for the community of public library users.

Although the virtual library may be replacing the physical library in some instances, public libraries still serve as a gathering place for the community. By partnering electronic classroom space, assistive technology, and Internet cafés with instruction, libraries empower library users to find government information more independently.

Academic Libraries

The academic library, both public and private, serves a diverse community of scholars, including experienced researchers and those new to the research process. Faculty and students from around the state or around the world are engaged in research and study on every conceivable topic, both theoretical and pragmatic. The virtual library has become a reality in the academic community, serving to make e-government information readily accessible to the community and beyond. Information professionals in both public services and technical services promote this accessibility through the library's online catalog, research guides, and course pages tailored to specific user groups. It is crucial in this environment that all academic libraries, whether or not they are government information depository libraries, incorporate e-government information into all their web, bibliographic, reference, information literacy, and programming services.

Promoting the awareness of government resources must relate to the academic library's current priorities and initiatives. Today more than ever, greater emphasis is being placed on librarians' increased classroom presence in academic environments. Outreach to faculty can begin with developing a departmental librarian liaison program and offering research workshops to teaching assistants. Incorporating online government resources through instruction and information literacy activities reinforces the value of this information as a significant and authoritative source of primary resources. Marketing government information expertise in the classroom and among other librarian/instructors in areas such as history, journalism, business, and political science will further promote integration of e-government sources into the research mainstream. Instruction in research methods can routinely incorporate sample searches that include government resources. Digital information packets, course-specific web-based bibliographies, and research guides can be delivered in the classroom, residence halls, remote computer clusters, and distance learning centers by e-mail, reference consultation, instant messaging, and virtual reference.

Institutions with distance learning programs are ideally suited to deliver e-government information to enrich the learning experience of distance learners. In addition, libraries can incorporate direct outreach to students, including online government information. New and returning students, international and multicultural groups, student athletes, undergraduates, and graduates may be targeted through orientation programs and customized tours based on research interests. Some libraries have instituted diversity librarian positions specifically to provide outreach services to meet the information needs of diverse student groups, including use of online government information. All academic library users, whether faculty or student, on-campus or remote, have access to the library's online catalog to access a wide range of research sources from government agencies. If provided through the library's catalog records, PURL links established by the GPO through the FDLP provide stable links that allow remote users access to full-text federal government resources.

There are additional opportunities if the academic library is on a campus with a library school. Graduate library education programs offer government documents specialists the opportunity to promote e-government resources through single instruction sessions or credit classes on government information resources for serving children and young adults, reference, collection development, and electronic resource management.

Publicly funded institutions have a community outreach responsibility that may extend to the entire state, although campus missions vary. Developing interinstitutional partnerships, offering workshops to a statewide audience, and sharing collections and expertise are a few instances of community outreach activities possible. For example, the business and academic communities share interests in economic and trade topics and need to hone their research skills using electronic resources from government agencies. Patent and trademark training attracts researchers in fields of engineering and medicine as well as inventors and entrepreneurs from the private sector. It is the responsibility of government depository libraries of all types to provide outreach and training opportunities to the community whose tax dollars support depository resources.

Special Libraries

Special libraries, either as independent institutions or within a larger organization, have their own constituency and may have a specialized research focus in areas such as business, law, and medicine. The research focus may range from theoretical to current practices and research-based to customer service–based activities. Many of the outreach methods utilized in academic libraries also apply in the special library setting, though services in these specialized libraries may be highly personalized and tailored to the individual requestor's needs. Academic instruction is replaced by customer-based services and digital delivery to satellite corporate offices. Web courses and instruction by e-mail support the delivery of digital government content to a client or branch office. Networking between like institutions supports specialized virtual reference and instant messaging programs and provides a method of sharing expertise.

Prison libraries represent a unique example of a type of special library that is required to provide access to judicial resources. The 1977 *Bounds v. Smith* (430 U.S. 817) decision affirmed that inmates in correctional facilities have a constitutional right to access to the courts though law libraries or an alternative avenue of legal knowledge. This does not guarantee that an on-site library exists, but it opens the possibility of partnerships with nearby law libraries that can provide limited delivery of services. Southern Illinois University School of Law Library in Carbondale, Illinois, located a few miles from the Marion Federal Correction Facility, has an excellent self-help collection of resources geared to nonlawyers (www.law.siu.edu/lawlib/) and a tradition of providing assistance to that population. Inmates who are nearing the end of their sentence are also anxious to find social services that can help prepare them for reentry in the workforce and provide access to other government benefits. Two examples of such web-based resources are the U.S. Department of Justice's Reentry (www.reentry.gov) and the Legal Action Center's National H.I.R.E. Network (www.hirenetwork.org).

School Libraries and Media Centers

The importance of e-government information literacy in school libraries and media centers is recognized by the inclusion of a program on this topic at the American Association of School Librarians' 2007 national conference: "Kids and Government Websites: Together @ your library." The program promises to share kid-friendly government websites available in all areas of curriculum and grade levels—sites that are authoritative, copyright free, and fun for kids. The benefits for media specialists listed in the program description include knowledge of e-government resources on other countries, statistics, careers, current affairs, and speech topics. "The more school media specialists know about government documents and websites, the better they will be able to assist students, teachers, and parents with information needs" (Williams 2007). Media specialists now have a rich and growing library of knowledge within easy access. Additional specific information on outreach to youth is available in chapter 6, which covers major resources for kids' online government information, including Kids.gov (www.kids.gov), the official children's gateway for the U.S. government and many others.

CONCLUSION

The wealth and variety of currently available e-government information benefit the many diverse populations in the United States. Libraries can improve services by routinely including e-government resources in library reference, instruction, programming, cataloging, and outreach activities. Uncovering the "hidden collection" of e-government information is the responsibility not only of documents librarians but of every librarian as the volume of digital resources from government agencies increases. Libraries of all types, including public, academic, special, and school, will find that using e-government information enhances their capacity to meet users' needs and helps them reach out to all user groups that have been underserved by the library community. The intrinsic value of these resources supports more efficient citizen-government interaction, improves quality of life, and documents the historic record. Librarians who realize their value will support activities within their libraries to make digital government information available to the communities they serve.

NOTES

1. On the National Bibliography, see U.S. Government Printing Office, Federal Depository Library Program, FDLP Desktop: National Bibliography Program, 2006, www.access.gpo .gov/su_docs/fdlp/cip/index.html. On the legacy collection, see U.S. Government Printing Office, Federal Depository Library Program, FDLP Desktop: GPO's Digitization and Preservation Initiatives, 2006, www.gpoaccess.gov/legacy/index.html.

2. See U.S. Department of Homeland Security, Federal Emergency Management Agency, Apply for Assistance, www.fema.gov/assistance/index.shtm; and U.S. Department of State, Citizenship and Nationality, http://travel.state.gov/law/citizenship/citizenship_782.html. Access the Newark Public Library Immigration Resources at www.npl.org/Pages/ InternetResources/SubjectGuides/immigrants.html.

3. For instructors' lesson plans, see Smithsonian Learn and Explore: Science and Technology for Educators, www.smithsonianeducation.org/educators/lesson_plans/science_technology .html.

4. U.S. Department of Health and Human Services, Administration for Children and Families, www.acf.hhs.gov/programs/add/; U.S. Department of Labor, Office of Disability Employment Policy, DisabilityInfo, www.disabilityinfo.gov; U.S. Department of Labor,

Find It by Audience—People with Disabilities, www.dol.gov/dol/audience/aud-disability .htm; Library of Congress, National Library Services for the Blind and Physically Handicapped, www.loc.gov/nls/; U.S. National Library of Medicine and the National Institutes of Health, MedlinePlus: Disabilities, www.nlm.nih.gov/medlineplus/disabilities.html.

5. See checklists of web design components for specific target groups at www.nlm.nih.gov/ pubs/checklist.pdf and www.utexas.edu/learn/accessibility/testing.html.

REFERENCES

American Association of Law Libraries. 2003. Washington Affairs Website. *State-by-State Report on Permanent Public Access to Electronic Government Information.* www .aallnet.org/aallwash/PPAreport.html.

GPO U.S. Government Printing Office. 2000. "Electronic Federal Depository Library Program: Transition Plan, FY 1996–FY 1998." www.gpo.gov/su_docs/ fdlp/retired/transit.html.

———. 2005. "2005 Minimum Technical Requirements for Public Access Workstations in Federal Depository Libraries." www.gpo.gov/su_docs/fdlp/ computers/mtr.html.

———. 2008. *Federal Depository Library Handbook.* Online ed. www.fdlp.gov/handbook/ index.html.

Hanson. Vicki L. 2004. "Accessibility: The User Experience: Designs and Adaptions." *Proceedings of the 2004 International Cross-Disciplinary Workshop on Web Accessibility.* New York: Association for Computer Machinery.

Mates, Barbara T. 2000. *Adaptive Technology for the Internet: Making Electronic Resources Accessible to All.* Chicago: American Library Association.

Schull, Diantha. 2004. "The Civic Library: A Model for 21st Century Participation." *Advances in Librarianship* 28. New York: Academic Press.

U.S. Department of Commerce, Economic and Statistics Administration, National Telecommunications and Information Administration. 2000. *Falling through the Net: Toward Digital Inclusion; A Report on Americans' Access to Technology Tools.* http://search.ntia.doc.gov/pdf/fttn00.pdf.

West, Darrell M. 2004. "E-Government and the Transformation of Service Delivery and Citizen Attitudes." *Public Administration Review* 64 (Jan./Feb.): 15–27.

Williams, Sandra. 2007. "Kids and Government Websites @ your library." Session description, American Association of School Librarians' 13th National Conference and Exhibition, conference website. www.eshow2000.com/aasl/conference_program .cfm.

Chapter 6   Reaching Out to Youth with Electronic Government Information

Karen Russ and Sarah Ziegenbein

The phrase "government publication" might bring to mind the image of endless transcripts of congressional testimony or statistics, but not resource materials for children. In fact, government agencies now offer a wide variety of material in different formats that can be used to supplement the educational experience for students and provide supporting materials for teachers. They can be widely used in libraries for children's websites or to support library programs for children. Materials include lesson plans and other activities designed for use in the classroom as well as activities students can explore independently. Some require a computer; others are to be printed for use in instruction. A growing percentage of these sites also include Spanish-language versions.

This chapter is a brief overview of selected recommended sites, highlighting our favorite U.S. government websites for children and adolescents. An explanation about technical requirements and accessibility for these online government resources for children precedes the discussion of two important gateways to kids' sites: Kids.gov and Ben's Guide. Finally, we discuss resources for perennial and emerging student needs such as science fair projects, primary source research, and finding online government materials.

Karen Russ has a BA in history from SUNY Fredonia and an MLS from SUNY Buffalo. She is currently the author of "What's Up?—Docs" for Arkansas Libraries. Russ has been active in GODORT since 1997, chairing both the Membership and Nominating Committees several times. She has also served as chair of the Government Documents Round Table of the Arkansas Library Association (ArLA) twice and as chair of the ArLA Conference Planning Committee for 2002. kmruss@ualr.edu

Sarah Ziegenbein has been government documents librarian at the Central Arkansas Library System since 1985. She has a BA in history from Georgia College at Milledgeville and an MLS from Florida State University. Ziegenbein has chaired the Reference Division of the Arkansas Library Association and the Government Documents Round Table, as well as the Arkansas Documents Consortium. She has also written articles for Arkansas Libraries. sarahz@cals.org

TECHNICAL ISSUES FOR ACCESSING CHILDREN'S GOVERNMENT WEBSITES

To make use of the websites discussed here, a certain amount of computer hardware and software is necessary. Because the equipment evolves as quickly as the websites, it is best to invest in the best equipment possible. The central processing unit (CPU) should be the most up to date, with as much memory as possible. It is also advisable to provide the highest-speed Internet connection possible. A dial-up modem will result in poor or no connection to most federal agency web pages; the detailed graphical interfaces cannot be supported on slow, aged equipment. Aim for the best audio and video cards possible to assure the best quality images and sound, because a growing number of websites include sound bytes with their graphics. Headphones are highly recommended, especially if there will be more than one computer in the area or if the computers are placed in a public area. If the computer will be alone in a secluded place, speakers are fine. Given the number of websites that offer the opportunity to download exercises or supplemental materials, flash drives or CD/DVD writable drives are suggested.

Printers are not required, but they are advantageous. A color printer is preferable. Except for the very detailed sites involving large maps, a basic printer that supports letter or legal size paper will suffice.

Software is as important as hardware. The latest edition of Adobe Reader should be installed and checked regularly for updates. Many sites do not offer backward compatibility, and if they do it is only for one or two upgrades of the reader. The machine should also be Javascript enabled. A few of the more developed websites require Adobe Flash Player or RealPlayer.

Although most sites operate nicely using Microsoft Internet Explorer or Netscape for web browsing, a few work better with Mozilla Firefox. Try to keep the latest edition of each browser installed on computers. Determining which is best for your library's and users' needs is a matter of trial and error. Regardless of which browser you use, pop-up blockers will be a problem. A large number of sites make use of pop-up windows to supplement materials, so you may need to disable your browser's pop-up blockers to allow some pages to operate to their fullest extent. The GPO publishes recommendations for workstation specification and minimum technical requirements for U.S. federal depository libraries that may be useful to all libraries accessing online government information. Technology, of course, costs money, and the U.S. Department of Education provides links to grant opportunities aimed at schools that will allow teachers to expand their classroom resources.[1]

An ongoing concern is the accessibility of websites for users with disabilities. Because all of these sites are supported by federal agencies, they are covered by the provisions of the Americans with Disabilities Act (ADA) of 1990, which requires that federal, state, and local governments provide qualified individuals with disabilities equal access to their programs, activities, or services, and this covers website design (see www.usdoj.gov/crt/ada/stdspdf.htm and www.ada.gov/websites2.htm). Unfortunately, many agencies offer only minimal compliance, and their websites are not accessible through the wide variety of software needed by various individuals with disabilities. A large number that use pop-up screens regularly cause problems with screen reading software. We recommend testing site compliance before any formal use, such as for assignments, to avoid frustration or disappointment later. Although many sites need additional progress in the area of accessibility, some offer specific sections for individuals with certain disabilities. Finding them is truly a matter of trial and error.

KIDS.GOV

USA.gov (www.usa.gov) is a general gateway to U.S. government websites and also state, local, and nongovernment websites. Several versions of USA.gov are available, including options for teachers and parents and for kids. The Kids section (www.kids.gov) is under the "For Citizens" tab on the home page banner, which also provides a link for "More Audiences," such as librarians and teachers. The site is designed intuitively, using colorful icons representing broad categories of information for the under-18 crowd. Games and other activities entertain while imparting useful information.

For those who know what subject interests them, selecting one of the images provides a list of websites on the topic, starting with government agency sites, federal and state. Some subjects then offer a list of nonprofit organizations' sites that have been investigated and approved by the creators of Kids.gov. Each section is arranged alphabetically by the name or topic of the site, not the agency producing it. The agency's name is in parentheses after the name of the site.

At a time when so many educators are concerned about student test scores in science and mathematics, the Science and Math link is an excellent place to turn. The math lessons are well hidden in fun activities like the "create your own code option" on CryptoKids or the flashcard-style math game at the Nez Perce National Historic Trail page. For youngsters who like nature, there are countless places to turn for scientific activities to pique their interests. If animals are the child's calling, start with Exploring Estuaries, from the EPA; here, the lives of birds, fishes, and other animals that live in or near rivers, ponds, and oceans can be explored through a virtual tour of several estuaries, and then games and activities reinforce the information just learned.

For those children whose minds drift farther from home, set off on a tour of the solar system with several sites sponsored by NASA. Rocket Science 101 recounts the creation of several rockets being used today for orbital and interplanetary spacecraft, including explanations of each part of the system and its purpose in the launch. Once in orbit, NASA's Kids Science News Network allows those in kindergarten through fifth grade to explore the astronauts' jobs in space and the interactions of various planets, moons, asteroids, and other heavenly bodies.

BEN'S GUIDE TO U.S. GOVERNMENT FOR KIDS

The other primary portal to children's content on the Web is Ben's Guide to U.S. Government for Kids (http://bensguide.gpo.gov), produced by the GPO. Many federal agencies could learn a great deal about developing websites for children by looking at Ben's Guide. The winner of numerous awards, this site introduces the design and function of the federal government using materials appropriate for age levels from kindergarten to twelfth grade. It also contains useful information for adults' reference.

Ben's Guide is an educational component of GPO Access, the GPO's free online service of official government information from all three branches of the U.S. government. Ben's Guide provides information and activities specifically tailored for educators, parents, and students in K–12. These resources can help teach students about our government and how it works. They can also teach about the primary source materials on GPO Access and how citizens can use GPO Access to carry out their civic responsibilities.

Ben's Guide was selected as a 2000 "Notable Children's Website," ranked in the top 2 percent of approximately 110,000 sites reviewed by BigChalk's Exceptional Websites thanks to its rich content and academic relevance. It was highlighted in the February 2001 issue of *Skewl Sites* newsletter as a top-notch resource to teach government topics and included in the *Scout Report* for January 21, 2000. Ben's Guide can be used on many levels—it is a gateway to government websites for children, an activity resource for teachers, and a reference tool. Users will notice some overlap with Kids.gov.

Ben's Guide is divided into four areas, for grades K–2, 3–5, 6–8, and 9–12. Each section explores community and government on a level and in terms appropriate for that grade level. More complex concepts are presented for each grade level.

Each area links to a section of Ben's Guide titled U.S. Government Websites for Kids (http://bensguide.gpo.gov/subject.html), which directs users to existing government and affiliated organization websites by agency or subject. Subjects are arranged by broad topic—for example, animals, agriculture, communities and people, crime and justice, environment. Interested students can explore the government websites listed to expand their knowledge in a specific area. Agencies with kids' websites are arranged by simplified name under the branch of government— for example, directing users to Congress, the courts, or the Agriculture, Education, Energy, or Health and Human Services departments. Independent establishments such as the Central Intelligence Agency, NASA, and the Peace Corps are also listed.

Ben's Guide also includes a section for parents and teachers, which enables them to explore ways to make effective use of the guide. The section on curriculum links directs the user to curriculum material already available at government websites or official partner sites. Lesson plans developed by government agencies generally have more than one access point—grade level, subject, geographic area, and others—making it easy for the teacher to locate a lesson plan or perhaps an activity to enrich an existing lesson plan.

SCIENCE FAIRS

Every year a certain number of students and parents groan when science fair projects come up. Picking a subject or experiment is not easy. Some topics are restricted or considered a pseudoscience and not allowed. A creative topic not only receives a better grade but will be more interesting to complete. If students use online government information to help pick a project, they are both encouraged and entertained. Start with Kids.gov and search "science fair projects." Although not every result will be on a .gov site, the .org and .com sites provided were selected for inclusion in Kids.gov on the basis of their quality of content.

If this is the student's first science fair entry, a stop at Science Buddies—Doing a Science Project (www.sciencebuddies.org/mentoring/science-projects.shtml) would be an excellent choice. From here, each step of the process is addressed with links to suggested topics, projects, research sites, and an Ask an Expert option. By asking questions at each step, students are guided to a selection of projects in their area of interest and skill level. The Science Buddies site provides guidance all the way from selecting a topic to putting the project results on display.

Science information for kids can be found on portals like Kids.gov, but a visit to almost any science-related federal agency student or children's site will also provide ideas for science projects. The Department of Energy's home page (www.energy .gov) links educators and students to curriculum plans and science fair projects and experiments. For example, the Department of Agriculture Science Fair site (www .ars.usda.gov/is/kids/fair/story.htm) offers project and experiment ideas covering a wide range of areas in botany, nutrition, chemistry, and zoology, The site also provides a well-written explanation of how to document the project, with information about writing the hypothesis, research procedure, and conclusion. To supplement the explanation of each section of the process, tips are provided on how to record information during the experiment for later analysis. The section on botany provides excellent reading material for preparing and presenting a top-quality experiment with results even if a student's project is on another subject.

PRIMARY SOURCE MATERIAL FOR KIDS

Government agencies can be rich resources for online primary source material for students, parents, and teachers. The use of primary sources is increasingly important in primary and secondary education, because it exposes students to multiple perspectives on events and issues. Prior to the electronic era, primary sources for younger students were limited to a few letters from a soldier overseas or maybe a diary in a local history collection. Students at the secondary level might have branched out and used an occasional editorial from the small town paper, but the options were few. In today's online world, materials like those in the Smithsonian museums' virtual exhibits offer invaluable resources for schools in rural areas or parents who are homeschooling.

The Smithsonian Institution's resources are a treasure trove for teachers, with lesson plans, activities, and other resources on subjects from art to zoology and all points in between. The Smithsonian is made up of museums, science centers, programs in conservation research, archives, and cultural and scholarly programs. According to its website, the Smithsonian archives hold an estimated 50,000 cubic feet of paper documents, 7 million still photographs, and thousands of film and audio recordings. Most of the museums, affiliates, and research centers have education directors and offices available to work with teachers. Some of the most appealing activities offered by museum education offices focus on classroom visits from schools in the Washington, DC, area. Many of them also provide material for distance learning, offering interactive electronic experiences that enhance a teacher's lesson plans. The Smithsonian website (www.si.edu) has separate pages for students and teachers. Pages for teachers present material in more detail than the students' pages and describe the student activities, whereas the students' pages have more online activities and content.

Find lesson plans via the handy tab at the top of the teachers' page, then select a topic or grade level or search by keyword. Many lesson plans developed by federal agencies use curriculum standards developed by national professional associations, allowing teachers to easily adapt the lesson plans to curriculum standards used in their own state. Often lesson plans begin by stating the applicable curriculum standard, skills addressed, interdisciplinary connections, length of time necessary for the lesson, additional materials required, and goal of the lesson. Necessary background information for the teacher's use is also provided, along with classroom activities. Many lesson plans are tied to specific Smithsonian exhibits and are linked to photos and primary materials used in the exhibit as well as the virtual exhibit. An effort is made to present balanced views.

An excellent example of a Smithsonian lesson plan is Lakota Winter Counts (http://wintercounts.si.edu/index.html), written by Anh-Thu Cunnion to accompany the exhibit curated by Candace Greene and provided by the National Museum of Natural History, one of the Smithsonian's affiliate museums: "Learn about Lakota life during the 19th century and the history of winter counts through interviews by contemporary Lakota community members, a searchable database of images from the winter counts, and anthropological data." Winter counts are histories or calendars used by the Lakota and other Plains Indians to record the years, using a picture to represent a major event of each year. The events chosen may not have been the most politically important event of that year but one that was memorable and widely known. That event might be a battle or treaty between two groups, or it could be an individual's death or some natural phenomenon. For instance, "The Year the Stars Fell" appears in several winter counts and was also widely known by non-Lakota people as the Leonid meteor storm of November 1833.

The National Archives and Records Administration also offers a wonderful assortment of historical, digital full-text materials. The educators' pages (www .archives.gov/education/) function as a digital classroom, offering complete lesson packets for teachers including activities for the students. The lessons are organized by eras in U.S. history and offer several events in each period. Each has primary documents, including photos, architectural drawings, and census forms, which can be incorporated into class discussions. Also provided are vocabulary lists, possible writing assignments, and presentation topics.

All public schools are required to observe Constitution Day (September 17), and the National Archives' materials on the Constitution provide educators with ideas that reach beyond just reading the document or making students memorize the Preamble. Part of the Teaching with Documents series is a set of lesson plans for students in grades 4–12. Supplementing the document online are worksheets that can be modified to reflect the involved grade level. To help with planning, each lesson even offers an estimate of how long each task will take to prepare and complete in class.

There is no need to abandon the Archives once Constitution Day has passed. The site also provides numerous activities on the student pages that allow individuals to pursue areas of personal interest. For those who might be visiting Washington, DC, in the near future, the link to Visiting the National Archives will help plan their trip. For those too far away to drop in, the Online Exhibits offer a chance to view dozens of thematic displays archived in the nation's capital as well as in presidential libraries or materials collections.

When you are searching for primary source materials, don't overlook the Library of Congress's American Memory project (http://memory.loc.gov/ammem/index.html), a treasure trove of photographs, maps, recordings, and art from America's past. Caution should be used when accessing this site, because the American Memory project is not designed specifically for children.

FINDING OTHER GOVERNMENT MATERIALS

At the beginning of this chapter we suggested going directly to government agencies for child-appropriate materials where a subject and agency obviously overlap, but if you have a topic and are unsure which agencies would be appropriate, start by consulting the *U.S. Government Manual* online (www.gpoaccess.gov/gmanual/index.html). Users may search the desired topic or agency to find an appropriate web page. Here is a sample of government websites beyond those reviewed above that offer suitable educational materials:

Environmental Protection Agency: www.epa.gov

Department of Health and Human Services: www.dhhs.gov

National Aeronautics and Space Administration: www.nasa.gov

National Air and Space Museum: www.nasm.si.edu

National Museum of American History: americanhistory.si.edu

National Museum of Natural History: www.mnh.si.edu

National Museum of the American Indian: www.nmai.si.edu

National Postal Museum: http://postalmuseum.si.edu

National Zoological Park: http://nationalzoo.si.edu

United States Mint: www.usmint.gov/index.cfm?flash=yes

FDLP libraries also welcome questions from the public. More than 1,250 public, academic, and other libraries offer access to government publications and assistance in their use. If you are not sure which library in your area is a federal depository, turn to the GPO depository library locator service (www.gpoaccess .gov/libraries.html). From this site, you can create a list of libraries by designating the state or area code in which you live.

If this piques your interest in using government materials with children and adolescents, you may wish to enhance your own skills by visiting the U.S. Department of Education website (www.ed.gov/index.jhtml), where separate sections for parents, teachers, students, and administrators are provided. Numerous links for lesson plans can be found here, but the real treasures are opportunities for further study, through either funding opportunities or fellowships. Teachers should explore the quick tips on topics such as multicultural teaching or classroom management or strategies for teaching children with special needs. The computer-savvy educator can also find links to web pages that assist effective use of computer technology in the classroom.

U.S. state and international government information online is equally kid friendly, current, authentic, and interesting to explore. Visit your state government pages and search under "kids" or "teachers" for resources. A quick search of the Web will also provide these resources. For foreign country information, check the Central Intelligence Agency's *World Factbook* (https://www.cia.gov/library/publica-tions/the-world-factbook/index.html). Each country's government section includes directory information on its foreign embassies in the United States, another good source of information. For international information, check under international governmental organizations, such as the United Nations' educational website for kids, Cyberschoolbus (www.un.org/Pubs/CyberSchoolBus/), which includes coun-try-at-a-glance and curriculum information.

CONCLUSION

Presenting government publications to children at an early age should not be intim-idating for the teacher, parent, or student. An early introduction to the government encourages future voters to be more informed citizens. Government documents also provide a wealth of information to support educational projects for teachers, parents, and students. As explored through the various sites described in this chapter, government documents can be used successfully with children and adolescents. Visit an agency online and encourage a child to explore the world.

NOTE

1. For GPO workstation technical requirements, see www.access.gpo.gov/su_docs/fdlp/computers/index.html. Explore the various options for Department of Education grant opportunities at www.ed.gov/fund/landing.jhtml?src=rt to see if your school is eligible for additional assistance.

Part II

Practices

Chapter 7 Collection Development

Handling Electronic Government Information through the Federal Depository Library Program and Beyond

Hui Hua Chua

T he explosion of e-government information from multiple sources such as the FDLP, government agencies, Internet archiving organizations, commercial vendors, and library and nonlibrary digitization projects has made collection development in the e-government information environment a challenging enterprise. Identifying, selecting, and providing access to government information now requires mastery of more complex tools and resources as well as an understanding of the new e-government information landscape. This chapter provides librarians, library and information science students, and library managers with an overview of online federal government information collection development.

FREE E-GOVERNMENT INFORMATION: SELECTING OR COLLECTING?

Free government information is widely available from many sources. As with print, a major source is still the 1,250 depository libraries participating in the FDLP. Equally important in offering access to government information are the originating agency's websites, websites of individuals or organizations, and library and nonlibrary digitization and preservation projects.

In practice, although information resources themselves may be available without charge, providing effective access to online government information, as with traditional printed resources, is costly for libraries and publishing agencies. There are costs for agencies in generating and making information available in the short and long term. There are costs to libraries in maintaining trained staff to manage collections, provide reference and instruction services for these collections, and create access points. A high degree of maintenance is required in all areas.

Hui Hua Chua is U.S. documents librarian at Michigan State University. She holds an MLS from Indiana University and an MA in history from the University of Auckland, New Zealand. She is active in GODORT. chua@mail.lib.msu.edu

What does it mean to "select" a freely available web-based resource? What constitutes a "library collection" in this context? What responsibilities does a library have for access, service, and archiving for the free electronic resources it selects or collects? These are the collection development questions raised by freely available web-based resources of all kinds, and the answers to these questions may be different for government information than for other resources. Additionally, different libraries pursue very different strategies and policies based on the needs of their users, the mission and priorities of their institutions, and available resources.

In the early years of the Internet, libraries were often reluctant to provide access to freely available web-based resources or to include catalog records for them in their library catalogs. Today few, if any, do not at least list some free electronic resources on their library web pages or web-based guides. Many libraries include bibliographic records with links to free government web resources in their library catalogs. Web guides represent the most common and most basic selection and access method for free government information. Such guides are relatively easy to implement, but they require time to identify suitable materials and place links on web pages. Cataloging resources requires more work from in-house technical services staff or the purchase of bibliographic records from a vendor, but it is also usually part of mainstream technical services processes in many libraries. If cataloging resources are limited, it may be that only a carefully selected set of resources can be added to the catalog. Selecting resources that already have catalog records in a bibliographic utility such as OCLC's WorldCat is one approach in this circumstance, but it limits resources selected to more mainstream materials. Another approach is to add never-cataloged online resources to the library catalog selectively, using records produced by the library itself. This method, however, requires greater cataloging expertise. A library's primary mission and clientele, as well as available resources and existing workflows, dictate the methods of access selected.

Planning for maintenance is as important as creating the original link or record. Link checking can be accomplished in various ways. Many integrated library systems can generate regular automated reports for links in catalogs. Links on web pages can be checked using web development software or stand-alone link-checking software. Information technology infrastructure and public service requirements for providing good user access to e-government information can also affect selection decisions and should be taken into account. For more on these topics, see chapters 2 and 9.

These methods of providing access to online government information integrate government information resources into a library's main resource discovery tools rather than segregating them from other resources. By providing such links, libraries continue to fulfill their role of identifying, evaluating, and providing access to valuable resources, selected from the vast array of information on the Internet. Costs in time and staffing for ongoing maintenance are balanced by providing users with the best current information and reduced user frustration with dead links.

Although the methods discussed above for providing access to e-government information meet short-term user needs, libraries selecting and providing access to freely available resources must also decide on a policy for ensuring long-term access to materials of enduring value to their users. Do libraries assume the same archiving responsibilities for their electronic selections as with print collections? Strategies vary widely. Some rely on the GPO or other (primarily federal depository) libraries for long-term preservation of e-government information from the depository program.

The GPO currently archives publications it catalogs with a PURL and plans to integrate preservation and archiving into its Federal Digital System (FDsys; www .gpo.gov/projects/fdsys.htm). Librarians should closely monitor development of this system, for its functionality and capabilities will affect the GPO's archiving activities.[1] These activities will have a considerable impact on decisions to select electronic-only depository materials. Libraries also need to track other FDsys issues that affect their decision to select electronic-only material, such as authentication of electronic document content and the multiple versions of a document. Organizations such as the Depository Library Council (DLC) and GODORT have produced valuable commentary and responses to earlier proposals and should also be monitored as FDsys becomes a reality.

Selecting only depository materials in electronic format has the advantage of not requiring local resources for digital archiving, allowing libraries to focus on providing access and service for its users. The University of Arizona is a federal depository library that has chosen this method as the primary means of selecting and providing access to e-government information. Its decision to become the first of many government information service centers was based on its analysis of its primary user population and their strong preference for web-based resources (Rawan, Malone, and Bender 2004). It does not archive electronic materials locally, relying on the GPO and other organizations, but it does provide access and reference help to users, support from library administration and staff, and collection management.

Still, some librarians argue that centralizing responsibility for digital preservation at the GPO makes government information vulnerable for financial, political, and technological reasons (Jacobs, Jacobs, and Yeo 2005). In this view, libraries have an ongoing responsibility to locally archive and preserve for permanent access their digital collections, in addition to selecting content using the methods described above. To accomplish this, many librarians have argued strongly for digital deposit of documents to allow libraries to preserve publications locally.

The GPO's first response to these requests was a pilot of the Lots of Copies Keep Stuff Safe (LOCKSS) model for digital preservation. This model creates multiple caches at different institutions, with content integrity maintained by constant cross-checking of material between caches and repair of content that is missing or corrupted. Local caches provide access to materials if the original content is not available. See more on LOCKSS in chapters 12 and 14.

The GPO has recently proposed wider dissemination of digital documents for local access, preservation, and archiving at federal depository libraries, though policy and operational details have yet to be finalized (GPO 2006d). An excellent resource for ongoing information about archiving and preservation of digital government information in general is the Free Government Information site (http://freegovinfo .info), which maintains news and commentary on these critical issues and should be checked regularly.

Although the GPO is an important player, some libraries and library consortia are also pursuing independent strategies for local or shared archiving of digital publications. The GPO's 2005 *Biennial Survey* indicated that 163 libraries were already archiving some federal government information content, with another 334 willing to host material (GPO 2006a). The scale of these initiatives varies greatly, and they are further discussed in chapters 3 and 12. Some libraries archive publications on a case-by-case basis on disks or local hard drives. Some like the New Mexico State Library systematically identify and capture regional federal agency documents overlooked by the GPO (Clark, Skeers, and Canepa 2006). Others such as the University of North Texas (http://digital.library.unt.edu/govdocs/) focus on entire collections from specific agencies such as the Congressional Research Service. Many state libraries such as the Arizona State Library (Pearce-Moses and Kaczmarek 2005) are involved in large-scale automated harvesting of entire government agency websites, or, in the case of the California Digital Library, websites of historical significance that are likely to be removed in a certain time frame, such as election-related websites (California Digital Library 2006). Other libraries purchase commercial online products with archival rights such as to the *U.S. Congressional Serial Set* to ensure permanent access to these collections or rely on print or microform versions for archival purposes. Libraries are most likely to rely on a combination of strategies rather than depend on a single method for best ensuring long-term access to electronic resources (Norris 2002).

The primary advantage of local or shared control of an archive is the greater assurance of permanent access to selected publications, so that libraries can ensure that their users still have access to critical materials when the original source is temporarily or permanently unavailable. Temporary lack of availability (e.g., due to system upgrades of GPO Access servers, which host core U.S. congressional and legislative publications), though not common, is frustrating for users. Deliberate removal of government information from agency websites, whether to ensure that only the most recent information or version of a publication is available or for political purposes, represents another compelling reason to maintain local or distributed archives.

Another advantage to locally hosted government information is that libraries can combine it with nongovernment information or add functionality such as data manipulation for statistical information to create rich information sources to better serve their users. An excellent example of such a project is the Counting California website (http://countingcalifornia.cdlib.org), which combines federal and California state statistical information in a common interface. The disadvantage is the financial, technological, and human resource cost. This, of course, has always been the difficulty, even with tangible collections.

Nonlibrary organizations also archive government information in digital format. Some like the Internet Archive (www.archive.org) include government information as part of larger archives. Others like the Memory Hole (www.thememoryhole .org), the Federation of American Scientists (www.fas.org), and George Washington University's National Security Archive (www.gwu.edu/~nsarchiv/) focus on fugitive or withdrawn government information or archive specialized collections. These organizations offer additional assurance of preservation, but libraries have little input into their archiving decisions and thus cannot readily rely on these sites for long-term access. The reliability and authenticity of information and publications on these sites must also be carefully evaluated, given that the provenance and version control of publications on these sites are not always clear. These sites may, however, offer the only alternative to remotely hosted government information that is suddenly unavailable. In some instances this has included information distributed through the federal depository program but not archived by the GPO. Examples include the National Institute of Medicine's *Magnuson Clinical Center's Medical Staff Handbook.*[2] In other cases, as with the declassified information on the National Security Archive website, they offer information not easily available elsewhere. Thus, librarians need to be aware of these sites and how they supplement a library's own selections or collections, though relying on them for permanent access to information of critical importance to a library's users is unlikely to be the best strategy.

Although there are clearly common practices in selection and provision of access to no-fee online U.S. federal government information, there is far less consensus regarding archiving. It is highly likely that libraries will pursue a combination of strategies for different types of e-government information, depending on their unique priorities, missions, and resources. A modest plan might include archiving significant publications locally in digital format, relying on print or microform versions for preserving other publications, while depending on remote archives for the rest.

E-GOVERNMENT INFORMATION RECEIVED VIA THE FDLP

A major source of U.S federal e-government information is still the FDLP. The GPO continues to collect and catalog e-government information from the federal government, as it does for tangible publications. Unlike tangible publications, electronic publications are freely available to all libraries regardless of depository status and to the public. Though it is possible to access the same electronic resources directly from federal agency websites, depository program tools offer an efficient method for libraries to identify, review, and select resources from a large, highly structured collection of free federal government information.

Selection tools from the GPO for depository materials are available to all libraries. These tools usually include publications in multiple formats such as the *Statistical Abstract of the United States,* which is available in print, CD-ROM, and online. This allows librarians to evaluate the various format options available to them and to select the most appropriate one for their users, but sometimes it makes it difficult to search for, review, and select specifically electronic information products. GPO selection tools often assume some understanding of the item number system or Superintendent of Documents Classification System (SuDocs), and most organize publications by the publishing agency rather than by subject, the traditional organization for selection and review tools in the wider library community. Those wishing to use GPO tools must familiarize themselves with at least the basics of government structure and the functions of various agencies and departments. Good resources for learning about government structures are the *U.S. Government Manual* and the "A-Z agency index" section of USA.gov (www.usa.gov). The *Federal Depository Library Handbook* offers guidelines and best practices for collection development of federal e-government information and related issues and is of great value to all libraries. GPO resources can also be supplemented with several other review and selection tools.

BUILDING A CORE COLLECTION

The GPO's Basic Collection—items all FDLP libraries are required to select—lists thirty-two publications or databases consisting of core reference titles such as the *Statistical Abstract of the United States* or databases such as GPO Access that include the official legal and administrative documents of the federal government. All are available in electronic format. A related list is the Essential Titles for Public Use in Paper Format. Despite its title, almost all titles included are also available in electronic format. Resources on these lists are valuable to libraries serving a wide range of users and should be considered for selection by all libraries.[3]

One common selection method is to review materials selected by similar libraries. In 2005, the GPO created lists of the most frequently selected depository titles by library type. Although created for a very different purpose, these lists allow those unfamiliar with government publications to use their peer institutions' selections to guide their own. Lists are available in the Essential Titles Spreadsheet on the Essential Titles List, Proposed Revision web page; electronic products available without charge exclusively to depository libraries are listed on the Depository Access to Online Subscription Services page.[4] This last web page includes valuable electronic resources such as STAT-USA (www.stat-usa.gov) and the National Climatic Data Center Online Document Library (www5.ncdc.noaa.gov/pubs/publications.html), which provide key trade and climatological statistics. Nondepository libraries could use the Subscription Services page to review fee-based products that depositories and the GPO have deemed sufficiently important to warrant free access through the depository program.

Appendix A of the *Federal Depository Library Handbook* (GPO 2008) recommends publications suitable for core collections in public, academic, and law libraries. Organized by item number, it provides a SuDocs classification number and title for each publication. Because no URLs are listed, selecting and providing access to the electronic versions of these publications is likely to be a time-consuming process.

Various notable documents lists are created annually by national and state government documents groups and can be used to identify recently published materials as well as older materials from prior lists. Librarians from ALA/GODORT select a list of notable international, federal, and state publications, which is published in the May 15 issue of *Library Journal*. State documents groups are a good resource for state government publications. Lists are generally published on the Web and can be found by searching state library or state library association websites. One example is the New York State Notable Documents (www.nysl.nysed.gov/edocs/notable.htm). Most publications on these lists are now mainly, though not exclusively, electronic.

Free government information resources are also regularly reviewed in standard collection development sources such as *Choice, Booklist, Library Journal*'s *NetConnect* supplement, and *School Library Journal*. These provide more evaluative information, are published regularly, and are usually already part of the standard reviewing repertoire of librarians. As such they are good selection tools for ongoing collection development.

BUILDING SUPPLEMENTARY COLLECTIONS

The GPO provides more comprehensive tools that include all publications available through the depository program. For those familiar with government information and structures these offer great detail and granularity, though without evaluative information or subject classification. Documents Data Miner 2 (DDM2; http://govdoc.wichita.edu/ddm2/) collates information from individual GPO publications and tools and is extremely useful for managing collections. It allows users to search or sort the *List of Classes* (a comprehensive list of materials available for selection from the GPO) by title, format, or publishing agency as well as to see which depository libraries in the same state or region have selected the same publication or publication set. Libraries can then use peer institutions' selections to aid their own selection decisions, though this method is time consuming, with more than 4,000 individual titles or series of electronic publications currently available for selection. This tool allows librarians to view a comprehensive list of available publication series, but it requires the ability to link the agency publisher with a subject area. Nondepository libraries must search this database regularly for new series or titles for addition to their selections, whereas the GPO automatically adds new publications on a similar topic from the same agency to depository libraries' selections based on their current recorded selections.

Libraries wanting to be highly selective in their selection of e-government information may wish to review the New Electronic Titles regularly and select materials on a title-by-title basis.[5] This list is based on electronic materials distributed through the depository system and cataloged by the GPO within a certain date range. Since the list always includes a URL, titles can be reviewed easily. Searches can also be conducted in the *Catalog of Government Publications* to find electronic publications by subject. This method offers the most control and specificity of selection for new materials, the main drawback being the large number of resources for review each month (nearly six hundred new titles in January 2008). New capabilities are planned for the *Catalog* that will allow users to save searches and receive automatic e-mail or RSS updates of new resources matching their search parameters, potentially automating some aspects of this selection method.

Subject-based bibliographies or lists can complement the Documents Data Miner 2, and several are available. Browse Topics (www.browsetopics.gov) features government information resources selected mainly by government information librarians by topic. Many libraries have also created subject guides that can be used for collection development purposes. These may include international, federal, state, and local government information resources as well as some fee-based sites. Examples include the University of Louisville's very detailed Government Resources pages, the Government Documents pages of the Tulsa City-County Library, and the University of Colorado, Boulder's Web Subject Guides. Many depository libraries have dedicated subject guides for government information, and local depositories or those of a similar size and type are most likely to list resources suitable for similar libraries. Depository libraries and their websites are listed in the *Federal Depository Library Directory.*[6]

Instead of selecting materials on a title-by-title basis, many large depository libraries wanting to develop comprehensive collections in a range of subjects simply select all publications from a specific agency or all electronic publications available from the GPO. This is an efficient selection method requiring less regular review of new materials. Libraries using this method frequently combine it with a purchase of bibliographic records for their selections from vendors such as Marcive or regular batch download of records from the Documents Data Miner 2, which provides records for no cost.

A major disadvantage of the selection tools and methods discussed above is the gap between publication of a resource and its appearance in a selection or review tool. Timeliness is critical for significant government publications. These are often featured prominently in the news media, generating interest and demand for the source publication. Waiting for the GPO to catalog such materials or for them to be reviewed leads to delays in availability to library users. Fortunately, there are many blogs that focus on new or "hot" government publications. Many are updated daily or several times a day. Docuticker (www.docuticker.com) is a selection of resources and publications from all levels of U.S. and international government. Many regional blogs, such as *New Mexico News Plus*, focus on government information of national significance as well as that of particular interest to New Mexico residents. Subject-oriented blogs such as the Documents section of *Jurist* (http://jurist.law.pitt.edu/gazette/) from the University of Pittsburgh provide links to government reports, legislation, court decisions, statistics, and regulations reported in the news from the United States and the world. Electronic mailing lists such as GOVDOC-L frequently report on major new publications, and USA.gov allows librarians to receive new publication notifications directly from an agency.[7] Many blogs and newsletters also offer RSS feeds that librarians can use to track sites and publications efficiently.

The GPO has proposed major changes in depository selection mechanisms. These would allow librarians to select the entire publication output of an agency or bureau or use collection development tools to select electronic materials by title, subject, geography, or agency more easily (GPO 2006b). If implemented, these changes will affect the selection tools offered to libraries as well as the organization of resources available through these tools. Librarians have provided feedback on the proposals, but final implementation decisions rest with the GPO. Given the potential effect of these new selection mechanisms on collection development, librarians should closely monitor the GPO's actions in this regard.

E-GOVERNMENT INFORMATION BEYOND THE DEPOSITORY PROGRAM

Many free e-government publications, either current or historical, never become part of the depository program. More and more historical government publications are being digitized by libraries, government agencies, and mass digitization projects such as the Google Books project but are not considered part of the depository program by the GPO, though the original print materials may have been.[8] Other publications fall outside the scope of the depository program or are simply overlooked by the GPO. The latter are generally referred to as "fugitive documents." This is a longstanding problem even in the print environment, with an estimate of about 50 percent of federal printed documents falling into this category. The exact percentage of fugitive online documents is unknown, but the print ratio offers a best-guess estimate for online publications (Baldwin 2003). The GPO's pilot web harvesting program was developed to address the issue of fugitive publications, though test results have been mixed (GPO 2006c). Librarians remain concerned about ongoing loss of information while the harvesting system is evaluated and implemented. Libraries should track this initiative but realize that they should still actively pursue identification, selection, and collection of fugitive material outside the depository system.

There are many libraries, government agencies, and other organizations digitizing historical government publications. The GPO also aims to digitize all historical government publications eventually (GPO 2006e). Projects range in scale from single works to mass collections of thousands of publications. The GPO has created the *Registry of U.S. Government Publication Digitization Projects* (www.gpoaccess .gov/legacy/registry/) to collect information on digitization projects with significant federal government information content.[9] This is a good starting point for discovering historical digitization projects, but librarians should also monitor federal agency websites and major review sources for other projects, particularly those that do not consist primarily of federal government publications, since these are less likely to be in the *Registry*. Librarians should certainly monitor mass digitization projects such as those from Google Book Search Library Project (http://books.google .com/googleprint/library.html) and the Open Content Alliance (www.opencontent alliance.org) as well as the participating library partners who may provide their own access points to the collections. Still, although these mass digitization projects promise large numbers of historical documents, their reliance on a few large collections means that historically nondepository documents such as U.S. congressional committee prints and historical fugitive documents will not always be included. In addition, access restrictions to materials, such as on post-1923 hearings on Google Books, and possible membership requirements or charges mean that libraries have to evaluate their reliance on these projects carefully.

Significant groups of publications that fall outside the depository program include those from agencies such as the Congressional Research Service[10] and unofficial government publications such as the *Taguba Report*,[11] which was classified though an unofficial version was made available by the news media. Other categories include publications from quasi-governmental organizations listed in the *U.S. Government Manual* such as the National Academy of Sciences and publications that cannot be distributed in the United States because the Smith-Mundt Act prohibits U.S. distribution of publications prepared by certain agencies for foreign audiences.[12] Publications created by government contractors rather than government employees, commonly known as contract publications, also fall outside the scope of the depository program. These primarily scientific and technical reports form a substantial body of government information not within the program. Several categories of publications fall into the area of gray literature, information that is not commercially published and often not easily available to the public, since it is largely designed for internal or specialized users. Finally, the GPO is also unable to keep up with the flood of electronic information published by individual agencies and may simply not be aware of many publications.

Librarians can identify nondepository and fugitive documents in several ways. Some categories of material or series such as CRS Reports are widely known to be outside the scope of the program. New reports in such series are often featured in the news media, new publication lists from agencies, and government information blogs monitoring depository publications.[13] Some nondepository materials are available for subscription or purchase from commercial vendors. These are an efficient alternative for securing access to nondepository materials, though libraries usually still have to search for specific publications that fall within the scope of their collection but are not available through the depository program, since not all materials are available for purchase.

The Thomas Branigan Memorial Library, a public library in Las Cruces, Mexico, actively selects and acquires Spanish-language e-government information. A librarian regularly selects an agency at random and searches its publication web page for suitable materials or uses a search engine to search for Spanish-language government publications on a specific topic. Suitable publications have a bibliographic record downloaded into the local library catalog from OCLC if a record is available. If not, the library creates an original record. The publication is then submitted to the New Mexico State Library for local archiving (Veatch and Veatch 2006). This is clearly a time- and resource-intensive process that requires local resources for cataloging as well as collaboration with another institution for preservation. Along with the benefits of local as well as wider access to the cataloged publication through OCLC, this work ensures future preservation of the publication.

Libraries may choose other strategies for dealing with nondepository or fugitive publications. Fugitive publications within the scope of the depository program can be reported to the GPO for cataloging and archiving via the GPO's Online Knowledge Base (www.gpoaccess.gov/help/index.html). Once cataloged by the GPO, other libraries are made aware of this material, and preservation by the GPO is more likely. A disadvantage is the processing and cataloging time. This is also not a viable approach for nondepository publications. For these, a library must choose the resources to allocate for identifying, providing access to, and archiving this material.

FEE-BASED E-GOVERNMENT INFORMATION

A wide range of commercial government information products are available. Some replicate content that is fully available for no charge on government websites. These include the many large aggregator databases aimed at general public or academic library audiences, such as Gale's General OneFile, EBSCO's MasterFile products, or Proquest's Research Library, which include several government information serials or publications.

Other vendors offer indexing or other tools that supplement or complement free online collections. An example is the American Statistical Index (ASI) component of the LexisNexis statistical database, which indexes federal statistical publications but provides only selected full-text content. The rest is often available online without charge from the agency. The ability to search across content from government and nongovernment sources is a feature of many of the aggregator and indexing tools, making it easier for users to access information from all sources. Many may also offer greater indexing and functionality for search, display, and retrieval than their free equivalents. Some, though not all, may provide use statistics that libraries require for reporting or assessment purposes.[14]

Commercial sources can also provide more comprehensive or exclusive access to some types of government information. Examples of such products are Proquest's Digital National Security Archive and Gale's Declassified Documents Reference System (www.galegroup.com). Although some of these documents are available on government agency Freedom of Information Act sites, these products offer more comprehensive collections than are available on agency websites.

Some vendors offer online products with archival rights. In this scenario, a library purchases the online content and pays a small annual fee for the vendor to host and provide access to the content or, upon purchase, receives copies of the online content for hosting and presentation on the library's own servers. The former scenario is far more common, with the library receiving only a copy of its purchase if it no longer wishes to pay the annual hosting fee, or if the vendor can no longer provide hosting. The prevalence of the remote hosting model of ownership is the most likely reason libraries may sometimes be willing to purchase ownership rights from vendors but be reluctant to archive freely available information. In this model, libraries can wait until digital preservation technologies and strategies are more stable and tested while securing ongoing access to core publications. This strategy does, however, presume the stability and continued existence of the vendor.

In summary, superior indexing and functionality, more comprehensive content, and ownership rights are some major reasons to purchase commercial versions of free government information, though each product still needs to be evaluated individually. Subscription costs and reliance on vendors for archiving are major drawbacks.

Although fee-based products can be costly, the most pressing challenge facing librarians trying to justify subscription or purchase costs can be the perception that all government information is available without charge on the Internet. This is clearly evident for products involving recent government publications, but the advent of mass digitization projects that promise free availability of massive collections of historical government publications has also convinced many that this is true for government publications of all time periods. As described above, though, there may well be access restrictions to online government information that make relying on these collections problematic as well as significant gaps in these collections' comprehensiveness.

Commercial products may also replicate a library's print or microform collections, whether acquired through the depository program or through purchase. Duplication of content, albeit in a different format, is often difficult to justify— but it may be necessary given the volatility of digital formats and the uncertainty regarding our ability to preserve born-digital content (Conway 1996).

The benefits of online products vis-à-vis their tangible equivalents and the functionality and content comprehensiveness of some commercial products over their free equivalents need to be understood clearly by library decision makers. Distinctions between the different types of government information (depository, nondepository, and fugitive) and their corresponding short- and long-term availability on government websites or through mass digitization projects need to be articulated clearly, so that the differences between free and commercial government information resources are recognized. With this information, collection and user priorities as defined in the library's collection development policies can be used to determine the best collection options for a library.

Identifying, selecting, processing, and archiving free resources is a time-consuming and resource-intensive process, requiring subject expertise and infrastructure. E-government information from government websites or the GPO may be free of charge, but providing and maintaining useful and meaningful short- and long-term access to it is not. Library workflows, processes, and staff, especially in large libraries, are often designed to manage commercial products rather than free electronic resources. These costs also need to be taken into account when comparing the costs of free government information with the cost of commercial products.

CONCLUSION

Although the quantity and form of available government information have changed dramatically in the past ten years, collection development processes for identifying, selecting, providing access to, and preserving government information are still of vital importance in the electronic era. A greater range of discovery and selection tools are available, from FDLP tools to blogs, but the challenges of building collections and providing access to nondepository and fugitive information have also increased. Strategies for locating and managing fugitive and gray literature, in particular, warrant close attention.

Given limited resources and the real costs of selecting, managing, and providing access to resources often perceived as free of charge, libraries have to weigh carefully the options for selection, collection, and, in particular, providing permanent access to online government information to their users. Will libraries rely on the GPO, other libraries and archiving organizations, local archiving, vendor products, print and microform formats or a combination of all these strategies? As mass digitization projects progress, librarians should continue to collaborate with digitizing and archiving organizations and use these resources fully to serve their users. But they must also continue to scrutinize and understand the details and complexities of these projects, paying particular attention to potential or actual access restrictions. Further research on these large-scale digitization projects and their impact on libraries' collections and services is needed.

NOTES

1. Another more regularly updated source of information on the FDsys is the Federal Digital System blog (http://fdsys.blogspot.com) maintained by GPO staff.
2. Paul Schaffer, e-mail to GOVDOC-L mailing list, July 24, 2006, http://lists1.cac.psu.edu/cgi-bin/wa?A2=ind0607D&L=GOVDOC-L&P=R163&I=-3.
3. Basic Collection, GPO 2004, www.access.gpo.gov/su_docs/fdlp/coll-dev/basic-01.html; Essential Titles for Public Use in Paper Format, GPO 2006, www.access.gpo.gov/su_docs/fdlp/pubs/estitles.html.
4. Essential Titles List, Proposed Revision, GPO 2006, www.access.gpo.gov/su_docs/fdlp/coll-dev/proposed-estitles.html; Depository Access to Online Subscription Services, GPO 2004, www.access.gpo.gov/su_docs/fdlp/coll-dev/pw-serv.html.
5. *Catalog of Government Publications: New Electronic Titles*, GPO, http://catalog.gpo.gov/F/?func=file&file_name=find-net&local_base=NEWTITLE.
6. University of Louisville, Government Resources, http://library.louisville.edu/government/subjects/subject.html; Tulsa City-County Library, Government Documents, www.tulsalibrary.org/govdocs/; and University of Colorado, Boulder, Web Subject Guides, http://ucblibraries.colorado.edu/govpubs/us/federal.htm. *Federal Depository Library Directory*, GPO 2006, http://catalog-gpo.gov/fdlpdir/login.jsp.
7. *New Mexico News Plus*, www.stlib.state.nm.us/services_more.php?id=361_0_13_0_M640; Federal Citizen Information Center, Office of Citizen Services and Communications, U.S. General Services Administration, 2006, Subscribe to Government Email Newsletters, http://apps.gsa.gov/FirstGovCommonSubscriptionService.php.

8. When the original publishing agency digitizes its own historical publications or a GPO partner conducts retrospective digitization, as with the Census Bureau's digitization of historical Census of Population and Housing volumes, these publications become available to the depository program through GPO cataloging. However, products of retrospective digitization from nonagency or nonpartner organizations such as Google Books are not made available in this manner. Information about Google Books is current as of December 2006.

9. The original registry was created by the ALA GODORT's Government Information Technology Committee, and this became the basis of the GPO's registry.

10. Comprehensive alert services for these reports are available through Gallerywatch (www .gallerywatch.com) for a fee, and OpenCRS (www.opencrs.com) offers a free RSS feed of new reports registered with their site, though this is a smaller, less comprehensive list.

11. This was a report by Maj. Gen. Antonio Taguba on the alleged abuse of detainees at the Abu Ghraib Prison in Baghdad: Antonio Taguba, *The "Taguba Report" on Treatment of Abu Ghraib Prisoners in Iraq*, available from http://news.findlaw.com/hdocs/docs/iraq/tagubarpt.html.

12. *U.S. Information and Educational Exchange Act of 1948*, Public Law 402, 80th Cong., 2nd sess. (January 27, 1948). Examples include publications from the U.S. Department of State's Bureau of International Information Programs.

13. These include many of the blogs and newsletters noted in the section on building supplementary collections. Additional monitoring resources include Secrecy News (www .fas.org/blog/secrecy/) and OpenCRS (www.opencrs.com).

14. Vendors such as Proquest and EBSCO, for example, provide statistical reports compliant with Project COUNTER's code of practice endorsed by many library associations, consortia, and individual libraries for measuring use of online information products and services; see www.projectcounter.org/articles.html.

REFERENCES

Baldwin, Gil. 2003. "Fugitive Documents: On the Loose or On the Run." *Administrative Notes* 24 (10): 4–8. www.access.gpo.gov/su_docs/fdlp/pubs/adnotes/ ad081503.html.

California Digital Library. 2006. The Web at Risk: A Distributed Approach to Preserving Our Nation's Political Cultural Heritage. www.cdlib.org/inside/ projects/preservation/webatrisk/.

Clark, Kirsten, Timothy Skeers, and Laurie Canepa. 2006. "New Mexico News Plus: Anticipatory Reference, Instruction, and Collection Development Tool." University Libraries, University of Colorado, Boulder. http://ucblibraries .colorado.edu/govpubs/conference/handouts/NewMexicoPlus.ppt.

Conway, Paul. 1996. "Preservation in the Digital World." www.clir.org/pubs/reports/ conway2/.

GPO U.S. Government Printing Office. 2006a. "Update for ALA January 2006." www.access.gpo.gov/su_docs/fdlp/events/ala_update06.pdf.

———. 2006b. FDLP Selection Mechanisms: Item Numbers and Alternatives. www .access.gpo.gov/su_docs/fdlp/selection/.

———. 2006c. "GPO Harvesting Pilot." www.access.gpo.gov/su_docs/fdlp/pubs/ proceedings/06fall/webharvesting.pdf.

———. 2006d. "Digital Distribution to Depository Libraries: Exploring the Issues." www.access.gpo.gov/su_docs/fdlp/council/fall06/digitaldistribution06.pdf.

———. 2006e. GPO's Digitization and Preservation Initiatives. www.gpoaccess.gov/legacy/index.html.

———. 2008. *Federal Depository Library Handbook.* Online ed. www.fdlp.gov/handbook/index.html.

Jacobs, James A., James R. Jacobs, and Shinjoung Yeo. 2005. "Government Information in the Digital Age: The Once and Future Federal Depository Library Program." *Journal of Academic Librarianship* 31 (3): 198–208.

Norris, Rebecca. 2002. "Obtaining Archival Copies of Online Only Depository Documents." University of Michigan University Library. www.lib.umich.edu/govdocs/godort/admin/coll/archdpos.htm.

Pearce-Moses, Richard, and Joanne Kaczmarek. 2005. "An Arizona Model for Preservation and Access of Web Documents." *DttP: Documents to the People* 33 (1): 17–24.

Rawan, Atifa, Cheryl Knott Malone, and Laura J. Bender. 2004. "Assessing the Virtual Depository Program: The Arizona Experience." *Journal of Government Information* 30 (5/6): 710–726.

Veatch, Jim, and Justine Veatch. 2006. *U.S. Government Information: Los Fugitivos.* University Libraries, University of Colorado, Boulder. http://uclibraries.colorado.edu/govpubs/conference/handouts/LosFugitivos.ppt.

Chapter 8 U.S. Government Printing Office Practices for Cataloging Electronic Resources

John A. Stevenson

The major challenges to managing e-government information resources are related to change. Not only has the nature of electronic resources changed greatly over the past decade, but cataloging rules and practices for electronic resources are also evolving.[1] In late 2007, the GPO began to test and implement the use of brief records for items being acquired, with the intent that any titles brought into the FDLP would be later cataloged to a higher standard, and it also expanded its use of abridged cataloging records.

In this chapter we describe essential principles guiding GPO cataloging practice since 1976 and seek to explain where GPO practices are going for librarians in technical and public services who work with the records. We include a brief history of the GPO's cataloging of electronic resources for the FDLP and outline critical MARC fields used in GPO records with examples. Observations as to the direction of future GPO practices conclude the chapter. This chapter addresses cataloging of all levels of government information (local, state, federal, and international), but its main focus is GPO cataloging of U.S. federal electronic resources. Additional specific information on new significant bibliographic initiatives not yet standardized in the GPO's policies and practices, such as the Functional Requirements for Bibliographic Records (FRBR) and Resource Description and Access (RDA) are covered in chapter 9.

John A. Stevenson is associate librarian and coordinator of the government documents and maps processing unit at the University of Delaware Library. He holds a BA in history from Binghamton University and an MLS from the University at Buffalo. He has been active in GODORT since 1991, serving as GODORT chair in 2004/5 and as Cataloging Committee webmaster, editing the online Toolbox for Processing and Cataloging Federal Government Documents. He contributed to two editions of the GPO's Superseded List: U.S. Documents That May Be Discarded by Depository Libraries, Annotated for Retention by Regional Depositories. *He has also served on the Depository Library Council to the Public Printer and in ALA's Map and Geography Round Table. varken@UDel.edu*

Although librarians know that not everything is online, it has been casually observed that almost any *worthwhile* title in the FDLP may be available online in some format. It is certainly true that current FDLP titles of significance are available online, and increasingly historically significant titles are online too. A library seeking to manage a large collection of federal electronic resources may find it cost effective to use records in its integrated library system (ILS), allowing users to find electronic resources as well as books in the library's catalog. High-quality catalog records for U.S. federal resources produced by GPO catalogers are readily available. Understanding the GPO's depository selection and cataloging practices for electronic resources supports effective use of the records in catalogs. All of the manuals and tools cited here are available through the ALA/GODORT Cataloging Committee Toolbox for Processing and Cataloging Federal Government Documents (ALA 1999).

The primary source for GPO cataloging practice is *Government Printing Office Cataloging Guidelines* (GPO 2002). The GPO uses MARC codes and content designators to create bibliographic and authority records that are used in OCLC, the GPO's own catalog, and library catalogs around the world. MARC is "a system of using brief numbers, letters, and symbols within the cataloging record itself to mark different types of information," with MARC 21 being the current standard (Furrie 2003). The MARC standards website at www.loc.gov/marc/ is an excellent resource.

The GPO has been producing MARC cataloging records for publications in OCLC since July 1976, when the Library of Congress recognized the GPO as the authority for cataloging federal government information (Wiggins 1998). OCLC maintains WorldCat, bibliographic utility and online union catalog of shared bibliographic records. In February 2000, the GPO became a member of BIBCO, the monograph component of the Program for Cooperative Cataloging (PCC). At the time, the GPO was already a member of CONSER (Cooperative Online Serials), NACO (Name Authority Cooperative), and SACO (Subject Authority Cooperative) (GPO 2002, vii). BIBCO and CONSER program participants contribute high-quality bibliographic records to national databases; NACO participants contribute authority name and subject records to national databases of similar high quality.

The GPO sometimes leads other cataloging institutions in innovative practices, such as its use of single records to describe what are called "dual distribution" publications. This practice was developed when the GPO began distributing some congressional publications in both paper and microfiche formats in the 1970s. It extended the practice to online titles in 1995, making single records describe titles made available as paper, microfiche, and remote electronic resources (GPO 2005a). In 2006, the GPO implemented a modern ILS using Ex Libris Aleph 500 software and loaded it with copies of the records it had produced since 1976. This online *Catalog of U.S. Government Publications* (GPO 2006a) provides no-fee access to the records cited in this chapter.[2]

A solid understanding of cataloging records is useful to anyone searching library catalogs, especially public service and information literacy librarians helping to locate materials for the public. One should recognize that records in OCLC and online catalogs (including the GPO's) that have not been updated since their creation may not reflect current cataloging practice. Government information specialists and technical services librarians will find that knowledge of current and past cataloging practices helps them improve searching in their library catalogs. Specific examples may be found in the discussion of the MARC fields.

GENERAL PRINCIPLES FOR CATALOGING IN THE FDLP

The GPO strives to produce records in a cost-effective way to fulfill its obligations under Title 44 *USC*. For maximum efficiency, it creates abridged cataloging records that are cataloged according to AACR2 as "modified first-level" or "minimum-level." Generally the GPO creates new records or adapts existing records based on the format that was distributed or made accessible via the FDLP.

Traditionally, depository titles ordered by agencies to be printed through the GPO are gathered for FDLP shipment and recorded on generic shipping lists that include GPO item numbers, SuDocs classes, and titles. Publications are moved to the FDLP distribution area, where titles are "thrown" by workers into the "lighted bins" of the GPO's automated depository distribution system. When an item number is being thrown, the lights turn on for libraries that select the item, and workers place single copies of titles into lighted shipment boxes.[3] Regional depository libraries' bins are collocated and receive copies of virtually all documents being distributed. For each shipment, a representative box of titles is sent to GPO catalogers. The exceptions are dual-distribution congressional materials, most of which are now cataloged before they are distributed to depository libraries using MARC records that describe the paper format and refer users to microfiche and online versions.

For titles available in a physical format but in the FDLP only in an online format, the GPO creates or adapts a record for the online version and adds appropriate links to records that describe a tangible manifestation with the same content. If the GPO has already cataloged the tangible equivalent of an online document, it adds the GPO depository item number, SuDocs classification number, title (if different), access information, and software requirements. Separate records are made for online and tangible versions if they are different editions of the same document; if one summarizes or abridges the other; if one is an expanded or enhanced version of the other; if the online version was cataloged before an optical disc version requiring special software; and for other reasons decided on a case-by-case basis (GPO 2002, 1).

Current GPO rules state that normally records are created for tangible versions; however, if the online version is cataloged before an equivalent tangible version is cataloged and the bibliographic details and content of the two versions are the same, information regarding the tangible version, including distribution information, is added to the record for the online version (GPO 2002, 1). In 2005, the GPO began cataloging dual-distribution titles (based on printed copies) when they were delivered to Congress rather than waiting until after the depository distribution of paper copies. For the first time, cataloging records (some with PURLs) became available through the *Catalog of U.S. Government Publications* and OCLC before paper copies were distributed to libraries.

GPO catalogers follow AACR2, chapter 12, and LCRI 12.0A when deciding whether to catalog a document as a serial or a monograph (GPO 2002, 2). Current GPO practice favors cataloging titles with editions issued on a regular basis as serials, including maps, as seen in the 2006 "Cataloging Practice for Nautical Charts." In December 2006, the GPO announced its intention to catalog all new serial titles (with the exception of U.S. congressional titles because of its congressional mandate and essential FDLP titles) using "Access Level" Serial MARC/AACR catalog record standards approved by CONSER beginning February 1, 2007 (GPO 2006c).

The GPO produces records for monographs with sufficient detail to allow positive identification of unique editions and titles and lists the kinds of monographs to which these rules apply. Its abridged records include reduced authority work and fewer name and subject added entries. Some descriptive cataloging elements are not provided or are less complete (GPO 2002, 5).

GPO catalogs only U.S. federal online files made available from federal Internet sites or nonfederal sites cooperating with the federal agencies that produced the file. For example, online files in the CyberCemetery, a partnership project with the GPO hosted by the University of North Texas, may be cataloged by the GPO while federal titles downloaded to servers at other organizations may not be. The GPO does not catalog files that are no longer available online. Sites providing access to multiple files, especially where the individual files would not be cataloged individually, are cataloged using collection level cataloging records, which describe the titles and provide subject access to them on one record as a single collection (GPO 2002, 63).

HISTORY OF CATALOGING ELECTRONIC RESOURCES IN THE FDLP

The GPO began distributing CD-ROM discs in 1988 with test disc no. 2 from the Bureau of the Census (Aldrich 1999, 248). Although this first disc was not cataloged by the GPO, the FDLP has distributed and cataloged hundreds of tangible electronic products since.

To provide users with complete information on system requirements while keeping cataloging requirements to a minimum, GPO records for tangible electronic resources have followed full-level cataloging rules, using encoding levels "blank" or "I" for existing and new records. Recognizing that tangible electronic formats have become commonplace, in 2007, the GPO began to apply abridged cataloging rules for CD-ROM and DVD-ROM discs, except for map products (GPO 2006c).

In the 1990s online publications flourished, but maintaining active links to publications was labor intensive as agencies posted, moved, and removed publications from websites without notice. Access to online electronic resources improved in 1994 when GPO catalogers began recording URL information in physical format records for serials. Maintaining URLs in records is time consuming. Concerns that catalogers would spend an increasing proportion of their time updating URLs in records instead of cataloging new electronic resources led the GPO to seek an alternative to unstable URLs. PURLs were developed by OCLC as an interim solution. Clicking on a PURL takes users to the PURL server, which redirects users to a registered URL. The GPO set up its own PURL server and started creating PURLs in 1998. When URLs change, the PURLs in GPO records remain the same while the GPO updates the PURL server to point to resources as needed.[4]

In 1996, GPO staff proposed to the Depository Library Council (DLC) that it create a database of very brief records for online electronic resources. Records would have consisted of a title, series tracing (where applicable), SuDocs class number, and hot-linked URLs. "This was intended to provide low-cost access, especially in view of the all too common practice of many agencies of taking the titles down after a brief time. The DLC favored full AACR2 cataloging so that titles could be included in online catalogs, rather than some kind of stand alone access" (Downing 1999). With the DLC's support, GPO staff began to add characteristics of the online version to the cataloging records created to describe tangible copies. This practice provided subject access to online titles and introduced electronic resources to libraries using the GPO's records. PURL referral statistics compiled by the GPO suggest that including PURLs in library catalogs results in the electronic resources being used.

GPO CATALOGING CIRCA 2006

Reductions in the number of titles distributed to libraries in tangible formats and a consequent reduced backlog of titles to be cataloged generally improved the timely availability of records. Although the tangible electronic resources constitute only a portion of the backlog, it is helpful to understand the process by which items are distributed and cataloged. The cataloging backlog reported for June 1, 2006, was 1,612 items, or roughly two months of work in a year that averaged more than nine hundred cataloging records produced per month (GPO 2006b). As online titles became more common for federal government information, catalogers also served as explorers and hunters, discovering and capturing fugitive titles from agency websites and bringing them into the FDLP.

The GPO reports that link checking for remote electronic resources is done on a regular basis and that PURLs are redirected when broken links are discovered or reported, but the task of maintaining an electronic collection supplied by agency servers is monumental. As noted in the *Report of the Task Group to Survey PCC Libraries on Cataloging of Remote Access Electronic Resources 2003*, "Most libraries do not review e-resources for content change. Obviously this would be a time-consuming process. Failure to review, however, results in records describing resources that may have changed considerably" (Byrd et al. 2004, 3).

Current GPO cataloging guidelines state that PURLs should link directly to the online file being cataloged wherever possible. PURLs should not be assigned to an agency's overall site or to a general site for publications, thereby avoiding multiple titles becoming associated with a single PURL. When a document is part of a database, the assigned PURL may point to a search screen, title listing, or other index (GPO 2002, 63). GPO practice is to archive electronic resources on its permanent access server at the time of PURL assignment.

In December 2006, the GPO announced its intention to follow CONSER principles and create access level serial records for new noncongressional electronic resources beginning in February 2007 and offered an example of an access level serial record to allow comparisons to be made (figure 8-1). Based on pilot project results, the PCC policy committee endorsed the streamlined treatment "to provide in an effective and timely manner a record that consistently ensures identification of and access to a serial title."[5]

The GPO participated in the pilot project, and results indicated a time savings of 30–35 percent in cataloging using these standards.[6] The sample access level record has fewer fields than the full level record (figure 8-2) and requires less time to create. CONSER and GPO instructions stress that correct information included in a record being adapted for an access level record should be retained, but the same information would not be keyed into a newly created access level record. The project's "Draft Cataloging Guidelines" and "Mandatory Data Elements" indicate what must be included in an access level record. Data that were more readily available from publishers, outdated quickly (source of acquisition), or redundant in other ways were considered aspects of cataloging that take unnecessary time and effort. Among the elements significant for government documents cataloging, fields such as 022 (ISSN) and 037 (source of acquisition) would not be included in a new access level record.

CRITICAL MARC FIELDS USED IN GPO RECORDS

035: System Control Number

Although the 035 field can be used for other control numbers, this repeatable field is used in the *Catalog of U.S. Government Publications* (CGP) to record the OCLC accession number generated by OCLC as each record is created in subfield "a." No indicators are used. Proper formatting requires that OCLC's MARC code in parentheses be followed immediately by the number:

> **035** __ **la** (OCoLC)41836073

MARC bibliographic standards allow for canceled or invalid control numbers to be recorded in a subfield "z," but CGP reflects the OCLC practice of using MARC field 019 to record the OCLC control numbers of duplicate records that have been deleted from WorldCat and replaced by current records.[7] Searching CGP for OCLC numbers retrieves records with OCLC numbers recorded in either the 019 or 035 fields.

In CGP, records created or adapted by the GPO from 1994 through 1995 generally include two searchable forms of the 035 field. Those with first indicator "9" (used here for previous system number) apply the "ocm" prefix to the OCLC number used in the WAIS-based CGP that preceded the current Aleph 500 software:

> **035** 9_ **la** ocm41836073
> **019** __ **la** 42295292

FMT SE

LDR 00000nas a22   3a 4500

001 __ 000595796

005 __ 20061213123022.0

006 __ m

007 __ cr

008 __ 061213c19uu9999dcuar ss   f0   0eng c

040 __ **la** GPO **lc** GPO

043 __ **la** n-us---

074 __ **la** 0718-H-05 (online)

086 0_ **la** J 38.16:

222 _0 **la** Annual firearms manufacturing and export report

245 00 **la** Annual firearms manufacturing and export report **lh** [electronic resource].

246 1_ **li** Web site index title: **la** Annual firearms manufacturers and export report

260 __ **la** [Washington, D.C. : **lb** Bureau of Alcohol, Tobacco, and Firearms].

300 __ **la** v : **lb** digital, PDF files.

310 __ **la** Annual

500 __ **la** Description based on: 1998; title from caption (viewed Dec. 13, 2006).

500 __ **la** Latest issue consulted: 2004.

538 __ **la** Mode of access: Internet at the Bureau of Alcohol, Tobacco, Firearms and Explosives web site. Address as of 12/13/06: http://www.atf.gov/firearms/stats/index.htm; current access is available via PURL.

550 __ **la** Issued by: Bureau of Alcohol, Tobacco, Firearms, and Explosives, 2003-

650 _0 **la** Firearms industry and trade **lz** United States **lv** Statistics.

650 _0 **la** Manufacturing industries **lz** United States **lv** Statistics.

650 _0 **la** Exports **lz** United States **lv** Statistics.

710 1_ **la** United States. **lb** Bureau of Alcohol, Tobacco, Firearms, and Explosives.

710 1_ **la** United States. **lb** Bureau of Alcohol, Tobacco, and Firearms

...

856 40 **lu** http://purl.access.gpo.gov/GPO/LPS68255

SYS 000595796

Figure 8-1 Sample GPO access level serial record

```
FMT SE
LDR    cas 2200481 a 4500
005 __ 20060516143333.0
006 __ m    a f
007 __ cr anu--------
008 __ 060330c19uu9999dcuar1 sss  f0   a0eng c
010 __ la 2006230165
022 0_ la 1931-8855
035 __ la (OCoLC)65339517
037 __ lb Bureau of Alcohol, Tobacco, Firearms and Explosives, 650 Mass. Ave.,
          NW, Washington, DC 20226-0013
040 __ la GPO lc GPO ld GPO ld NSD ld DLC ld GPO
042 __ la lcd la nsdp
043 __ la n-us---
050 00 la HD9744.F55
074 __ la 0718-H-05 (online)
082 10 la 683.4 l2 14
086 0_ la J 38.16:
222 _0 la Annual firearms manufacturing and export report
245 00 la Annual firearms manufacturing and export report lh [electronic resource].
246 1_ li Web site index title: la Annual firearms manufacturers and export report
260 __ la [Washington, D.C. : lb Bureau of Alcohol, Tobacco, and Firearms]
300 __ la v. : lb digital, PDF file
310 __ la Annual
500 __ la Description based on: 1998; title from PDF caption (ATF website, viewed
          Mar. 30, 2006).
500 __ la Latest issue consulted: 2004.
550 __ la Issued by: Bureau of Alcohol, Tobacco, Firearms, and Explosives, 2003-
538 __ la Mode of access: Internet at the Bureau of Alcohol, Tobacco, Firearms,
          and Explosives web site. Address as of 3/30/06: http://www.atf.gov/
          firearms/stats/index.htm; current access is available via PURL.
650 _0 la Firearms industry and trade lz United States lv Statistics.
                                                                    (cont.)
```

Figure 8-2 Sample GPO full level electronic resource serial record

---

650 _0 **Ia** Manufacturing industries **Iz** United States **Iv** Statistics.

650 _0 **Ia** Exports **Iz** United States **Iv** Statistics.

710 1_ **Ia** United States. **Ib** Bureau of Alcohol, Tobacco, Firearms, and Explosives.

710 1_ **Ia** United States. **Ib** Bureau of Alcohol, Tobacco, and Firearms

...

856 40 **Iu** http://purl.access.gpo.gov/GPO/LPS68255

SYS 000588786

Figure 8-2 (cont.) Sample GPO full level electronic resource serial record

Because all these fields are included in the OCLC number index, this record can be retrieved in CGP by searching for the OCLC number as "41836073," "ocm41836073," or the obsolete "42295292."

074: GPO Item Number

This repeatable field is used to record GPO item numbers actually used in distribution or dissemination online. Item numbers, with their associated titles, and the corresponding formats typically used for each in the FDLP are updated monthly in the *List of Classes of United States Government Publications Available for Selection by Depository Libraries*.[8] The GPO maintains a public database of item numbers and the depository libraries that select them. The inclusion of item numbers in MARC records allows the batch loading of records into library catalogs and supports the use of locator software, such as the "Locate in a Library" component of CGP. Locator software compares item numbers in MARC records to the selection profiles of depository libraries, allowing users to identify libraries likely to hold specific titles.

GPO depository item numbers should only be recorded in records for those formats distributed or disseminated through the FDLP. The presence in a record of both a 074 field and a 500 field with a shipping list number is the equivalent of the "black dot" in the printed *Monthly Catalog of United States Government Publications*, indicating titles distributed to depository libraries. Many GPO records from the mid-1970s lack 074 fields and shipping list numbers, making the depository status of those titles difficult to determine. In early records lacking 074 fields, depository item numbers may sometimes be found in 500 field notes. Contemporary OCLC records with the GPO's symbol in 040 (cataloging source) fields lacking item numbers usually represent formats not included in the FDLP but to the records of which GPO catalogers have added 765–787 linking entry fields. For titles being cataloged as part of their broader mission and not for the FDLP, the GPO uses a dummy item number, 3000-A, for internal use in ACSIS (the GPO's Acquisitions, Classification, and Shipment Information System), but this item number should not appear in MARC records (GPO 2002, 79).

Item number searches in catalogs are complicated by changes in formatting that have occurred over time. After the introduction of a standard "style" for item numbers in 1990, some titles were still cataloged with multiple item numbers in a single subfield "a" separated by commas. Records created before 1990 may include 074 fields with single-digit item numbers or lack leading zeroes in the second numeric sequence on longer item numbers. For example,

Current	Obsolete
074 __ **Ia** 0084	**074** __ **Ia** 84
074 __ **Ia** 1025-A-01	**074** __ **Ia** 1025-A-1, 1025-A-2 (MF)
074 __ **Ia** 1025-A-02	

No indicators are used with the 074 field. Subfield "a" is used for the item number of actual physical distribution, and subfield "z" is used for invalid item numbers. "Because it represents an actual occurrence, the item number recorded in the catalog record is the one used to distribute a document, not the one it should have been distributed under. The item number remains unchanged even if the SuDocs class is corrected" (GPO 2002, 76). For libraries batch loading records, these rules may result in libraries receiving records for unselected items distributed in error, and libraries selecting misclassified items may identify missing titles by reading corrections published in *Administrative Notes Technical Supplement* (ANTS).

The GPO's practice for catalogers to qualify item numbers for online and microfiche formats aids staff in some libraries in processing the records. The code in the *List of Classes* for "online electronic format" is EL, but "(online)" qualifies the item number in the 074 field. Other electronic format designations included in the *List of Classes*—for example, (E) for miscellaneous electronic products, (CD) for CD-ROM, DVD for optical/recordable discs, and (FL) for floppy diskettes—are not qualified in MARC records. In records representing multiple formats, such as congressional hearings, four 074 fields are common, where the first and third fields represent tangible formats (actual or planned distribution) and the second and fourth indicate access to an online version of the title. For example (OCLC record no. 66525874),

074 __ **Ia** 1039-A
074 __ **Ia** 1039-A (online)
074 __ **Ia** 1039-B (MF)
074 __ **Ia** 1039-B (online)

Cataloging records for serial titles may have more than one valid 074 field. Each represents the GPO item number used during a period of issuance. GPO policy is to arrange the items chronologically, with the earliest item assigned to the first 074 field.

If a title is withdrawn from the program, as in figure 8-3, 074 fields are removed by GPO catalogers and a 500 note added. Although the example document was originally cataloged with item numbers and a microfiche distribution note, the title was withdrawn from the FDLP at the request of the Senate's Committee on Finance before tangible distribution took place. Libraries loading new and updated records without checking them may have the original version (suggesting distribution), since updated records lacking 074 fields may not be included in a library's batch.

An example of a title that was withdrawn *after* FDLP distribution is shown in figure 8-4. This version in CGP has the item number added back in, a mistake that violates GPO cataloging policy.

086: Government Document Classification Number

This repeatable field is regularly used to record government document classification numbers for federal publications of the United States and Canada but can be used for documents of any country with a government documents classification scheme. The first indicator should be coded "0" for the SuDocs Classification System or "1" for Government of Canada Publications: Outline of Classification. For other government documents classification numbers, the indicator is left blank and the source of classification specified in a subfield "2." Valid SuDocs classification numbers are entered in subfield "a," and incorrectly assigned SuDocs class numbers, including those appearing on microfiche headers or on depository shipping lists, are recorded in subfield "z" (GPO 2002, 8).

When the GPO began cataloging online titles for which no tangible format was distributed to depository libraries, catalogers sought to save time by assigning the ACSIS publications ID numbers (generated by the GPO's internal system) after the SuDocs stem appropriate to the publishing agency, such as PR 42.2:2002010107 (OCLC record no. 48960581). In 2002, GPO cataloging guidelines stated that, when a publication is part of a numbered series or represents a different edition of

---

035 __ la (OCoLC)63031273

040 __ la GPO lc GPO ld GPO

042 __ la pcc

043 __ la n-us---

050 14 la KF26 lb .F5 2004v

086 0_ la Y 4.F 49:S.HRG.108-791

110 1_ la United States. lb Congress. lb Senate. lb Committee on Finance.

245 10 la FDA, Merck, and Vioxx : lb putting patient safety first? : hearing before the Committee on Finance, United States Senate, One Hundred Eighth Congress, second session, November 18, 2004.

260 __ la Washington : lb U.S. G.P.O., lc 2005.

300 __ la iv, 921 p. : lb ill. ; lc 23 cm.

490 1_ la S. hrg. ; lv 108-791

500 __ la This document has been withdrawn from the federal depository library program at the request of the publishing agency on 6/20/06.

Figure 8-3 Example of a title withdrawn from the FDLP, 074 fields removed by the GPO

---

035 __ **Ia** (OCoLC)34871921

037 __ **Ia** Catalog no. 64601 H **Ib** IRS

040 __ **Id** SLU **Id** GPO

074 __ **Iz** 0956-J

086 0_ **Ia** T 22.2/15:7233

245 00 **Ia** 75 years of IRS criminal investigation history, 1919-1994.

246 18 **Ia** IRS criminal investigation history, 1919-1994

246 3_ **Ia** Seventy-five years of IRS criminal investigation history, 1919-1994

250 __ **Ia** Rev. 2-96.

260 __ **Ia** [Washington, D.C.?] : **Ib** Dept. of the Treasury, Internal Revenue Service, **Ic** 1996.

300 __ **Ia** 202 p. : **Ib** ill. ; **Ic** 23 cm.

490 __ 1_ **Ia** Document ; **Iv** 7233

500 __ **Ia** "Special Agent, U.S. Internal Revenue."

500 __ **Ia** Cover title.

500 __ **Ia** Not distributed to depository libraries.

506 __ **Ia** "For confidential use of authorized Internal Revenue Service officials only and not for publication."

Figure 8-4 A title that was withdrawn *after* FDLP distribution is shown in CGP with the item number added back in, a mistake that violates GPO cataloging policy.

a title previously distributed and cataloged with a Cutter number, GPO catalogers should assign SuDocs class numbers that place the title with its series (GPO 2002, 66–67). Currently, the GPO assigns appropriate Cutter numbers, such as PREX 23.14:T 24, to titles regardless of their format. This practice eliminates the confusing and artificial GPO practice of assigning different SuDocs classification numbers to the same title for different formats and helps libraries collecting nondepository tangible copies of a title assign official SuDocs numbers even if the title is online-only in the FDLP.

088: Report Number

This repeatable field is used to record report numbers other than the standard technical report numbers (STRNs) issued by NTIS that are recorded in a 027 field. No indicators are used. Subfield "a" is used to record valid numbers. GPO cataloging guidelines instruct catalogers to omit field 088 "from original records; retain in existing & cloned records if used in accordance with GPO [cataloging guidelines] for full-level; record STRNs in 027 field even if also found outside technical report page" (GPO 2002, 8). Many library catalogs are not configured to index or display this field. Fortunately, GPO catalogers frequently record technical report numbers lacking an STRN in a 500 field general note, making them searchable in many additional library catalogs, as in this example from OCLC record 67775338:

>**088 __ la** PNW-GTR-670
>**500 __ la** "PNW-GTR-670."

110: Main Entry—Corporate Name (710—Added Entry—Corporate Name)

The nonrepeatable 110 field uses only the first indicator to record the type of corporate name main entry element (corporate author), with the second indicator undefined. According to AACR2, an agency or government name qualifies as a main entry (in the 110 field) on a MARC cataloging record if the title is issued by the corporate body about itself or fulfills a specific mission charged to it, such as a commission report. If the name is not appropriately assigned to the 110 field, catalogers assign it to the 710 field as a corporate name access point for the record. Most library catalogs also search the 710 field as author. GPO cataloging practice is to include an agency's name either in the 110 or 710 fields. Valid values for the first indicator in both fields are "0" for a corporate name beginning with a personal name in inverted order; "1" for a jurisdiction name; or "2" for a name transcribed in direct order. Because most U.S. federal publications have values of "1" or "2," it is easy to search for records using keywords or phrases from agency names (examples from OCLC record nos. 71313458 and 66385554):

>**110 1_ la** United States. **lb** President (2001- : Bush)
>**110 2_ la** Library of Congress. **lb** Copyright Office

Only persons responsible for authoring a document are included in the 110 field of AACR2 records. Principal investigators may be recorded in the 110 fields if it is clear that they are the authors of a document. Personal authors, including program directors, who are the primary authors of documents are recorded in the 100 field for main entry/personal name instead of the 110 field for main entry/corporate name (GPO 2002, 9).

245: Title Statement

This nonrepeatable field is used to record the title, subtitle, and statement of responsibility of a work and should always have two indicators. The first indicator can generate a title added entry: "1" generates an added entry and "0" indicates that no added entry should be generated in the catalog display. The second indicator, which may range in value from 0 to 9, records the number of nonfiling characters in the title subfield "a" so that articles such as "the" (value: 4) are not indexed in a browsing list of titles.

Nonrepeatable subfields "a" and "b" are used for the title and remainder of the title or subtitle, respectively, and subfield "c" is used to record the statement of responsibility for the title. The 245 field, subfield "h," is used to record general material designation (GMD) values such as "microform." Records from the mid-1990s that have not been updated may contain obsolete GMD values, but the GPO's current policy states that all electronic resource records created by the GPO on or after December 1, 2001, will use the GMD of "electronic resource" instead of "computer file" (GPO 2002, iv).

Searching CGP for the GMD "electronic resource" as a title phrase retrieves more than 34,000 records for electronic resources, more than 31,000 of which include "http" in an 856 field, meaning that they provide a link to an online resource. Valid title statement subfield codes are listed as follows (LC 2005):

|a: Title (NR)

|b: Remainder of title (NR)

|c: Statement of responsibility, etc. (NR)

|f: Inclusive dates (NR). The period during which the entire content of the described materials was created.

|g: Bulk dates (NR). The time during which the bulk of the content of the described materials was created.

|h: Medium (NR)

|k: Form (R). A term that is descriptive of the form of the described materials, determined by an examination of their physical character, the subject of their intellectual content, or the order of information within them.

|n: Number of part/section of a work (R)

|p: Name of part/section of a work (R)

|s: Version (NR). The name, code, or description of a copy of the described materials that was generated at different times or for different audiences.

|6: Linkage (NR). See Control Subfields

|8: Field link and sequence number (R). See Control Subfields

300: Physical Description

This repeatable field is used to record a physical description of the described item. No indicators are used, but subfields allow recording of the extent, physical details, accompanying materials, and more. Used for many years to describe tangible electronic resources in the FDLP, the extent of remote electronic resources went unrecorded until the GPO's 2005 implementation of "MARC Field 300 for Remote Electronic Resources" (GPO 2005b). This option is outlined as AACR2, 2002 Rev. rule 9.5C3, and allows inclusion of the extent of the item and details such as file type in bibliographic records for monographic remote electronic resources. Use of this field helps users of the records distinguish between records describing extensive hearings and reports and records describing summaries of larger titles. Knowing at once that an electronic resource has several hundred pages may deter users from giving up if downloading is slow.

The diversity of electronic resources being cataloged for the FDLP is illustrated by the examples of GPO practice in the MARC field 300 of cataloging records shown in figure 8-5.

500: General Note

GPO catalogers record a variety of important notes in subfield "a" of this repeatable MARC field. Alphanumeric version designations and report numbers are frequently recorded in a 500 field instead of the 088 field reserved for report numbers. Because many library catalogs do not index or display the 088 field but may allow searching and viewing of 500 field notes, their use may improve access. Searching by values recorded as notes, such as "November 2006," may help identify the record associated with a particular disc or report when other words are not unique.

Paired with a GPO item number, a shipping list number noted in this field can help verify a title's distribution. The GPO ended its use of two-digit fiscal years for shipping lists on October 1, 1999 (GPO 1999). Since new records recording old shipping list numbers using current formatting (e.g., "1997-0358-P" instead of "97-358-P") have been created since 2000, the phrase "shipping list" is a more reliable search term to retrieve records of titles the GPO distributed in tangible formats.

530: Additional Physical Form Available Note

This repeatable field records availability information for a different physical format in which the described item is available. The GPO generally uses this field to note the availability of an online version in a record for a paper or microfiche edition:

> 530 __ |a Also available via Internet from the NASA Technical Report Server web site. Address as of 8/24/05: http://ntrs.nasa.gov/archive/nasa/casi.ntrs.nasa.gov/19900011329%5F1990011329.pdf; current access is available via PURL.

Note that when a record for an online electronic resource is created and description for a tangible copy is added later, GPO catalogers use the generic MARC 500 field to record tangible depository distribution of the title (OCLC record no. 37845611):

> 500 __ |a Also distributed in paper to depository libraries, shipping list no.: 1998-0030-P.

533: Reproduction Note

No indicators are used in 533 fields. Subfield "a" records the type of reproduction, "b" the place of reproduction, "c" the agency responsible for reproduction, "d" the date of reproduction, and "e" the physical description of reproduction.

Chiefly used by the GPO for microfiche, this repeatable field records descriptive data for a reproduction of an original item when the 300 field of the bibliographic record describes the original item and additional data need recording. In

PDF FILES

Monographs:

Unnumbered pages:	**300** __ **la** [190] p. : **lb** digital, PDF file.[1]
Numbered pages:	**300** __ **la** 16 p. : **lb** digital, PDF file.[2] [one level]
Mixed pagination:	**300** __ **la** iv, 38 p. : **lb** digital, PDF file.[3] [two levels]
	300 __ **la** iii, 8, 2 p. : **lb** digital, PDF file.[4] [three levels]
	300 __ **la** 1 v. (various pagings) : **lb** digital, PDF file.[5] [more than three levels]

Serials:

Open:	**300** __ **la** v. : **lb** digital, PDF file.[6]
Closed:	**300** __ **la** 3 v. : **lb** digital, PDF file.[7]

INTEGRATING RESOURCES

Closed items: **300** __ **la** 178 p. : **lb** digital, PDF file. [AACR2 example][8]

HTML FILES

Monographs: **300** __ **la** 1 electronic text : **lb** HTML file.[9]

Serials: **300** __ **lb** HTML file. [note that the **la** portion of the field, extent of item, will be left blank for HTML files at CONSER's recommendation][10]

COMBINATIONS OF HTML AND OTHER FILE TYPES

Monographs: 300 __ **la** 1 electronic text, (xiii, 69 p.) : **lb** HTML, digital, PDF file. [AACR2 example]

300 __ **la** 1 electronic text : **lb** HTML, digital, PDF file.[11]

300 __ **la** 1 electronic text : **lb** HTML and Java file.[12]

Open serials: **300** __ **la** electronic text, v. : **lb** HTML, digital, PDF file.[13]

Closed serials: **300** __ **la** 4 v. : **lb** HTML, digital, PDF file. [recording PDF extent only][14]

NOTES
Full records as follows. Note that CGP may be searched by OCLC record no. via the advanced search option

1. OCLC record no. 70919957.
2. OCLC record no. 66900449.
3. OCLC record no. 67519509.
4. OCLC record no. 62717289.
5. OCLC record no. 62867280.
6. OCLC record no. 54759886.
7. OCLC record no. 53073732.
8. GPO (2005b, 1).
9. OCLC record no. 67541592.
10. GPO (2005b, 2).
11. OCLC record no. 70921281.
12. OCLC record no. 67721432.
13. OCLC record no. 76819842.
14. OCLC record no. 70912586.

Figure 8-5 Examples of GPO practice for the MARC 300 field, by format

OCLC record 61356516, the 300 field describes the title as "1 v." (1 volume) while field 533 notes that this consists of one microfiche (1 sheet):

> **533** __ **la** Microfiche. **lb** [Washington, D.C. : **lc** National Aeronautics and Space Administration, **ld** 1990]. **le** 1 microfiche.

538: System Details Note

This repeatable field is used to record technical information about the item. For tangible electronic resources, the GPO uses this field to record system requirements, including software and peripheral components. For remote electronic resources, the mode of access and file type are generally included. When computer software is being cataloged, this field is used to record the computer programming language used. No indicators are required. Subfield "a" is used for system details (examples from OCLC record nos. 41585326, 57125422, and 37845611):

> **538** __ **la** Written in dBase and ASCII formats.

> **538** __ **la** System requirements: Microsoft.NET Application Framework Redistributable package; DVD-ROM drive.

> **538** __ **la** Mode of access: Internet from the BJS web site. Address as of 8/13/03: http://www.ojp.usdoj.gov/pub/bjs/ascii/apvsvc.txt; current access is available via PURL.

580: Linking Entry Complexity Note

This repeatable field is used to record "a description of the complex relationship between the described item and other items when an intelligible note cannot be generated from data in the linking entry fields 760–787" (LC 2005). It is most often used for cataloging serials and integrating resources. No indicators are used. Subfield "a" is used to record the related title and a statement describing the relationship (OCLC record no. 50443596):

> **580** __ **la** Formed by the union of: United States government annual report; and: United States government annual report. Appendix.

> **580** __ **la** Continued by online version.

765–787: Linking Entry Fields

Specific GPO policies on linking notes are in *Government Printing Office Cataloging Guidelines*, and additional information about the fields can be found in *MARC 21 Concise Format for Bibliographic Data*, "Linking Entry Fields (76X-78X)," on the Library of Congress website. These optional repeatable linking entry fields are used as necessary to inform users of publications related to the one described in the record being viewed, which are generally integrating resources and serials. They are optional MARC 21 fields that may be used to link catalog records for various types of related publications. Linking note fields (530 and 580) are also optional MARC 21 fields, which may be used in conjunction with or in place of linking entry fields. At the GPO, serial catalogers are to use linking fields as instructed by the CONSER instructions, whereas map and monograph catalogers use the additional forms available field (776 field) to link records for monographic online files with records for tangible versions. The GPO cataloging manual describes the basic sub-field elements and delimiters for linking fields 765–787, noting they are used only if the publishers of related documents differ (GPO 2002, 75, 81–82):

> |a Main entry heading
> |b Edition
> |c Qualifying information
> |d Place, publisher, date
> |g Relationship information
> |h Physical description
> |s Uniform title
> |t Title
> |w Record control no.
> |z Intl standard book no.

GPO catalogers record the OCLC number and LCCN of the titles being linked to in subfield "w" to make identification easier.

765: Original Language Entry

Used to record information concerning the publication in its original language when the item being cataloged is a translation, this field can be coded to generate a "translation of" note for display. The GPO's record for the French edition of the *International Journal of Government Auditing* includes this field (OCLC record no. 37958291):

> **765** 0_ |t International journal of government auditing |x 0047-0724 |w (DLC) 2003230468 |w (OCoLC)32365802

767: Translation Entry

Used to record information about a version of a publication translated into a language other than the original when the item being cataloged is in the original language or is another translation, this field can be coded to generate a "translated as" note for display. The GPO's record for the English edition of the *International Journal of Government Auditing* includes three examples of this field pointing to translated editions (OCLC record no. 32365802):

767 1_ **lt** Revue international de la verification des comptes publics
    lw (OCLC)37958291

767 1_ **lt** Revista internacional de auditoria gubernamental
    lw (OCLC)40186186

767 1_ **lt** Internationale zeitschrift für staatliche finanzkontrolle
    lw (OCoLC)40155738

775: Other Edition Entry

This field is used to record another available edition of a title; the first indicator can be coded to generate an "other editions available" note for display. For example, OCLC record no. 56555375 has a 245 field with the title and 775 fields with OCLC numbers corresponding to its partner publications, and its partner publication OCLC record no. 56610657 shows the reciprocal link back.

245 00 **la** Military review Brazilian **lh** [electronic resource] : **lb** revista profissional do Exército dos EUA.

. . .

775 1_ **lt** Military review Hispano-American **lw** (DLC) 2004231925
    lw (OCoLC)56610657

245 00 **la** Military review Hispano-American **lh** [electronic resource] :
    lb revista profesional del ejército de EE. UU.

. . .

775 1_ **lt** Military review (Online) **lw** (OCoLC)37904438

775 1_ **lt** Military review Brazilian **lw** (DLC) 2004231924
    lw (OCoLC)56555375

776: Additional Physical Form Entry

Used to record the availability of other formats of items, field 776 requires the additional forms availability note (field 530). The first indicator can be coded to generate an "available in other form" note, as in the GPO's record for the English edition of *Military Review* (OCLC record no. 56610657), which points to other editions that are not translations:

776 1_ **lt** Military review (Edición hispanoamericana) **lw** (DLC)sn 79009309
    lw (OCoLC)5348508

780: Preceding Entry

Field 780 is used to record information concerning the immediate chronological predecessor of a title; the first indicator can be coded "0" to display a note labeling this field. Typical uses include recording the preceding title of a periodical that has had a name change or the preceding titles of a serial that has been formed by the union of several other titles. The text of the note is determined by the value in the second indicator position, as follows (adapted from LC 2005):

00 Continues

01 Continues in part

02 Supersedes

03 Supersedes in part

04 Formed by the union of . . . and . . .

05 Absorbed

06 Absorbed in part

07 Separated from

785: Succeeding Entry

Field 785 is used to record information concerning the immediate chronological successor of the title; the first indicator can be coded "0" to display a note labeling this field. Typical uses include recording the succeeding title of a periodical that has had a name change or the succeeding titles of a serial that has split into or merged with other titles. The text of the note is determined by the value in the second indicator position, as follows (adapted from LC 2005):

00 Continued by

01 Continued in part by

02 Superseded by

03 Superseded in part by

04 Absorbed by

05 Absorbed in part by

06 Split into . . . and . . .

07 Merged with . . . to form . . .

08 Changed back to

787: Nonspecific Relationship Entry

Field 787 is used to record information concerning a work related to the item when the relationship does not fit any of those defined in fields 760–785. The GPO has used this field for titles associated with *Index Medicus*, a well-known medical index issued as a serial, in OCLC record no. 01752728:

787 1_ **lt** List of journals indexed in Index medicus **lx** 0093-3821 **lw** (DLC)
73642296 **lw** (OCoLC)2760305

787 1_ **It** Cumulated index medicus **Ig** 1960-2000 **Ix** 0090-1423 **Iw** (DLC) 62004404 **Iw** (OCoLC)1565584

856: Electronic Location and Access

This field is used to record the information needed to locate and access an electronic resource. Modern catalogs allow users to link to resources by clicking through this field. The standardized interface and powerful indexing of a modern ILS make it possible to identify specific electronic resources by searching subjects and keywords.

The use of field 856 has evolved, but the GPO has always used subfield "u" to record the URL. Current GPO practice is to assign unique PURLs linking the record directly to a copy of the electronic resource, either on an agency server or to a copy harvested and archived on the GPO's permanent access server. If a title moves from its current URL, the PURL is redirected to the new URL or to an archived copy on the GPO's permanent access server. If the title is withdrawn by the agency, the GPO retains its archived copy, deactivates the PURL, and notes that the title was withdrawn.

Field 856 indicators and coding are critical for proper linking and display. Since the GPO's PURL server is an HTTP server, the GPO uses first indicator "4" for HTML and a second indicator reflecting whether the item is being cataloged as the online electronic resource itself (value = 0), an electronic version of a tangible item (value = 1), or a related resource (value = 2). Because the GPO describes paper, microfiche, and electronic titles on the paper format record of the same title, noncatalogers may be confused about the format of the title being described and linked to via multiple 856 fields.

The GPO's previous practice was to use first indicator "7" with a subfield "2" to specify "http" as an access method. Because many records with the earlier coding use URLs instead of PURLs, CGP displays URLs with this coding only in the MARC view. GPO catalogers assign PURLs only to complete versions of resources, not to tables of contents or generic web pages of the publishing agency, even if the URL is printed in the publication.

Cataloging in Publication (CIP) records created by the Library of Congress that include a link to an electronic table of contents submitted before the book was published are problematic when the GPO edits these records to include linking fields to records cataloged as other formats. Although including a subfield 3 designating the URL a link to "table of contents," the Library of Congress use of field 856 with first indicator "4" and second indicator "1" suggests to noncatalogers that the table of contents is an electronic book. Because the 856 field has indicators "4" and "1," the record is included in the Internet Publications logical base. GPO policy does not allow catalogers to remove valid URLs from records, but additional 856 fields with PURLs may be added to records linking to electronic resources.

The record in figure 8-6 describes a printed book and was adapted by the GPO for its National Bibliography. The table of contents page states: "Contents data are machine generated based on pre-publication provided by the publisher. Contents may have variations from the printed book or be incomplete or contain other coding."

035 __ **la** (OCoLC)57514688
040 __ **la** DLC **lc** DLC **ld** GPO
042 __ **la** pcc
043 __ **la** n-us--- **la** a-ja---
050 00 **la** U270 **lb** .C38 2005
082 00 **la** 355.4 **l2** 22
100 1_ **la** Cavaleri, David P., **ld** 1961-
245 10 **la** Easier said than done : **lb** making the transition between combat
operations and stability operations / **lc** by David P. Cavaleri.
260 __ **la** Fort Leavenworth, Kan. : **lb** Combat Studies Institute, **lc** 2005.
263 __ **la** 0503
300 __ **la** p. cm.
440 0_ **la** Global war on terrorism occasional paper ; **lv** 7
530 __ **la** Also available via Internet from the Combined Arms Research Library
web site.
504 __ **la** Includes bibliographical references.
...
776 1_ **la** Cavaleri, David P., 1961- **lt** Easier said than done : making the transition
between combat operations and stability operations **lw** (OCoLC)58804128
856 41 **l3** Table of contents **lu** http://www.loc.gov/catdir/toc/ecip056/2005001079
.html

Figure 8-6 Example of a paper format book record adapted by GPO for its national bibliography

The GPO's record for the online PDF version of the title (figure 8-7) links to the file via a PURL. Field 856 indicators are coded "4" and "0" because the record describes the electronic resource itself and the PURL in subfield "u" points directly to that resource. Although describing a PDF file, this record lacks a 300 field description of extent because it was created before the GPO adopted the practice of creating a field 300 for digital, PDF files.

Because many government publications are corrected by errata, the GPO now assigns a PURL for each online erratum and adds it to the record for the title, allowing users to read the original document and the corrections. GPO policy is to assign erratum PURLs a second indicator value of "2" for "related resource" with the result that an erratum's PURL may not display near the PURL for the edition it corrects in CGP. The logic to this coding is that the table of contents is a portion of the document, whereas errata published discretely are not.[9]

035 __ **la** (OCoLC)58804128
040 __ **la** GPO **lc** GPO
043 __ **la** n-us--- **la** a-ja---
074 __ **la** 0359-C (online)
086 0_ **la** D 110.15:7 **lz** D 110.2:T 68
100 1_ **la** Cavaleri, David P., **ld** 1961-
245 10 **la** Easier said than done **lh** [electronic resource] : **lb** making the transition between combat operations and stability operations / **lc** by David P. Cavaleri.
246 30 **la** Making the transition between combat operations and stability operations
260 __ **la** Fort Leavenworth, Kan. : **lb** Combat Studies Institute Press, **lc** [2005]
440 _0 **la** Global war on terrorism occasional paper ; **lv** 7
538 __ **la** Mode of access: Internet from the Combined Arms Research Library, Command & General Staff College web site. Address as of 4/5/05: http://www.cgsc.army.mil/carl/download/csipubs/cavaleri.pdf; current access is available via PURL.
500 __ **la** Title from title screen (viewed on April 5, 2005).
504 __ **la** Includes bibliographical references.
710 2_ **la** U.S. Army Command and General Staff College. **lb** Combat Studies Institute.
776 0_ **la** Cavaleri, David P., 1961- **lt** Easier said than done : making the transition between combat operations and stability operations **lw** (OCoLC)57514688
856 40 **lu** http://purl.access.gpo.gov/GPO/LPS59578

Figure 8-7 Example of an online book record created by GPO for its national bibliography

GPO 856 Locator Link

The GPO includes a special 856 field in CGP records that allows users to link to a database of depository libraries selecting the item described in the record. These 856 fields lack first and second indicators and display to the public in CGP but are not intended for use in the catalogs of other libraries and do not appear in OCLC. In CGP, OCLC record no. 61356516 includes an 856 field with item number 0830-D. Users clicking on this URL are taken to a search page where postal state code, area code, or city name criteria may be entered to find libraries currently selecting item 0830-D:

856 __ **l3** (MF, online) **lu** http://catalog-web2.gpo.gov/LocateLibraries/locate.jsp?ItemNumber=0830-D&SYS=000579607

CGP includes a version of this 856 field for each item number associated with a record. For example, the CGP record for the *U.S. Congressional Serial Set* (OCLC record no. 03888071) includes seven locator link fields, one for each GPO item number associated with this title.

FUTURE CATALOGING PRACTICES AND CONCLUSIONS

The *Government Printing Office Cataloging Guidelines* will evolve, with incremental updates appearing on the GPO's National Bibliography program web pages as changes are implemented.[10] Assuming that Congress authorizes funding for current plans, the GPO will abandon its policy of using a single record to describe multiple formats and create records for each format of a title in 2008 in support of FDsys.[11] Cataloging separate formats on separate records also follows the Program for Cooperative Cataloging policy for BIBCO (cataloging monographs) and CONSER (cataloging continuing resources).

Instead of combining paper, microfiche, and remote electronic resource formats on a single record, catalogers will create individual records describing each format of a title produced or pointed to by the GPO. The creation of separate records for each manifestation will follow the FRBR model as applied through RDA rules when they are adopted. The FDsys tracking of all manifestations of federal titles handled by the GPO will result in GPO catalogers creating more records for formats not distributed to depository libraries. Use of access level serial records and abridged records for monographs may help achieve this.

GPO representatives have indicated that the GPO item number structure should change to feature greater specificity for the selection of tangible items and to offer broad categories for online electronic resources. The *List of Classes* will change considerably as new items are established for general online classes for particular agencies and older series are abolished. Complications arise when older titles from abolished series are digitized and assigned SuDocs numbers in a currently valid general publications classification because their original series no longer has a valid unique classification. This results in records with 086 field values that do not match the SuDocs classes of printed publication sitting (perhaps uncataloged) in depository collections. Once used as a roadmap to guide people through collections of printed depository materials organized by SuDocs classification, the *List of Classes* may become a more esoteric tool for collection management, relying more on GPO item numbers to control the flow of MARC records into catalogs for FDLP titles available online from agency and GPO archive servers.

Now, in the twenty-first century, monographic microfiche have almost disappeared from the FDLP, replaced by electronic resource files, but nearly six hundred libraries still select the microfiche edition of some dual-distribution titles (congressional titles distributed in both paper and microfiche formats). Processing and providing access to these materials will undergo dramatic changes when format-specific records following GPO cataloging rules become the norm. Whereas currently a single record provides access to online, paper, and microfiche formats, three records will be needed. Since SuDocs numbers are generally the same for all manifestations of a title, considerable effort may be needed to ensure that the right records are loaded for each title distributed or made available via the Internet. Many regional and selective depositories use vendor-supplied records based on the shipment of paper format congressional publications to provide access to microfiche and online versions, and format-specific cataloging will complicate the processing of these materials. Item qualifiers for all FDLP formats might aid libraries and vendors processing cataloging records in distinguishing one record from another.

The library locator feature of CGP and other databases created with GPO records will fail more frequently as long-established GPO item numbers are abolished. Although GPO item numbers were created to facilitate the distribution of materials, database vendors soon discovered that these numbers could be used to direct users from the MARC records to libraries likely to hold selected materials using a union list of item selection profiles. Library locator features work because of the general stability of depository library item profiles over time. As FDLP staff correct the *List of Classes* and move large numbers of items into appendix II, "Classes No Longer Active," users looking for libraries likely to hold abolished items are increasingly directed to the list of regional depository libraries. Although the roughly 1,200 selective depository libraries nationwide hold a large number of titles, when locator software fails to find a match CGP users are referred to the fifty-two regional depository libraries when seeking materials with brand new or abolished item numbers. Although regional library staff may refer people to the closest depository holding the title, there seems to be no easy solution, especially since the GPO began to set holdings in OCLC for over half of the regional depository libraries.[12] Increasingly sophisticated union catalogs and federated searching with new technologies may help the public locate government information resources in libraries.

Electronic information managers in libraries and at the GPO face many challenges. The GPO *List of Classes* and depository distribution system, designed to make tangible distribution of depository materials foolproof, need major overhauls. GPO and librarians are looking at ways to better meet user and library needs, such as allowing selection of very specific tangible products while offering a broader range of online electronic resources. It will be interesting to see if the FDLP and its library partners and vendors are able to adapt the depository system to facilitate the distribution of records for online titles by subject content rather than provenance.

NOTES

1. The GPO's current cataloging guidelines follow the AACR definition of electronic resources, which states, "Material (data and/or program[s]) encoded for manipulation by a computerized device. This material may require the use of a peripheral directly connected to a computerized device (e.g., CD-ROM drive) or a connection to a computerized network (e.g., the Internet)."

2. To search OCLC numbers in the *Catalog* to view the records, readers may wish to bookmark the advanced search options page for searching: http://catalog.gpo.gov/F/?func=find-d-0& local_base=GPO01PUB&clear_level=2.

3. See the Library Programs Service Web Tour, www.access.gpo.gov/su_docs/fdlp/pr/lpstour/ index.html.

4. On PURLs, see Downing (1999) and LC (1996).

5. See GPO, "GPO Cataloging Guidelines Draft for Review," posted December 13, 2006, http://listserv.access.gpo.gov/archives/gpo-fdlp-l.html; and Mechael D. Charbonneau, "New CONSER Standard Record Approved," posted November 20, 2006 to PCC List, www.loc.gov/acq/conser/pdf/alr/CONSERRecordApproved.pdf.

6. CONSER, "Access Level Record for Serials Working Group Final Report," July 24, 2006, www.loc.gov/acq/conser/alrFinalReport.html.

7. See "019 OCLC Control Number Cross-Reference," *Bibliographic Formats and Standards*, OCLC, www.oclc.org/bibformats/en/0xx/019.shtm.

8. Access the *List of Classes* at www.access.gpo.gov/su_docs/fdlp/pubs/loc/index.html.

9. Telephone conversation with Jennifer K. Davis, manager, Bibliographic Control, Library Technical Information Services, GPO, June 14, 2006.

10. Other sources of information are the online proceedings of the DLC, especially because the GPO updates its handouts before DLC and ALA conferences. The GPO posts cataloging changes to GOVDOC-L and autocat lists for feedback. Concerned stakeholders, such as GODORT and other ALA groups, provide formal, written feedback on the GPO's cataloging proposals, which can be found on their websites.

11. The GPO depends on having an approved legislative branch budget for any initiative requiring financial support and is currently operating only on a continuing resolution.

12. FDLP-L announcement posted February 1, 2005, available from http://listserv.access.gpo .gov/archives/gpo-fdlp-l.html.

REFERENCES

ALA American Library Association. 1999–. ALA/GODORT Cataloging Committee Toolbox for Processing and Cataloging Federal Government Documents. Ed. John A. Stevenson and the Cataloging Committee of the American Library Association's Government Documents Round Table. www2.lib.udel.edu/godort/cataloging/toolbox.htm.

Aldrich, Duncan M. 1999. "Things Change: The FDLP Setting and Early Partnership Efforts." *Proceedings of the 8th Annual Federal Depository Library Conference*. Washington, DC: U.S. GPO.

Byrd, Jacqueline, et al. 2004. *Report of the Task Group to Survey PCC Libraries on Cataloging of Remote Access Electronic Resources 2003*, rev. 2004. Library of Congress. www.loc.gov/catdir/pcc/archive/tgsrvyeres_final.pdf.

Downing, Thomas A. 1999. "GPO's Cataloging of Electronic Government Serials: Evolving Challenges and Practices." *CONSERline*, January. www.loc.gov/acq/ conser/conserline/conserline-13.html#gpo.

Furrie, Betty, in conjunction with the Data Base Development Department of the Follett Software Company. 2003. *Understanding MARC Bibliographic: Machine-Readable Cataloging*, 7th ed. www.loc.gov/marc/umb/um01to06.html#part1.

GPO U.S. Government Printing Office. 1999. "Depository Administration Branch Update," *Administrative Notes* 20 (16): 34. www.access.gpo.gov/su_docs/fdlp/pubs/adnotes/ad102599.html.

————. 2002. *Government Printing Office Cataloging Guidelines.* Prepared by Steven R. Uthoff. 4th ed. Washington, DC: Cataloging Branch, Library Programs Service, U.S. GPO. Last updated March 25, 2002. www.gpo.gov/su_docs/fdlp/cip/gpocatgu.pdf.

————. 2005a. "National Bibliography Policy: Separate Records for Titles in Multiple Formats" (draft). January 11. www.access.gpo.gov/su_docs/fdlp/cip/SeparateRecord.pdf.

————. 2005b. "GPO Cataloging Practice: MARC Field 300 for Remote Electronic Resources." September 16. www.access.gpo.gov/su_docs/fdlp/cip/marc_field_300_91905.pdf.

————. 2006a. *Catalog of U.S. Government Publications* (OCLC numbers used as reference points). http://catalog.gpo.gov/F/?func=find-d-0&local_base=GPO01PUB&clear_level=2.

————. 2006b. "GPO Cataloging Practice: ALA 2006 Update." June 19. www.access.gpo.gov/su_docs/fdlp/cip/gpo-catalog-prac.pdf.

————. 2006c. "GPO Cataloging Guidelines Updates." December. www.access.gpo.gov/su_docs/fdlp/cip/proposal_access_level_dec06.pdf.

LC Library of Congress. 1996. "Defining a Uniform Resource Name Field in the USMARC Bibliographic Format." Discussion paper no. 96. May 6. www.loc.gov/marc/marbi/dp/dp96.html.

————. 2005. *MARC 21 Concise Format for Bibliographic Data.* www.loc.gov/marc/bibliographic/.

Wiggins, Beecher. 1998. "The Program for Cooperative Cataloging." *Proceedings of the Taxonomic Authority Files Workshop, Washington, DC, June 22–23.* www.calacademy.org/research/informatics/taf/proceedings/wiggins.html.

Chapter 9   Bibliographic Control and Processing of Electronic Government Information in Libraries

Elaine Winske

Bibliographic control: what does it mean and how does it relate to the processing of e-government information in libraries? Lois Chan defines bibliographic control as "the operations by which recorded information is organized or arranged according to established standards and thereby made readily identifiable and retrievable" and lists indexing, classification, and descriptive and subject cataloging as related activities (Chan 1994, 3). This definition correlates with the statement in the *Federal Depository Library Handbook* that a major technical services goal is to organize and maintain information resources in a manner that promotes efficient retrieval and use (GPO 2008, 82). Both statements support the concept that the ultimate goal of bibliographic control is the identification and ultimate retrieval of information. Processing bibliographic data in an online catalog, usually in an integrated library system (ILS), completes the bibliographic control process by providing the information necessary for local access. Maintaining bibliographic data in an ILS for depository materials is an ongoing library issue.

In this chapter, we focus on the steps of the bibliographic control process after cataloging: access to bibliographic data customized for the ILS and the maintenance of that access. The chapter provides an overview of current practices and standards, offers information about new developments in bibliographic control, and addresses local bibliographic control issues for e-government information. Significant issues addressed include how bibliographic data are added to a library's ILS, shelf listing requirements, what oversight must occur to complete the initial bibliographic control process, and what catalog maintenance is necessary for access that meets

Elaine Winske received her MLS from Southern Connecticut State University. She joined Florida International University as head of the documents section, Biscayne Bay Campus, in 1990 with responsibilities for both public and technical services. In 2004 she transferred to the University Park Campus as head of the authorities and database maintenance unit. Winske now also serves as assistant head of the cataloging department and co-project coordinator for ALEPH.

Federal Depository Library Program (FDLP) requirements for bibliographic control. Continuing developments and changes in standards and policies for bibliographic control, such as the Functional Requirements for Bibliographic Records, the development of new cataloging rules, and metadata issues are also discussed. Creation of bibliographic data in the MARC 21 format and the cataloging policies of the GPO are covered in chapter 8.[1]

IMPACT OF TECHNOLOGY ON BIBLIOGRAPHIC CONTROL

Bibliographic control is one of the essential library services under scrutiny specifically because of developments associated with digital technology, such as new and varied metadata schemas other than MARC used for the representation and communication of bibliographic data. In 2000, at the Library of Congress Cataloging Directorate's Bicentennial Conference on Bibliographic Control for the New Millennium, Clifford Lynch stated:

> We are entering a new world where content will be predominantly digital, and where it will be used, not just located, using electronic information systems. We cannot and must not attempt to map the future of bibliographic control without recognizing this. Continuing to ignore developments outside of the traditional scope of bibliographic control . . . runs the very real risk that our traditional practices may be discarded as unaffordable and of insufficient value in light of what the new technologies can offer. . . . we must concentrate on determining what bibliographic control practice can uniquely contribute, and where, when and how this contribution matters most. . . . we must understand the changing context, and the economics, capabilities and limitations of the alternatives. (Lynch 2000, 4)

In the past decade there have been many developments related to bibliographic control. The following list gives some perspective to the scope of those developments:

- Functional Requirements for Bibliographic Records (FRBR) model, final report from an IFLA Study Group (www.ifla.org/VII/s13/frbr/frbr.pdf) and ongoing developments from IFLA's FRBR Review Group (www.ifla.org/VII/s13/wgfrbr/)

- Report from the second worldwide review of Functional Requirements for Authority Data (FRAD), by an IFLA working group presenting the model that extends FRBR concepts to authority data (www.ifla.org/VII/d4/FRANAR -ConceptualModel-2ndReview.pdf)

- *Guidelines for Authority Records and References* (GARR), 2nd ed. rev., 2001 (www.ifla.org/VII/s13/garr/garr.pdf)

- 2005 establishment of IFLA Working Group on Functional Requirements for Subject Authority Records (FRSAR; www.ifla.org/VII/s29/wgfrsar.htm)

- Revision of "Statement of International Cataloguing Principles" (known as the Paris Principles); in process, latest draft 2006 (www.d-nb.de/standard isierung/pdf/statement_draft_apr2006.pdf)
- Implementation of the CONSER Access Level Record for Serials (www.loc .gov/catdir/cpso/conser.html). *Note:* The GPO participated in pilot project.
- Recommendations from the Library of Congress Working Group on the Future of Bibliographic Control; final report issued January 2008 (www.loc .gov/bibliographic-future/)
- Development of Resource Description and Access (RDA), the new cataloging standard that will replace AACR2, scheduled for release 2009 (www.collectionscanada.gc.ca/jsc/rda.html)

A significant policy change not yet mentioned is the Library of Congress's June 2006 decision not to create or update series authority records and not to provide controlled series access points in its bibliographic records for resources in series (LC 2006). This highly controversial decision shifted the burden for series authority control. The Program for Cooperative Cataloging (PCC) continues to wrestle with the consequences of this decision; OCLC has implemented changes to deal with it; and the GPO along with many others will continue series authority work.[2]

It is increasingly difficult to keep up in this environment of bibliographic change triggered by new technologies. Opportunities to increase and improve services are accompanied by the responsibility of assessing how they can best be applied considering existing practices. As Lynch concluded,

> Redesigning bibliographic control for the new millennium will call for a new dialog among all parties and perspectives [stakeholders] concerned with information finding that is grounded in a study of how the full array of tools and techniques now available can be applied to find information most effectively, and not in the inherent correctness or superiority of any one approach. (2000, 5)

Libraries must manage change and work toward achieving bibliographic control through an optimum application of new and existing technologies.

STANDARDS FOR BIBLIOGRAPHIC CONTROL

Bibliographic control includes identifying, describing, analyzing, and classifying materials, whether tangible or electronic, so that they may be effectively organized, stored, retrieved, and used when needed. The use of standards for these activities increases the effectiveness of the information retrieval process and optimizes the transfer and sharing of bibliographic data.

Bibliographic control is governed by three types of standards:

- standards for *content* data in bibliographic records (including subject, location, and description and access data)

- standards for the *display* of bibliographic data
- *communications* standards for systems that serve as "carriers" of bibliographic data

Adherence to these standards increases the usability of bibliographic data by improving information retrieval and the ability to transfer and share data. Although not everyone needs to master the skills necessary to apply these standards, an awareness of the underlying principles contributes to the effective processing of government information.

Standards for Content Data

One of the three types of content is *subject content* (subject headings). The application of standards for subject headings creates data that provide access points identified through the subject analysis process. Subject heading thesauri serve as standards for subject access content. With the exception of NASA technical reports, the GPO assigns Library of Congress Subject Headings (LCSH) to all records and retains and corrects headings in records input by designated members (GPO 2002, 164). Other specialized subject heading schemes and descriptor thesauri used for documents include Medical Subject Headings (MeSH), the *NASA Thesaurus*, and the ERIC descriptors.[3] The GPO retains NASA and MeSH terms in selected records.

Location content is the classification data added to a bibliographic record (call number information). For tangible materials, the call number is also a shelf location that allows users to retrieve materials within the library. Two prominent classification systems standards are the Library of Congress Classification (LCC) and the Dewey Decimal Classification System (DDC). The GPO uses the Superintendent of Documents Classification System (SuDocs) specifically created for FDLP materials. "An Explanation of the Superintendent of Documents Classification" (www .gpo.gov/su_docs/fdlp/pubs/explain.html) provides a good overview of SuDocs, and the *GPO Classification Manual* (www.access.gpo.gov/su_docs/fdlp/pubs/classman/ index.html) describes how to assign them.

The third type of content data is *description and access content*, which provides descriptive information such as title, statement of responsibility, publisher, and pagination. It also supplies controlled access points for entities such as authors, editors, performers, titles within a collected work, series, and uniform titles. The current standard for description and access is AACR2 (www.aacr2.org) (see figure 9-1). Data for description and access account for the highest percentage of content data in a bibliographic record.

To remain useful, standards must continue to evolve. The Anglo-American Cataloguing Rules (first developed in 1968), along with the second edition, constituted major revisions of the standard for cataloging rules, but the current rules do not adequately address the description of digital collections or facilitate access to data through new technologies. As a result, a new standard is currently under development by the Joint Steering Committee (JSC) for Development of RDA: Resource Description and Access, scheduled for release 2009. Since RDA is primarily being developed for use in libraries, a strong consideration in its development is the

Content data are in italics and MARC 21 **content designators** are bold.

Author main entry showing authorized form of heading:

100 1_ **la** *Lee, T. M.* **lq** *(Terrie Mackin)*

Transcribed data showing title and statement of responsibility:

245 10 **la** *Influence of evaporation, ground water, and uncertainty in the hydrologic budget of Lake Lucerne, a seepage lake in Polk County, Florida /* **lc** *by T.M. Lee and Amy Swancar.*

Descriptive 500 note justifying additional access point (AACR 2 rule 21.29F):

500 __ **la** *"Prepared in cooperation with the Southwest Florida Water Management District."*

Descriptive 530 note for availability in another form:

530 __ **la** *Also available via Internet from the USGS web site. Address of 9/21/02: http://fl.water.usgs.gov/Abstracts/wsp2439_lee.html; current access is available via PURL.*

Added entry access point showing authorized form of heading for second author:

700 1_ **la** *Swancar, Amy.*

Access point for authorized form of corporate name appearing in descriptive note:

710 1_ **la** *Southwest Florida Water Management District (Fla.)*

Figure 9-1 AACR2 description and access content in MARC 21 format.

need to minimize changes to bibliographic data cataloged according to earlier cataloging rules. In addition, the JSC is consulting many groups in order to broaden the applicability of the standard to metadata schemas used by other information management organizations while trying to follow a strong mandate to align RDA with FRBR and FRAD (JSC 2007, 1–2; IFLA FRBR 1998; IFLA FRAD 2007). By consulting with groups outside the library community, the JSC expects the new standard to serve information management organizations other than libraries. It is challenging to develop RDA to address all of these considerations. Another form of outreach is the monitoring of ongoing developments in bibliographic control such as the revision process for the Paris Principles and their relation to RDA and the Library of Congress's report on the future of bibliographic control (IFLA 2006; LC 2008).

JSC also launched a joint initiative with representatives of the publishing industry to create a common framework for resource categorization. The first version of the RDA/ONIX framework was released in August 2006. It identified and defined two sets of attributes, one for intellectual or artistic content and one for means/methods by which the content is carried (Dunsire 2007, 1–2). Previously, RDA lacked agreement on terminology standards that clearly separated the concepts for carrier and content.

Because the new structure for RDA more closely aligns it with the conceptual models in FRBR and FRAD, we include a brief overview of FRBR along with an explanation of how FRBR and RDA may impact GPO cataloging production and policy. The development of the FRBR entity-relationship model had two objectives (IFLA FRBR 1998, 7). The first was to provide a well-defined framework for relating bibliographic data to the needs of the data users. Defining entities and their attributes as well as the relationships between the entities meets this first objective of FRBR.

Entities, which represent objects of interest to data users, are grouped as follows (IFLA FRBR 1998, 12):

Group 1: Products of intellectual or artistic endeavor (work, expression, manifestation, and item)

Group 2: Those responsible for the intellectual or artistic content, the physical production and dissemination, or the custodianship of the entities in Group 1 (person and corporate body)

Group 3: Subjects of works (concept, object, event, and place plus Group 1 entities or Group 2 entities)

Attributes are a set of characteristics associated with an entity that enable data users to formulate queries as well as interpret responses to queries. *Relationships* depict links between entities and assist users in making connections between entities. To operate correctly, the entities on both sides of the relationship must be explicitly identified (IFLA FRBR 1998, 56–57). Barbara Tillett's "Family of Works" diagram is a visual representation of FRBR relationships (Tillett 2004, 4; see also Tillett 2003; 2001, 23).

The second objective of FRBR, recommending a basic level of functionality with specified data requirements for bibliographic records, was accomplished in two steps. The first step mapped the attributes and relationships to four fundamental user tasks; *finding* material that goes with the search criteria, *identifying* or confirming the identity of material found, *selecting* material most appropriate to specific information needs, and *obtaining* access to or locating selected material (IFLA FRBR 1998, 97–98). The mapping of attributes and relationships to user tasks showed the role, or "value," of the attribute/relationship in carrying out the user task. The assessment of value was based on the knowledge and experience of the study group members and consultants. Criteria were developed for assessing the values for each user task. Mapping charts were used to identify minimum data requirements by analyzing the value assessed to an attribute in meeting a user task (IFLA FRBR 1998, 5, 88–96).

These mapping charts served as the "frame of reference" for the second step, defining a set of basic requirements for national bibliographic records. For example, the attributes *title of work* and *form of work* mapped to the task of *selecting a work* with a high value. The two relationships that mapped to that task with a high value were *person/corporate bodies responsible for the work* and *entities treated as subject of the work*.

Because of the importance of these attributes in selecting a work, they qualified as minimum data requirements. The results of the analysis were consolidated and grouped according to descriptive elements and organizing elements; see figures 9-2 and 9-3 for simplified lists of elements.[4] The lists from these groupings became the recommendation, with the following comment concerning national bibliographic data:

> While the recommended basic level of functionality and the basic data requirements will be applied as the norm for records included in the national bibliography, they will not necessarily be applied as an absolute requirement. . . . national bibliographic agencies may choose to include certain categories of material in the national bibliography that they treat as "listed" materials only. . . . for those categories of material they may

---

Title and statement of responsibility area
- title proper (including number/name of part)
- parallel title(s)
- s/r identifying individual(s) and/or group(s) with principal responsibility for the content

Edition area
- edition statement
- additional edition statement

Material (or type of publication) specific area
- numbering (serials)
- mathematical data statement—coordinates (cartographic work)
- mathematical data statement—scale (cartographic image/object)
- musical presentation statement—type of score (musical notation)

Publication, distribution, etc. area
- place of publication, distribution, etc.
- name of publisher, distributor, etc.
- date of publication, distribution, etc.

Physical description area
- specific material designation
- extent
- dimensions

Series area
- title proper of series
- parallel title(s) of series
- first statement of responsibility relating to the series

Figure 9-2 Descriptive elements of FRBR basic level national bibliographic record

---

Name headings

- name heading(s) for person(s) and/or corporate body(ies) with principal responsibility for the work(s)
- name heading(s) for person(s) and/or corporate body(ies) with principal responsibility for the expression(s)

Title headings

- title heading(s) for the work(s)
- addition to uniform title—language
- addition to uniform title—other distinguishing characteristic
- addition to uniform title—medium of performance (music)
- addition to uniform title—numeric designation (music)
- addition to uniform title—key (music)
- addition to uniform title—statement of arrangement (music)

Series headings

- heading for the series

Subject headings / classification numbers

- subject heading(s) and/or class number(s) for the principal subject(s) of the work(s)

Figure 9-3 Organizing elements of FRBR basic level national bibliographic record

establish a minimal level of functionality and minimal data requirements that do not conform with those recommended for the basic level record. By the same token, it is recognized that national bibliographic agencies may choose to provide a fuller level of treatment than the basic requirement to certain categories of material. (IFLA FRBR 1998, 116; and see 112–115 for a complete listing of basic data elements)

The identification of basic data requirements is useful only to the extent the requirements are incorporated into the cataloging rules and the basic data are correlated with a description standard. The Library of Congress's decision not to continue series authority work is particularly disappointing considering the FRBR recommendation of name, title, series, and subject headings as basic level organizing elements for national bibliographic records.

In the context of FRBR, current cataloging occurs at the manifestation level. Strictly speaking, this means titles available in more than one format would have a separate catalog record for each format. The increase of titles in multiple formats coupled with the inability of current standards to group and organize them effectively created a confusing display of these records in the OPAC. To alleviate that confusion, the practice of using a single catalog record for titles in multiple formats was adopted by many practitioners. There has been an ongoing debate over the single-record versus separate-record approach ever since. With the incorporation of concepts presented in FRBR, RDA will support a separate-record approach. Traditionally the GPO was a leader in using the single-record approach for titles in different formats; however, it has changed this policy and now catalogs a separate record for each tangible format (see chapter 8). Eventually the GPO will also catalog a separate record for each title also available in electronic format.

The establishment of relationships between manifestations and works is expected to provide a structure that enables a less confusing collocated display for multiple records for the same title. At the end of 2001, nearly 80 percent of the "works" in OCLC's WorldCat existed in one manifestation, that is, one title, one format (Storey 2003, 3). Under RDA rules, complex relationships of manifestation to work will only need to be described for the 20 percent of the works that have more than one manifestation. How the establishment of these relationships will impact the GPO's cataloging production is unknown. The prevalence of multiple formats for government information indicates that the percentage of records requiring a manifestation-to-work relationship is higher than 20 percent. As the GPO implements the policy to catalog titles in differing formats on separate records, its catalogers will be adding linking fields for records in another format (GPO 2002, 81–89). How manifestation-to-manifestation and manifestation-to-work relationships will be expressed in GPO records remains to be determined. Just as the usefulness of linking fields for records in another format is dependent on the functionality in the local ILS, the ability to collocate records according to FRBR relationships will also be dependent on the library's local ILS functionality.

Standards for Bibliographic Data Display

The standard for bibliographic description developed from a resolution at an international meeting in Copenhagen in 1969. The first standard, ISBD (M): International Standard Bibliographic Description for Monographic Publications, was published in 1971. Currently there are eight standards for bibliographic descriptions (see IFLA 2007). The backbone of each standard is the specification of data elements.

The descriptive elements as defined in ISBD were a resource for the development of FRBR attributes. Inherent in the specification of elements in ISBDs are aspects governing data display (see figures 9-4 and 9-5). The data display aspects allow the ISBD standard to double as a display standard and broaden its applicability. ISBD (CF): International Standard Bibliographic Description for Computer Files, created in 1990, was replaced by ISBD (ER) International Standard Bibliographic Description for Electronic Resources in 1997 (IFLA 1997, 2–3).

Standards for the Bibliographic Data Communication

MARC 21 is the current standard for the representation and exchange of data in an ILS. In addition to the MARC format for bibliographic data, there are MARC

Punctuation	Area	[MARC subfield]
	Title proper	‡a
[ ]	General Material Designation (GMD)— optional	‡h
=	Parallel title	‡b
:	Other title information	‡b
	Statements of responsibility	
/	First statement	‡c
;	Subsequent statement	‡c

Figure 9-4 ISBD punctuation: title and statement of responsibility area

With title proper, GMD, and statement of responsibility:
‡a PubMed ‡h [electronic resource] / ‡c NCBI ; National Library of Medicine.

With title proper, GMD, other title information, and statement of responsibility:
‡a Description of Senate Finance Committee chairman's mark relating to technical correction provisions ‡h [electronic resource] : ‡b scheduled for markup before the Senate Committee on Finance on June 19, 1997 / ‡c prepared by the staff of the Joint Committee on Taxation.

Figure 9-5 Display showing ISBD punctuation: title and statement of responsibility area. Note that punctuation precedes the element it is "announcing." MARC subfield delimiter and code follow the mark of punctuation.

standards for authority data, classification data, community information, and holdings data. MARC is not a cataloging content standard but a framework standard to which cataloging content has to be added; that is, bibliographic material is cataloged according to cataloging rules and presented in MARC format (Gorman 2000, 4). Although MARC format is just a "container" for bibliographic content, its structure is crucial to accessing and transferring content. The MARC Standards website (www.loc.gov/marc/) hosted by the Library of Congress provides access to all MARC standards. Librarians may consult the standards or refer to this chapter as a reference when working to understand and improve their libraries bibliographic record loads. The OCLC version of the bibliographic format standard, *Bibliographic Formats and Standards* (www.oclc.org/bibformats/en/), gives examples of data input based on content and display standards. With its extensive examples and excellent navigation features, this is a good resource on MARC for catalogers and noncatalogers.

Coding for the MARC bibliographic standard is very detailed because it provides specifications for both bibliographic data exchange between systems and encoding the data elements/content that describe, retrieve, and control bibliographic data (MARBI 1996, 2, 4). The FAQ section of the MARC Standards website links to related information on the XML and SGML versions of MARC, the mapping of MARC to metadata schemas and vice versa, and the guidelines for coding electronic resources in a MARC format record. The increasing number of metadata schemas provides libraries with more options for resource description than ever before, but the issues surrounding metadata are highly complex. The following comments from the Bicentennial Conference on Bibliographic Control for the New Millennium emphasize the importance of content standards for interoperability between metadata schemas:

> To the extent that we choose to abandon or downplay content rules, we choose to limit what we can do, what functions we can support with our metadata. . . . mapping between metadata schemes always results in loss: loss of data, loss of meaning, loss of specificity, loss of accuracy. . . . The application of content rules usually requires human judgment in conjunction with an examination of the resource itself. . . . Specifically, mapping will not necessarily allow metadata that was designed to operate in one context—in support of a given set of functionality—to operate in another context, in support of a different set of functionality. (Wendler 2000, 2–3)

The absence of content standards for other metadata schemas strongly indicates that MARC functionality cannot currently be replaced.

A MARC record consists of these three elements:[5]

- record structure: an implementation of the Information Interchange Format standard (ANSI/NISO Z39.2)
- content designation: the framework that permits the computer to interpret the bibliographic data
- content: data elements mandated by content standards outside the MARC standard

A thorough knowledge of content and display standards such as AACR2, LCSH, and ISBD is a prerequisite to working in the MARC format.

MARC 21 Fields and Content Designation

The general structural features of a MARC 21 record are as follows:

- ANSI Z39.2 and other relevant ANSI standards are implemented.
- All information in a record is stored in character form and coded in Extended ASCII.

- *Tag* for a field is stored in the directory entry for the field, not in the field itself.
- *Field length* can be calculated from the directory entry or from the field terminator character; *record length* can be calculated from the leader or the record terminator character; *location of each variable field* is explicitly stated in the directory entry.

MARC records consist of two types of variable fields: variable *control fields* and variable *data fields*. Each field may have more than one value or data element. The difference in structure accommodates the intended data content. The *levels of content designation* (MARBI 1996, 9) or parts of a field are as follows:

Field tag: a three-digit number at the beginning of the field that represents the name of the field:

Blocks of Tags by Function

0XX Control information, numbers, and codes	6XX Subject access fields
1XX Main entry	7XX Added entries other than subject or series; linking fields
2XX Titles and title paragraph (title, edition, imprint)	8XX Series added entries; location, and alternate graphics
3XX Physical description, etc.	
4XX Series statements	9XX Reserved for local implementation
5XX Notes	

Parallel Blocks for Content Designation

X00 Personal names	X40 Bibliographic titles
X10 Corporate names	X50 Topical terms
X11 Meeting names	X51 Geographic names
X30 Uniform titles	

"Further content designations (indicators and subfield codes) for data elements subject to authority control are defined consistently across the bibliographic and authority formats" (MARBI 1996, 7).

Indicators: These are two positions immediately following a field tag that may or may not be assigned/used. Indicators can be used as "filing indicator" in the title field to permit proper indexing of titles with initial articles; or to identify the standard used for the data content:

086 0_ (Government documents classification number field, first indicator "0") indicates SuDocs is the location content standard

650 _0 (Subject added entry, topical subject, second indicator "0") indicates LCSH is the subject content standard

The *subfield code* identifies distinct data elements in a field and makes it possible for them to be manipulated separately. A *subfield delimiter* precedes the subfield code to distinguish the code from "content."

The *field terminator* follows the last data element in the field and is essential to the structural integrity of the record. A *record terminator* shows the end of a record.

Content designator is an inclusive term used for the "tags, codes and conventions [levels of content designation] established explicitly to identify and further characterize the data elements within a record and to support the manipulation of that data."[6] The structure for data content in both types of variable fields plays a significant role in accessing data in a MARC record. Without separately coded data elements, not all data elements would be retrievable. For instance, library catalogs that allow searching limited by language or by format (e.g., serials, online electronic resources, videos) would not be able to do this without coded data content from a variable control field.

Control fields provide two levels of content designators: a three-digit tag representing the field name and a field terminator. The control fields have "tags" that begin with 0. They are structurally different from the data fields and do not make use of indicator positions or subfields. They contain coded "content" in a preset length. The fields provide information for the record as a whole, special bibliographic characteristics, additional material characteristics, and physical description. An accepted notation form for fixed field data is "nnn/nn/x," where nnn represents the tag number, nn represents the position number, and x represents the value. Control fields precede data fields and are also called "fixed fields" because field length is set, unlike the variable length of data fields. For example, the 245 title field varies depending on the length of the title. Examples of the "fixed" lengths for control fields:

- Leader is always 24 positions (00–23).
- 008 field for material characteristics is always 40 positions (00–39).

    Note: Positions 18–34 are format-specific values based on type of record code in the Leader (000/06). The Leader and the 008 field are not repeatable. A Leader with record type "a" refers to language material in print or electronic (000/06/a), so positions 18–34 of the 008 field on that record would be based on the book format. If the language material is electronic, a 006 field is used to show the additional material characteristic of a computer file/electronic resource (006/00/m).

- 006 field for additional material characteristics is always 18 positions (00–17).

    Note: The 006 field works like a subset of the 008 field.[7] The first position (00) is coded for the type of record. The format used to code positions 01–17 is determined by the type of record code in the 00 position, and the coding is the same as the coding for 008 positions 18–34.

- The length of the 007 field for electronic resources is always 14 positions (00–13).
- The length of the 007 field for maps is always 8 positions (00–07).

  Note: The first position (00) of the 007 field indicates the category of material. The rest of the coding is specific to that material category, just as the rest of the coding in the 006 field is specific to the record type code in the first position (00).

The *Leader* is the first and most important variable control field. Because it is a variable control field, no indicators are assigned and there are no subfield codes. The three-digit tag for the Leader is 000, but it is usually referred to as the "Leader" except in the notation form for fixed fields. The Leader has 24 positions. It provides information for data content (e.g., status, type of record, bibliographic level, and encoding level) that is valuable for record processing.

The *Directory* is a system-generated index to the variable fields immediately following the leader in a bibliographic record. When a bibliographic record is updated in an ILS, the system automatically updates the directory and the leader. MARC records outside a system that supports the MARC format may not be modified without destroying the record integrity, that is, field and record length mentioned in the record structure section. If records must be changed outside an ILS, MARC editing software can convert data to a readable form to make changes and reconstruct the directory entry and leader fields when the record is reconverted to the MARC format.

The structure of the *variable data fields* uses all four levels of content designators: the three-digit tag, the two indicator positions, subfield codes, and the field terminator. Indicators are defined in conjunction with a specific tag. For example, a first indicator "1" in a 100 field indicates that the type of personal name entry is a surname. A first indicator "1" in a 110 field indicates that the type of corporate name entry is a jurisdiction name.

MARC 21 and ILS Indexes/Indexing

The use of content designators in variable data fields and coded content in variable control fields supports the bulk of the indexing of bibliographic data in the ILS. Both public and technical services staff need a thorough knowledge of indexing. Not knowing what MARC fields or subfields are included in a particular index makes it impossible to rely on the search results. For example, is the "remainder of title" (245 or 246 fields, subfield b) included in the title index in an ILS? Is the 246 "varying form of title" field included in the title index? If not, a search for "remainder of title" data would not retrieve any records even though the bibliographic record was in the database. Most online catalogs now include "remainder of title" information (subtitle and other title) in the title index so the record would be retrieved when searching this information; however, OCLC "derived" searching does not include "remainder of title" information in the title indexing, limiting the records retrieved.[8] Although many indexes are standard across ILSs, new indexes may be created for special needs. Several of the Florida State University Libraries use the Florida Public Documents Classification System (086 __ . . . 12 fldocs) and had a separate call number index created for it. Most ILSs also have existing indexes that could be searched with a string of text to retrieve a "set" of records. The Florida State University Libraries used the 035 control number field for this purpose in their old ILS. After the migration to a new ILS, the nonconforming 035 fields were converted to a new TKR, or "tickler," field that served the same purpose. Other libraries have used a 590 note field. The field used is immaterial; what counts is the ability to retrieve a set of records for a specific purpose. Ideally, the field should not display to the public, because its content and form would not be meaningful to the end user.

BIBLIOGRAPHIC CONTROL AND DEPOSITORY REQUIREMENTS

Making depository materials available for the free use of the general public is one of a library's legal responsibilities associated with depository status (GPO 2008, 25). Bibliographic control and processing are the technical service functions responsible for adding content data to the catalog so the information in depository materials can be identified and accessed. The *Federal Depository Library Handbook* acknowledges the role bibliographic control and processing have in meeting this requirement with the statement that acceptable technical service occurs when users can easily locate and retrieve, at no cost, the government information products available at their depository library (GPO 2008, 82). Since e-government resources are accessed remotely, the inventory control activities required for tangible products are not pertinent to this chapter (GPO 2008, 81–82). Other bibliographic control activities apply equally to tangible and e-government resources. Three technical service operations are addressed here: batch loading of records into the ILS; processing activities necessary to review records and provide any local or system specific information to further support the ability to search or retrieve records; and bibliographic control maintenance needed to reflect any changes in availability.

Record Loading and Preload Considerations

Within the scope of this chapter, the first bibliographic control activity specifically discussed is the addition of records cataloged by the GPO to the ILS. The most common method of adding records to the ILS is the batch loading of records purchased from a private vendor. Before records can be loaded into the ILS, there must be an agreement on what records should be loaded. This is usually based on the depository library's item selection profile. If the responsibility for loading records is outside the area for processing, it is crucial to have good communication between the areas. A good working relationship with the area responsible for loading records can facilitate the development of an efficient workflow and procedures.

Load decisions based on ILS configuration and local processing must be made prior to loading bibliographic records into the online catalog. How does the ILS provide access "limited to" online resources? The ILS could limit searching to an online "format"—probably based on complex coding from MARC control fields. A second possibility is the use of a virtual database based on collection information from a holdings record. This is advantageous for multiple campuses, special libraries, or certain collections such as periodicals or online collections, but it requires creation of a holdings record. Florida International University (FIU) creates holdings records with collection/location information that reflects FDLP materials in both online and tangible formats (figure 9-6). It also uses only one holdings record for online materials from two depositories. This eliminates redundant holdings statements when both depositories select the same item number, resulting in a less cluttered OPAC display. Institutions with multiple campuses or depositories may want to consider this option. Another consideration is whether to create item records. Some ILSs, when creating an item record, can assign a processing status to the item. This provides another means to retrieve sets of records to facilitate processing. If this flexibility can be used in a local ILS, the details need to be worked out with those responsible for loading records.

Another significant consideration is whether data in the MARC record can be manipulated prior to loading. Sorting records can improve loading of collection information. The GPO's policy of using multiple item numbers on a record to show titles distributed in multiple formats is helpful but incomplete. Only two qualifiers for the 074 item number field are used: (online) and (MF) (GPO 2002, 76–80). If

Tag	Indicators	Sub library	Collection	Call number
852	3_	lb FIELR	lc ELRUS	lh HE 20.3627:

Value	Description/Public Display
852	Location/Call number field
3_	SuDocs classification
lb FIELR	Online
lc ELRUS	Electronic Resources—U.S. Documents
lh HE 20.3627:	same

Figure 9-6 Explanation of OPAC location display

the qualifiers used in bibliographic records could be expanded to incorporate the fuller range of qualifiers used in the *List of Classes*—(P) for paper, (CD) for CD-ROMs, (DVD) for optical/recordable discs, and (FL) for floppy diskettes—it would go a long way toward simplifying the loading of accurate location information in the MARC holdings 852 field. Because "(online)" is a qualifier, the policy works for online publications. However, the use of multiple item numbers still makes it necessary for FIU to manipulate records with MARC editing software prior to loading in order to create records sets for online publications. FIU creates a set of records for online-only publications and a set of records distributed in other formats but also available online. Although the concept of creating sets of records for online publications to load appropriate location information in the MARC holdings record is simple to grasp, in practice it is cumbersome.

Government documents staff may not be responsible for batch loading records, but loading specifications should be established in coordination with government documents staff and based on local procedures and workflow. The depository requirements already discussed help determine

- how to create sets of records to load appropriate location information in the MARC holdings record
- whether to create MARC holdings records
- whether to create item records
- whether to assign a processing status to an item record
- whether to load bibliographic records as suppressed
- what matching criteria to use if records are overlaid
- when to overlay existing records
- what tracking fields to add to facilitate the review/processing of records

The batch loading of records is even more complex when there are existing records needing replacement in the catalog. The overlay of existing records should occur when full catalog records must replace a temporary shipping list record, or when a "changed" record, updated by the GPO, must overlay an existing record. Coding "c" in the leader Record Status (000/05/c) indicates a record correction or revision. Most loading software could use this coding to create a set of "changed" records in order to review loads and improve load specifications. It is easy to load records with inappropriate MARC holdings location information and time consuming to remove bad location information, so great care should be taken in the development of load specifications

Processing

There should be a set of checks for any batch-loaded records based on a profile to ensure that there are records for materials received and no records for materials not received. Since the bibliographic record provides access for online publications, there is a guaranteed match between records received and materials accessed. Despite this match, it is still essential to review the record load. The easiest way to accomplish a review is to generate a set of records for the load. For database maintenance purposes, FIU uses a TKR field with a specific text string that identifies the "source" of all batch-loaded records. Every record in the March 2006 load, for example, has the source TKR slm063. For government documents record loads, FIU also uses a processing TKR (figure 9-7). These fields may be searched alone or in combination with other indexes to provide information useful for processing (figure 9-8). The working index for reviewing online records is generated by a combined search for

Source data	10/05 monthly load	TKR __ la (Source)SLM05A
	03/06 monthly load	TKR __ la (Source)SLM063
Processing data	date of 10/05 load	TKR __ la (DGPO)mrcv UP 20051016
	date of 03/06 load	TKR __ la (DGPO)mrcv UP 20060305

Figure 9-7 Text strings retrievable through the local TKR index. The concept of tracking record loads by "source" data that would always identify the record load and by "processing" data that is removed after the record is processed is effective for many things. The fields used to do this are dependent on local indexing and ILS functionality.

Search	Database	No. of records
TKR=slm063*	FIU01	572
TKR=slm063* and URL=http://purl.access*	FIU01	531
TKR=mrcv up 20060305* and URL= http://purl.access*	FIU01	284

NOTE

The asterisk (*) is a truncation symbol used in Boolean searches for variant endings.

Figure 9-8 FIU search and results for information about March 2006. The TKR index indexes the TKR field FIU uses for text strings to retrieve sets of records. The first search uses the text string that retrieves a set of records for the whole load based on the source file. The second search combines the first search with a search of the URL index using the starting text for the GPO PURL in the 856 field. The third search retrieves records with online access that need to be reviewed by the University Park Campus by searching the TKR index for the Campus text string for the load and by searching the URL index for the starting text for the GPO PURL. FIU has two campuses with two FDLP designations. One record is shared by both campuses but separate TKRs are loaded for each campus so that each has the ability to track its own processing.

the processing TKR and the beginning of the GPO PURL address. Loads often have a high percentage of records with an 856 field, 93 percent in the March load. More than 46,000 records with a PURL were loaded into the FIU database through March 2006.

The ability to search and retrieve this type of record set makes the review of records for appropriate location information possible. It can also point out unforeseen load issues that may be resolved by changing load specifications. There could be overlooked circumstances that do not provide online collection information. For example, a combined search for the March 2006 load and U.S. online collections retrieved 463 records, opposed to the 531 records with PURLs. That FIU creates only one online holdings record per title even if multiple records exist could account for some discrepancy. The review process should resolve the discrepancies. Location information should be corrected in the reviewed records. Any load issues should be conveyed to the area responsible for loading records and possible revision of load specifications discussed.

The review process confirms that records are loaded according to local specifications such as holdings records with appropriate collection/location information and item records with appropriate material type, loan information, and processing status. It should also resolve any bibliographic data issues (regarding, e.g., valid PURLs, superseded publications, duplicate records) according to local procedures. The background in standards and coding in this chapter provides basic knowledge of the bibliographic record fundamental to the review of records for local bibliographic control and conducive to improving ILS searching. This background also highlights the value of bibliographic standards, their contribution to the quality of bibliographic data in an ILS, and the ability to access it using MARC format functionality.

Bibliographic Control Maintenance

Updating cataloging records to reflect changes in data or availability is a challenging part of the bibliographic control process and involves many issues. Records may be manually updated based on the changes in *Administrative Notes Technical Supplement* (ANTS), or updated changed records can be batch-loaded into the ILS. Many changes stem from online availability added to records per current GPO cataloging practices (GPO 2002, 62). Records for online publications no longer available online also need to be updated. Records can be identified through a manual workflow based on ANTS, or if changed records are loaded they can be identified by searching the note the GPO adds to the record (GPO 2002, 65, 67; and see figure 9-9). Records no longer available online can be reviewed and edited according to local policies and procedures (e.g., suppress online copy statement if still available in another form, suppress record, allow record to display as no longer available).

Other bibliographic control/processing issues not specific to online publications may affect processing because of online availability. Policies for multipart items may require records to be updated. Sometimes duplicate publications are

Search	Database	No. of records
WNO=no longer available via	FIU01	138
WNO=no longer available via and TKR=slm063*	FIU01	5

NOTE

The asterisk (*) is a truncation symbol used in Boolean searches for variant endings.

Figure 9-9 FIU search and results for records no longer available via the Internet. The first search searches the keyword note index (WNO) for the text string "no longer available via." The second search combines the first search with a search that limits the number of titles no longer available via the Internet to the March 2006 load by combining the keyword note search with a search for the source data TKR for the March load.

distributed under different item numbers or call numbers. Some GPO item numbers and call numbers permit human interpretation, but the correlations and associations are not readily discernable to an ILS. Corrected prints supersede the original print and should trigger the local procedures for superseded records (GPO 2002, 79, 96–104, 156). Corrections in the form of errata need a local policy to connect the original document being corrected with the errata. These bibliographic control issues need to be included in the review process, whether relating to new records or to changed records. Not all issues are reported in ANTS. When problems such as duplicate records are identified, they should be reported to askGPO (http://gpo .custhelp.com/cgi-bin/gpo.cfg/php/enduser/ask.php) for resolution (GPO 2008, 8). If a bibliographic record has been merged with another, the OCLC number from the merged record will be moved to an 019 field in the "valid record." Loading problems for merged records affect only libraries receiving changed records. It is possible to create a set of records with 019 fields, or the ILS may have a special 019 report. Once an invalid record has been identified—a record that has an invalid OCLC number from an 019 field in the valid 035 field—local procedures for updating/replacing the record should be followed.

Technology has made it easier for libraries to do business with the GPO. E-mail, discussion lists, and problem-reporting systems have dramatically improved communication between depository libraries and the GPO. It has also improved the functionality of the *Federal Depository Library Handbook*. The new handbook not only consolidates depository information and requirements into one publication but also provides an abundance of links to depository resources, making it an invaluable tool. For example, it includes links to each of the following resources, which have also contributed to improved communication: a discussion list for announcements; Reporting Errors on GPO Access web page for errors such as broken links; the PURL search form; and the Knowledge Base, also part of askGPO that tracks and archives reported problems.[9] This level of interaction has improved the quality of bibliographic control by making it easier to report problems and reducing the time required to resolve them.

CONCLUSION

The direction of bibliographic control is a hot topic in the library world because of rapid advances in new technologies. The overview of current standards in this chapter emphasizes how well they have served libraries by contributing to the quality of bibliographic data and the ability to access that data. Bibliographic control initiatives reflect a proactive response to this environment of change via FRBR and RDA, among others. The Library of Congress Working Group on the Future of Bibliographic Control in its final report in 2008 emphasized the importance of cooperation among libraries and other organizations. Despite the potential elusiveness of online information and the awkward task of batch loading records with appropriate collection/location information, the review of new records for local bibliographic control purposes can be straightforward and valuable. One change that would improve the loading of holdings information is the use of additional qualifiers for GPO item numbers. Librarians who develop good ILS skills can better assist in the development of local policies and procedures that take advantage of the full functionality of the ILS. Current technologies facilitating communication can be effectively used to resolve problems and share their resolution. The use of online technologies facilitates the expeditious processing of e-government information and provides library end users with the best possible access to this information through high-quality bibliographic control and processing.

NOTES

1. MARC format used in this chapter refers to MARC 21. For more information, see the Library of Congress's MARC standards website at www.loc.gov/marc/.

2. For more information about the Program for Cooperative Cataloging, see www.loc.gov/catdir/pcc/.

3. For more information about Medical Subject Headings (MeSH), see the National Library of Medicine website at www.nlm.nih.gov/mesh/; for the *NASA Thesaurus*, see the products list on NASA's Scientific and Technical Information website for the full text of both volumes and a monthly list of new terms; for the *Thesaurus of ERIC Descriptors*, see www.eric.ed.gov/ERICWebPortal/Home.portal?_nfpb=true&_pageLabel=Thesaurus&_nfls=false; and for a factsheet about ERIC descriptors, see www.csa.com/factsheets/supplements/ericthes.php.

4. Some FRBR descriptive and organizing elements are considered core elements only under certain conditions, which are elaborated in the FRBR report. For a complete list of elements and explanations, see IFLA FRBR 1998, 112–115.

5. See MARBI 1996, "MARC 21 Formats: Background and Principles," section 3: Structural Features.

6. Ibid., 1.

7. OCLC, Summary of Leader and 008 field bytes, *Bibliographic Formats and Standards*, www.oclc.org/bibformats/en/fixedfield/008summary.shtm.

8. OCLC derived search examples may be found in Connexion: Searching WorldCat Quick Reference at www.oclc.org/support/documentation/worldcat/searching/refcard/#derived.

9. GPO-FDLP-L, http://listserv.access.gpo.gov; GPO Access, Reporting Errors on GPO Access, http://origin.www.gpoaccess.gov/help/report_errors.html; PURL search form, http://purl.gpo.gov/maint/display.html; GPO Access, Online Knowledge Base, http://origin.www.gpoaccess.gov/help/.

REFERENCES

Anglo-American Cataloguing Rules. 2002. 2nd ed. rev. Chicago: American Library Association.

Chan, Lois Mai. 1994. *Cataloging and Classification: An Update.* 2nd ed. New York: McGraw Hill.

Dunsire, Gordon. 2007. "Distinguishing Content from Carrier: The RDA/ONIX Framework for Resource Categorization." *D-Lib Magazine* 13 (1/2). www.dlib .org/dlib/january07/dunsire/01dunsire.html.

Gorman, Michael. 2000. "From Card Catalogues to WebPACS: Celebrating Cataloguing in the 20th Century." www.loc.gov/catdir/bibcontrol/gorman_paper .html.

GPO U.S. Government Printing Office. 2002. *Government Printing Office Cataloging Guidelines.* Prepared by Steven R. Uthoff. 4th ed. Washington, DC: Cataloging Branch, Library Programs Service, U.S. GPO. Last updated March 25, 2002. www.gpo.gov/su_docs/fdlp/cip/gpocatgu.pdf.

———. 2008. *Federal Depository Library Handbook.* Online ed. Washington, DC: U.S. GPO. www.fdlp.gov/handbook/index.html.

IFLA International Federation of Library Associations. 1997. *International Standard Bibliographic Description for Electronic Resources.* Munich: K. G. Saur. www.ifla.org/ VII/s13/pubs/isbd.htm.

———. 2007. Family of ISBDs. www.ifla.org/VII/s13/pubs/cat-isbd.htm.

IFLA FRAD 2007. *Functional Requirements for Authority Data: A Conceptual Model,* draft, April 1. www.ifla.org/VII/d4/FRANAR-ConceptualModel-2ndReview.pdf.

IFLA FRBR, Study Group on the Functional Requirements for Bibliographic Records. 1998. *Functional Requirements for Bibliographic Records: Final Report.* Munich: K. G. Saur. www.ifla.org/VII/s13/frbr/frbr.pdf.

IFLA Meeting of Experts on an International Cataloguing Code. 2006. "Statement of International Cataloguing Principles." Draft, April 3. http://www.ddb.de/standard isierung/pdf/statement_draft_apr2006.pdf.

JSC Joint Steering Committee for Development of RDA. 2007 "Executive Summary of the Meeting of the Joint Steering Committee, October 15–20, Chicago, IL." *News and Announcements.* www.collectionscanada.ca/jsc/0710exec.html.

LC Library of Congress, Cataloging Policy and Support Office. 2006. Series at the Library of Congress, June 1. www.loc.gov/catdir/cpso/series.html.

LC Library of Congress, Working Group on the Future of Bibliographic Control. 2008. *On the Record: Report of the Library of Congress Working Group on the Future of Bibliographic Control.* www.loc.gov/bibliographic-future/news/lcwg-ontherecord -jan08-final.pdf.

Lynch, Clifford. 2000. "The New Context for Bibliographic Control In the New Millennium." www.loc.gov/catdir/bibcontrol/lynch_paper.html.

MARBI. 1996. "MARC 21 Formats: Background and Principles." www.loc.gov/ marc/96principl.html.

Storey, Tom. 2003. "Understanding FRBR, the New Bibliographic Model." *OCLC Newsletter* 262.

Tillett, Barbara B. 2001. "Bibliographic Relationships." In *Relationships in the Organization of Knowledge,* ed. Carol A. Bean and Rebecca Green, 23. Boston: Kluwer Academic.

———. 2003. *The FRBR Model: A Presentation.* www.loc.gov/catdir/cpso/frbreng.pdf.

———. 2004. "What Is FRBR? A Conceptual Model for the Bibliographic Universe." Washington, DC: Library of Congress, Cataloging Distribution Service. www.loc .gov/cds/downloads/FRBR.PDF.

Wendler, Robin. 2000. "Musings on Priscilla Caplan's 'International Metadata Initiatives: Lessons in Bibliographic Control.'" www.loc.gov/catdir/bibcontrol/ wendler_paper.html.

Chapter 10   Integrating Online Government Documents into Library Reference Services

Grace-Ellen McCrann

The U.S. federal government is the largest publisher in the world, and it would be hard to find a subject/field in which the federal government does not have some degree of interest. There are approximately 1,250 federal depository libraries in the United States, but the current online availability of so much federal information now makes many government documents available to any library, federal depository or not. In August 2000, Francis J. Buckley, then federal Superintendent of Documents, sent a letter to library directors announcing the beginnings of a transition from a mostly print depository system to a primarily electronic program (Buckley 2000). Since that letter, the federal government and especially the GPO have rapidly increased free online access to government documents and information. In 2006, for example, an astonishing 93 percent of the documents included in the FDLP were available online (GPO 2006).

Such a large quantity of online government information creates positive opportunities for libraries that want to incorporate government information into their reference collections. The wide range of interests addressed by federal agencies and departments, the two houses of Congress, and the executive branch make U.S. government documents valuable reference resources for almost any library and for almost any patron.

Brady, McCord, and Galbraith (2006) describe the accelerating change in patron usage from print to electronic formats as a "cultural shift." How is the profession changing as part of this shift? The implications of the movement away from print to online access began to be recognized as early as the October 2000 Federal Depository Library Conference, held just a few months after Superintendent Buckley's announcement. While discussing the changing depository environment, John Shuler of the University of Illinois, Chicago, spoke of librarians' "shift in focus from depository librarianship to government information specialists" (Cheney 2004). Traditionally, the term "government documents" has been used for titles that were part of the FDLP. Because so many depository and nondepository government titles are now freely available online, in this chapter we use "government documents" as well as "government information" to describe the full range of online government resources.

For librarians who have not been exposed to them, the very thought of government documents can often be a bit intimidating (Downie 2004, 38). Traditionally, not all that many libraries collected government documents (except IRS forms, of course). Documents were often kept in specialized collection areas and shelved using the SuDocs call number/classification system, which looked nothing like Dewey or Library of Congress classifications.[1] Now, online government information has broken through these barriers. There are no unusual call numbers, and online resources are available to any library with an Internet connection.

The merging of government documents and general reference service points has already occurred in many libraries that at one time had separate government documents collections (Frazer et al. 1997; Salem 2006). One initiative that is furthering the integration of these resources into the realm of reference is Government Information Online (GIO; http://govtinfo.org), a free national online information service supported by nearly thirty public, academic, and state libraries throughout the United States. GIO combines the concepts of collaborative, chat, and e-mail reference and answers questions about government resources from all users.[2]

In this chapter we offer practical help and suggestions for librarians who have not had much prior experience with government information, whether they are in a recently merged government information and general reference environment, are new to the profession, or see the proliferation of online government information as a new patron resource.

COLLECTION DEVELOPMENT

Although government documents might be a somewhat unfamiliar resource, the principles of good collection development are the same. Collection development is one of the underpinnings of library reference services. If a library does not own, know about, or have access to a resource, then that resource is unavailable to its librarians or patrons for consultation. For collection development of government information, think about the word *DOCS*.

Define your Audience.

Organize your Resources.

Collect your Documents.

Select your Subjects.

Expanding current collection development practices to include e-government information is the first step in integrating those resources into reference services. For example, public libraries may select online local and state government documents of current interest to meet user needs, and academic libraries serving a large science and engineering department can provide online access to documents from NASA or the USGS.

When librarians are deciding how to spend reference book budgets, they familiarize themselves with what is available and often check recommendations in *Choice* or *Publishers Weekly*, read book reviews, or look at RUSA reference recommendations. Including online government documents in library reference services takes a similar commitment of time and interest. The following are a few suggestions for keeping current in the world of government documents as an aid to the selection and collection development process. Note that the GPO's online resources are excellent places to start, but libraries should be aware that there is much more government information than is included in the FDLP.

Browse the GPO List of Classes. The GPO *List of Classes* (http://purl.access.gpo .gov/GPO/LPS1480) is arranged by federal agencies because SuDocs call numbers for government documents represent the publishing agency rather than the subject categories, as with the Dewey and Library of Congress classification systems (e.g., call numbers for all Department of State documents regardless of topic begin with S, for State). The arrangement of resources by SuDocs call numbers/federal agencies makes this list easy to browse. Call numbers may not matter in online documents, but browsing through the list agency by agency gives a quick overview of much of what the government publishes. Also, the GPO currently assigns all online documents, e-journals, and websites a SuDocs number in their cataloging records.

Search the GPO Online Catalog. The GPO's online *Catalog of U.S. Government Publications* (http://catalog.gpo.gov/F) contains records for about half a million document titles published from July 1976 onward. Updated daily, the catalog includes links to online versions from a title's MARC-view cataloging record. The advanced search option allows keyword searching, and it is possible to limit results to titles with online versions by clicking on "Internet Publications" at the top of the screen.

Subscribe to the GPO "New Titles by Topic" e-Mail Alert Service. The GPO offers an e-mail alert service by topic when new documents are published. Topics range from education and health care to statistics, the environment, and Spanish-language publications. Find out more and subscribe (it's free) at http://bookstore.gpo.gov/ alertservice.jsp.

Consult the GPO New Electronic Titles Website. Every month the GPO lists new electronic and tangible electronic titles added to the GPO catalog (http://catalog .gpo.gov/F/?func=file&file_name=find-net&local_base=NEWTITLE). This is a good site to browse the latest online titles.

Join GODORT. If you are an ALA member join GODORT, even if you are not a depository librarian (www.ala.org/Template.cfm?Section=godort). GODORT is a community of people who work with, are interested in, and often love government documents. Non–documents specialist librarians will benefit from GODORT members' willingness to share their expertise.

Join a Local Documents Interest Group. Many state and regional library organizations sponsor special interest groups, and there's often a government documents group.

Subscribe to GOVDOC-L. GOVDOC-L is an electronic discussion forum about government information and documents. Depository librarians and others who share an interest in government information subscribe. Find out more and subscribe at http://govdoc-l.org.

Check GODORT's Annual Notable Governments Documents List. GODORT has produced an annual Notable Government Documents List since 1984. The list is currently published each year in the May 15 issue of *Library Journal.*

OUTREACH—INTERNAL

Although any reference librarian certainly can individually recommend government websites and online documents as part of a reference transaction, the value of such online resources is expanded if accessing online government information becomes part of a library's reference policies. So, if at all possible, get colleagues involved. One recommended ALA RUSA core competency for reference librarians is "Dissemination of Knowledge: Goal: A librarian shares expertise with colleagues and mentors newer staff."[3] It is particularly important to share knowledge of government information and how to access it. These have not traditionally been required of reference librarians but now are critical skills.

Most libraries do not have a large number of print primary sources applicable to ready reference. That many government documents are primary sources is a strong selling point. Do patrons want to see statistics about a state's population, get information about product recalls, compare nursing homes, find a city zip code, or obtain an obscure tax form? All these reference needs can be filled using online government information.

Another reason for reference librarians to become familiar with online government documents is that many federal agencies are moving from print, or even a combination of print and online resources, to "born-digital" resources. As a result, public libraries especially are seeing increased patron traffic requesting online government information. High-profile examples of born-digital resources include the FEMA forms required for dealing with the aftermath of Hurricane Katrina and Medicare prescription drug coverage enrollment forms (Bertot 2006). In recent years the IRS has cut back significantly on the numbers of printed tax forms sent to libraries, and in August 2006 the EPA announced that it is closing some EPA libraries, which were open to the public, and moving toward providing public access to environmental information through electronic means (Office of Environmental Information 2006).

All these actions are pushing patrons toward online government information. Since government documents have traditionally been a somewhat specialized resource, information about them needs to be proactively made part of a library's professional development activities. Strategies and resources for sharing expertise internally include the following:

> *Regular Updates.* Internal discussion lists or regular e-mail can notify reference librarians about specific online government information that can be useful and timely in reference transactions.

Workshops/Meetings. Professional development days or regular reference staff meetings are opportunities to share information about interesting or topical online government.

Bookmarks/Favorites on the Reference Desk Computers. Between January and April each year, the IRS website should certainly be part of the bookmark lists on reference desk computers. The IRS homepage offers both forms and instructions online. IRS forms are one government resource that appeals to patrons at almost any kind of library, but just as with regular collection development, librarians should tailor their reference desk bookmarks to their patron base. (See the Ready Reference Suggestions section at the end of this chapter.)

Library Displays. Traditional methods work too. Displays quickly reach both library colleagues and patrons.

GODORT Handout Exchange and Clearinghouse (www.lib.umich.edu/govdocs/godort.html). The government documents depository community has produced some wonderful handouts to introduce, update, or remind librarians about government documents. Many of them permit noncommercial copying and adaptation under a Creative Commons Attribution Noncommercial Share Alike 2.5 License. Under the terms of this license the original author must be cited when the information is used.[4]

OUTREACH—EXTERNAL

Patrons often do not know that the answer they want is contained in a government document. Outreach and teaching activities such as the following raise patrons' awareness of these resources.

Include Government Information in the Catalog

Cataloging is an integral part of library public services, and online government information should be included in a library catalog. If patrons cannot easily find an item in the catalog, then for all intents and purposes that library doesn't own that title—even if there are fifteen copies on the shelf. Online or print government documents often have long, complicated titles, which can be a barrier for patrons. But many documents also have common/short titles or popular names, like "Public Law 107-13" or the "9/11 Commission Report." Catalogers should be encouraged to include common/short titles in the catalog record for added title access (field 246).

The MARC catalog record format standard also includes a field (856) for a website's URL. URLs included in an 856 field become live links to that website or document in online catalogs. Libraries should include online documents with live links in library catalogs so that physical and virtual patrons can find them. The successful inclusion of online government documents in reference services is a collaborative endeavor and means changes in workflow and job responsibilities for reference, administration, and technical services/cataloging (Buttlar and Garcha 1998). The concept of a "hot government document" may be an oxymoron to some, but when a newly released federal report is the top story on television newscasts, this media attention attracts patron interest. Many of these reports are released electronically, and librarians can take advantage of online access to make the information available to patrons quickly. The *Taguba Report*—the report of the investigation into the alleged abuse of prisoners of war at Abu Ghraib Prison in Baghdad, Iraq—is one example. This report was available online almost as soon as it was released, and within hours many libraries provided a link to the online version.[5]

Use the Library Website to Promote Government Information

Two excellent examples of library websites that promote government information are Documents Center, maintained by the University of Michigan (www.lib.umich .edu/govdocs/), and Country Resources: The Green Boxes, maintained by Indiana University, Bloomington (www.libraries.iub.edu/index.php?pageId=1765). Jakob Nielsen's (2002) top two categories for homepage usability are "Make the Site's Purpose Clear: Explain Who You Are and What You Do" and "Help Users Find What They Need," and both of these websites fulfill these usability requirements. Both sites identify the author, the purpose, and the content of their web pages, have good internal navigation, and give a creation/update date for each page. Web page design is individual, but libraries can use these two websites as models of clear, current, and comprehensive online government information resources.

Take Advantage of Anniversaries of Historical Events

Librarians often look for an idea that will create interest in their collections and introduce patrons to online government information. In the case of historical event celebrations or memorials, government documents are often an integral part of the history being commemorated. Government information is not just congressional hearings and reports from commissions; it encompasses resources such as the American Memory collection at the Library of Congress (http://memory.loc.gov/ ammem/index.html). Such online collections are full of unbelievable treasures on topics from fifty years of Coca-Cola advertisements (part of the Library of Congress motion picture archives), to Works Progress Administration posters, to Thomas Edison's 1910 film "The Stenographer's Friend."

The City College of New York provides a good example of this tactic. CCNY drew heavily on e-government information and documents to create a website to commemorate the sixtieth anniversary of the D-Day invasion of Normandy. The website includes photographs taken of the landings of U.S. troops on Omaha Beach posted on the Web by the Naval Historical Center. The navy also assigned combat artists to accompany the troops as they landed in France, and these first-person sketches and artwork are available online. Also included or linked are an interview with Charles Chibitty, a Comanche code talker who landed on Utah Beach a day or two after D-Day; a transcript and image of General Eisenhower's Order of the Day for the Normandy invasion; and the Eisenhower Presidential Library's digitized image of the handwritten note composed by General Eisenhower in case the invasion failed.[6] Talk about primary sources!

Offer Public Workshops

Academic librarians can make short presentations at departmental meetings. Public librarians can offer local schools workshops for teachers. Any type of library can offer workshops. A hint about workshops: target the presentation to the audience. Don't call it a government documents workshop. Instead invite patrons to "Learn More about Social Security," or "Find Help for Small Businesses on the Web," or attend the workshop "Census Statistics You Can Use in Research Papers."

Include Online Government Documents in Information Literacy Sessions

Many academic librarians teach library instruction sessions to college students and faculty. Some libraries refer to this as BI (bibliographic instruction); others title these sessions IL (information literacy) or simply instruction. Whatever the name, most college libraries have such programs, and online government information should be part of the agenda (Downie 2004; Sheehy and Cheney 1997).

READY REFERENCE RESOURCES

The following represents a wide range of selected online government information sites that are particularly suitable as ready reference resources. Libraries will need to choose the reference resources most suitable to their populations and patron base. Also visit the GODORT website Frequently Used Sites Relating to U.S. Federal Government Information at www.library.vanderbilt.edu/romans/fdtf/ for good ready reference links by subject.

Search Engines and Portals

- USA.gov, the "U.S. Government's Official Web Portal," is more than just a search engine. It searches government and military websites as well as state government websites. Patrons can find the latest news about the U.S. government, links to government information by topic, and answers to frequently asked questions about government services (e.g., contacting public officials, getting or renewing a passport, applying for government jobs). Topics are also organized by specific user groups, such as kids, parents, seniors, and veterans. (www.usa.gov)

- Google U.S. Government Search is a standard search engine that searches .gov and .mil websites. Federal, state, and international government websites, as well as some nongovernment websites, are included in this database. To narrow search results to government sites, either add .gov to the search keywords or click on the link "Search Government Sites." For example, using taxes and .gov as search terms produces websites for the IRS as well as the Vermont and Oregon tax departments and the Ministry of Taxes in Azerbaijan. An advanced search feature allows users to limit searches in many ways, such as by language, region, or specific web page. The Google U.S. Government Search homepage also includes links to latest government news, the *Washington Post*, the White House, *Government Executive* magazine, and the American Armed Forces Information Service. (www.google.com/ig/usgov/)

- Science.gov is a searchable and archived portal for government science information and includes government information arranged by topic (e.g., Astronomy, Earth and Ocean Sciences, Health and Medicine, Science Education). Websites of current interest are featured, such as the website for methicillin-resistant *Staphylococcus aureus* (MRSA) disease. A Special Collections area links to National Science Portals, Science Conferences, and Taxonomies and Thesauri. (http://science.gov)

- Regulations.gov is a portal where patrons can comment on federal regulations and search for regulations by agency, document type, or keyword. (www.regulations.gov/search/index.jsp)

Documents/Websites Arranged by Subject

There are several websites (often maintained by depository libraries) that arrange online government documents/websites by subject. Libraries may want to bookmark these sites on their reference desk computers.

- Browse Topics. This website is a partnership between the GPO and Oklahoma State University. Topics are available alphabetically, from "Accounting and Auditing" through "Zip Codes." (www.browsetopics.gov)

- Government Databases by Subject. Maintained by Indiana University-Purdue University Indianapolis. (www.ulib.iupui.edu/subjectareas/gov/dbsubject/)

- Government Documents. Maintained by The City College of New York, Government Documents Division. (www.ccny.cuny.edu/library/Divisions/Government/GOVPUBS.html)

- Government Information on the Web Subject Index. Maintained by St. Mary's University, Austin, Texas. (http://library.stmarytx.edu/acadlib/doc/us/subjects/submain.htm)

- Subject Indexes to Government Information on the Internet, by Stephen J. Woods. Maintained by Idaho State University. Links and brief description of the subjects indexed on various library websites. (www.isu.edu/library/documents/subinst.htm)

- Government Information on the Internet by Subject. Maintained by the University of Idaho Library. (http://db.lib.uidaho.edu/govdocs/index.php3)
- Frequently Used Sites Related to U.S. Federal Government Information. Maintained by GODORT, hosted by Vanderbilt University. This searchable resource site lists popular resources by topic and agencies by level of government. It includes resources for government information librarians such as blogs, electronic discussion lists, indexes, and citation guides. (www.library .vanderbilt.edu/romans/fdtf/index.shtml)
- Documents Center. This central reference and referral point for local, state, federal, foreign, or international government information, maintained by the University of Michigan Library, provides a searchable reference and instructional tool for government, political science, statistical data, and news. (www.lib.umich.edu/govdocs/)

Citing Online Government Documents

Once patrons begin to use online government documents as part of their research, they will need to know how to cite them in bibliographies.

- Brief Guide to Citing Government Publications. Maintained by the Government Publications Department, Regional Depository Library, University of Memphis. (http://exlibris.memphis.edu/resource/unclesam/citeweb.html)
- Citing Online Government Information Sources using MLA (Modern Language Association) Style. Maintained by the University of Nevada, Reno, Libraries. (www.library.unr.edu/subjects/guides/government/cite.html)
- "Citing Records in the National Archives of the United States." National Archives General Information Leaflet No. 17. (www.archives.gov/publica tions/general-info-leaflets/17.html)

Budget of the U.S. Government

- Budget of the United States Government: Main Page. Search the latest edition of the federal budget at this website and browse or search federal budgets from FY 1996 to the present. (www.gpoaccess.gov/usbudget/index .html)

Census Data

- The U.S. Census Bureau website provides census data, information categorized under People and Households (e.g., state median income, poverty tables) and Economic Indicators (e.g., housing starts, new home sales, manufacturers' shipments, inventories and orders, retail trade quarterly reports). (www.census.gov)

- American Fact Finder has information, statistics, and maps about the Federal Decennial Census, the American Community Survey (yearly data on areas of 65,000 population or more), the Population Estimates Program (population estimates made between the decennial censuses), the Economic Census (taken every five years), and the Annual Economic Surveys (data derived from the Annual Survey of Manufactures, County Business Patterns and Nonemployer Statistics). (http://factfinder.census.gov)

Charities

- Search for Charities (online searchable database of organizations eligible to receive tax-deductible charitable contribution). Maintained by the IRS. (www.irs.ustreas.gov/charities/article/0,,id=96136,00.html)
- Rules for Charitable Contributions. Maintained by the IRS. (www.irs.ustreas .gov/charities/article/0,,id=96102,00.html)

Children/Youth

- America's Story from America's Library, the Library of Congress's entertaining and educational media for youth, has something of interest for all ages. (www.americaslibrary.gov)
- Ben's Guide to the U.S. Government for Kids—that's Ben as in Ben Franklin—is maintained by the GPO. (http://bensguide.gpo.gov)
- Youth Education: Fun and Games. Previously called Money Central Station, these are games and activities to teach children about money, maintained by the U.S. Bureau of Engraving and Printing. (www.moneyfactory .gov/newmoney/main.cfm/learning/fun/)
- NASA's page for students. Maintained by NASA. (www.nasa.gov/audience/ forstudents/index.html)
- Teaching with Documents—Lesson Plans includes links to reproducible primary documents from the National Archives. Topics include images of the American Revolution, 1912 political cartoons, Watergate, and much more. (www.archives.gov/education/lessons/)
- Toy Hazard Recalls. Maintained by the U.S. Consumer Product Safety Commission. (www.cpsc.gov/cpscpub/prerel/category/toy.html)
- Infant/Child Product Recalls (not including toys). Maintained by the U.S. Consumer Product Safety Commission. (www.cpsc.gov/cpscpub/prerel/ category/child.html)

Congressional Record, via GPO Access

- The *Congressional Record* is published every day Congress is in session and records the debates and proceedings of both the Senate and the House of

Representatives. GPO Access includes a database that searches the *Record* from 1994 to the present. (www.gpoaccess.gov/crecord/)

Copyright

- The U.S. Copyright Office website contains an excellent introduction to the basics of copyright, a page of FAQs, and a list of the current copyright fees. Search copyright records from 1978 to the present and find out how to register a work or record a document. (www.copyright.gov)

Countries of the World

- *Background Notes*, from the U.S. State Department, includes information on foreign countries' political conditions, economy, history, land, people, and foreign relations, updated every few years. (www.state.gov/r/pa/ei/bgn/)
- *World Leaders*, online directory previously known as *Chiefs of State and Cabinet Members of Foreign Governments*. The CIA continuously updates this most current directory available on this subject. (https://www.cia.gov/library/publications/world-leaders-1/index.html)
- *World Factbook.* The print version of this CIA document is updated yearly, but the online database version is updated continuously. Each country's entry includes a simple map, a short history of the country, and detailed data on the country's geography, people, government, economy, communications, transportation, military, and transnational issues. The site also includes a section on world flags. (https://www.cia.gov/library/publications/the-world-factbook/index.html)

Grants and Contracts: Elementary and Secondary Levels

- Find Programs by Title. Almost $38 billion of U.S. government grant money was distributed in fiscal year 2006 through the U.S. Department of Education. Local schools can use this agency's website to find out what monies and programs are available. (www.ed.gov/programs/find/title/index.html?src=fp)
- Grants.gov. Central storehouse of information on federal grants. Use this site to find and apply for federal government grants. (www.grants.gov)

Health

- Medicare. Patrons can compare Medicare prescription drug plans, find plans in their state that match a prescription drug list, and access information about lowering prescription costs during Medicare's coverage gap period. From the U.S. Department of Health and Human Services. (www.medicare.gov/default.asp)

- Nursing Home Compare. This Department of Health and Human Services website contains detailed information about every Medicare and Medicaid certified nursing home in the country. (www.medicare.gov/NHCompare/Home.asp)

Internet Hoaxes and Urban Legends

False information and rumors can spread like wildfire through the Internet. Here are two reliable government sites to help you check out these rumors.

- Internet Hoaxes: Identifying Hoaxes and Urban Legends, from the U.S. Department of Homeland Security. Defines and gives sample Internet and e-mail hoaxes and urban legends. (www.dhs.gov/xcitizens/general _1165337828628.shtm)
- Hoaxbusters, from the U.S. Department of Energy. Information about Internet hoaxes and chain letters and how to recognize them. (http://hoax busters.ciac.org)

Small Business Sites

- Business.gov (Doing Business with the U.S. Government). Maintained by the U.S. Small Business Administration. The U.S. federal government is the largest purchaser of goods and service in the world, and you don't have to be a huge corporation to do business with it. For small businesses, the Small Business Guides site is a great place to start. (www.business.gov/guides/)
- SBA Programs. Maintained by the U.S. Small Business Administration. The Small Business Administration is set up specifically to offer help and assistance to small businesses. This site links patrons to available SBA programs. (www.sba.gov/aboutsba/sbaprograms/gc/index.html)
- Small Business/Self-Employed Virtual Small Business Tax Workshop, maintained by the IRS, offers a small business/self-employed online classroom with step-by-step information about federal tax obligations. (www.irs.gov/businesses/small/article/0,,id=97726,00.html)

Social Security

- Social Security Claims. Maintained by the Social Security Administration, allows user to apply for and check application status for retirement/disability/spouse's benefits. (https://s044a90.ssa.gov/apps6z/ISBA/main.html)
- Benefit Calculators, by the Social Security Administration. Calculator for social security retirement benefits. (www.ssa.gov/planners/calculators.htm)
- Retirement Planner, by the Social Security Administration. Detailed information about social security retirement benefits under law. (www.ssa.gov/retire2/index.htm)

- *Online Social Security Handbook*, by the Social Security Administration. A basic guide to the benefits and programs. (www.ssa.gov/OP_Home/hand book/)

Statistics

- The National Center for Education Statistics is the primary federal entity for collecting and analyzing data related to education. Its website offers data, fast facts, and tools such as a school, college, and library search tool. (http:// nces.ed.gov)
- National Center for Health Statistics website, by the Centers for Disease Control and Prevention. (www.cdc.gov/nchs/)
- *Statistical Abstract of the United States*, by the U.S. Census Bureau. The website of the *Statistical Abstract*, the annual national data book produced since 1878, is the best megasite for statistics generated across the U.S. government. Patrons can find everything from public high school graduates by state to federal drug seizures by type of drug or details on congressional campaign finances. The bicentennial edition, *Historical Statistics of the United States: Colonial Times to 1970*, is also available online. For further information, users can check the detailed and copious references. (http://purl.access .gpo.gov/GPO/LPS2878)
- Zip Code Statistics, provided by the U.S. Census Bureau. Statistics by zip code about people, housing, the labor force, personal income, and households. (www.census.gov/epcd/www/zipstats.html)

Student Aid

- Federal Student Aid. Higher education gets more expensive all the time. The federal government offers several student aid programs, and this website, maintained by the U.S. Department of Education, provides information on Pell Grants, Stafford Loans, PLUS Loans, Federal Supplemental Educational Opportunity Grants, Federal Work Study, and Perkins Loans. Patrons can also fill out the online Federal Student Aid application at this site. (www.fafsa.ed.gov)

Technical Documents

Some government agencies are better than others when it comes to digitizing technical and scientific documents and making them available on the Web. Two of the best are NASA and the USGS.

- NASA Technical Reports Server. Patrons can search/browse NASA documents on this website. If there is an online version of the document, the link is included in the record. (http://ntrs.nasa.gov)

- USGS Publications Warehouse. Patrons will find more than 70,000 bibliographic records in this database. As with the NASA site, if there is an online version of the document, the link is included in the record. There is also a link to recently published titles by month. (http://infotrek.er.usgs.gov/pubs/)

Vital Records

- National Center for Health Statistics. This site by the Centers for Disease Control and Prevention provides links by state for birth, death, marriage, or divorce records. (www.cdc.gov/nchs/howto/w2w/w2welcom.htm)

CONCLUSION

Online government documents are free resources with significant content value that can improve library reference services. As Low (1966) reminds us, even with technical innovations, the core public service mission of reference librarians will not change. Government information belongs to the people, an idea echoed in the title of the GODORT journal, *DttP: Documents to the People.* Making online government documents part of your reference services really will be bringing documents to the people.

NOTES

1. For more information about the SuDocs Classification System, see the GPO's "An Explanation of the Superintendent of Documents Classification System," www.access.gpo .gov/su_docs/fdlp/pubs/explain.html.
2. Similar to general library reference, online government reference incorporates new technologies. For more information, see chapter 2. The following sources are recommended for technology related to reference: blogs/weblogs (Clyde 2004; Pomerantz and Stutzman 2006); establishment of a reference Facebook community (Matthews 2006); and chat/virtual reference (Francoeur 2001; Ronan 2003; Johnson 2004).
3. More information is available in the "Professional Competencies for Reference and User Services Librarians," written by the ALA RUSA Task Force on Professional Competencies, 2003, www.ala.org/ala/rusa/protools/referenceguide/professional.cfm.
4. Check the specifics of this license at http://creativecommons.org/licenses/by-nc-sa/2.5/.
5. The full report by Maj. Gen. Antonio Taguba, *The "Taguba Report" on Treatment of Abu Ghraib Prisoners in Iraq,* is available from http://news.findlaw.com/hdocs/docs/iraq/tagubarpt.html.
6. CCNY Libraries, Government Views of D-Day, 2006, www.ccny.cuny.edu/library/Divisions/Government/DDay.html; Naval Historical Center, The Invasion of Normandy, 2001, www.history.navy.mil/ac/d-day/exdday/exdday.htm; Naval Historical Center, Normandy Invasion June 1944—The "D-Day" Landings 6 June 1944, 2004, www.history .navy.mil/photos/events/wwii-eur/normandy/nor4.htm; Rudi Williams, "Comanche Code Talker Charles Chibitty," 2002, available at Defend America, www.defendamerica.mil/profiles/nov2002/pr111202a.html; National Archives, "General Dwight D. Eisenhower's

Order of the Day" (1944), 1999, www.ourdocuments.gov/doc.php?flash=true&doc=75; Dwight D. Eisenhower, "Our Landings in the Cherbourg-Havre Area Have Failed, 1944," Eisenhower Presidential Library, www.eisenhower.archives.gov/dl/DDay/InCaseofFailureMessage.pdf.

REFERENCES

Bertot, John Carlo, et al. 2006. "Drafted: I Want You to Deliver E-Government." *Library Journal* 131 (13): 34–37.

Brady, Eileen E., Sarah K. McCord, and Betty Galbraith. 2006. "Print versus Electronic Journal Use in Three Sci/Tech Disciplines: The Cultural Shift in Process." *College and Research Libraries* 67 (4): 354–363.

Buckley, Francis J. 2000. "SuDocs Letter to Directors: Changes in FDLP." *Administrative Notes* 21 (13). www.access.gpo.gov/su_docs/fdlp/pubs/adnotes/ad091500.html.

Buttlar, Lois, and Rajinder Garcha. 1998. "Cataloguers in Academic Libraries: Their Evolving and Expanding Roles." *College and Research Libraries* 59 (4): 311–321.

Cheney, Debora. 2004. "Government Information Reference Service: New Roles and Models for the Post-Depository Era." *DttP: Documents to the People* 32 (3): 33.

Clyde, Laurel A. 2004. "Library Weblogs." *Library Management* 25 (4/5): 183–189.

Downie, Judith A. 2004. "The Current Information Literacy Instruction Environment for Government Documents (pt 1)." *DttP: Documents to the People* 32 (2): 36–39.

Francoeur, Stephen. 2001. "An Analytical Survey of Chat Reference Services." *Reference Services Review* 29 (3): 189–203.

Frazer, Stuart L., et al. 1997. "Merging Government Information and the Reference Department: A Team-Based Approach." *Journal of Government Information* 24 (2): 93–102.

GPO U.S. Government Printing Office. 2006. "GPO Depository Library Council Update." October. www.access.gpo.gov/su_docs/fdlp/pubs/adnotes/ad09_10_1506.html#7.

Johnson, Corey M. 2004. "Online Chat Reference: Survey Results from Affiliates of Two Universities." *Reference and User Services Quarterly* 43 (3): 237–247.

Low, Kathleen. 1996. "The Future of Reference Librarians: Will It Change?" *Reference Librarian*, no. 54: 151.

Matthews, Brian S. 2006. "Do You Facebook? Networking with Students Online." *College and Research Libraries News*, May, 306–307.

Nielsen, Jakob. 2002. "Top Ten Guidelines for Homepage Usability." *Jakob Nielsen's Alertbox*, May 12. www.useit.com/alertbox/20020512.html.

Office of Environmental Information. Environmental Protection Agency. 2006. "EPA FY 2007 Library Plan: National Framework for the Headquarters and Regional

Libraries." August 15. www.epa.gov/natlibra/Library_Plan_National _Framework081506final.pdf.

Pomerantz, Jeffrey, and Frederic Stutzman. 2006. "Collaborative Reference Work in the Blogosphere." *Reference Services Review* 23 (2): 200–212.

Ronan, Jana Smith. 2003. *Chat Reference: A Guide to Live Virtual Reference Services.* Westport, CT: Libraries Unlimited.

Salem, Joseph A., Jr. 2006. "The Way We Work Now: A Survey of Reference Survey Arrangement in Federal Depository Libraries." *Reference Librarian*, no. 94: 69–94.

Sheehy, Helen M., and Debora Cheney. 1997. "Government Information and Library Instruction: A Means to an End." *Journal of Government Information* 24 (4): 313–330.

Chapter 11 Government Information Instruction in the Information Literacy Environment

Barbara Miller and Barbara J. Mann

The plethora of information now freely available to anyone who has an Internet connection includes a vast amount of government information. Once largely limited to physical resources housed in depository library collections, government information is now more readily available to all libraries due to the digitization of existing information as well as the creation of new, "born-digital" information. This environment creates a need for incorporating government information into all library information literacy instruction, whether it be for patrons, students, or peers.[1]

Information literacy instruction refers to teaching information seekers how to locate, evaluate, and use various types of information effectively, efficiently, ethically, and legally. The information literacy push encourages librarians to switch from finding information for the constituencies they serve to teaching all users how to find and evaluate the information. In libraries, the information literacy initiative has had a major impact on government information instruction. Despite a growing emphasis on taking an information literacy approach to library service, government

Barbara Miller holds a BA and MA in anthropology from the University of Illinois Urbana-Champaign and an MSLS from the University of Tennessee. She is associate professor and documents librarian in the documents department at Oklahoma State University Libraries. She has taught information literacy at OSU. She is active in service to GODORT, notably as chair of GODORT Bylaws and Conference Committees and as coordinator of the State and Local Documents Task Force. She has also served as GODORT chair for the Oklahoma Library Association and is currently the OLA Education Division chair. Miller has served as past secretary of Oklahoma ACRL Council of Instruction Librarians and is the current legislative liaison for Oklahoma ACRL. barbara.miller@okstate.edu

Barbara J. Mann is assistant director for public services and instruction and information literacy librarian at the University of Maryland University College. She received her MLIS from the University of South Carolina. She is active in GODORT, RUSA, and ACRL. Mann was coauthor, with Andrea M. Morrison, of International Government Information and Country Information: A Subject Guide *(2004). In addition, she has authored articles and reviews and served as conference presenter on topics of information literacy and reference services.*

information courses in graduate library degree programs are still apt to focus on teaching future librarians how to find this information and omit any instruction on how to apply information literacy instruction methods to government information. In the past, many libraries had a separate government documents department, and reference service and library instruction were handled there as a discrete, insular unit. Today many library reference and instruction departments have integrated government information into their reference and instructional services. In the past, nondepository libraries (e.g., public libraries, smaller or specialized libraries, or even branches of university libraries not physically connected to the depository collection at their institution) also depended on depositories for help. Now that all librarians have access to a vast and rapidly increasing collection of government information on the Web, they need to know how to locate and use it themselves as well as how to teach others to do likewise.

NEW NATURE OF INSTRUCTION

The information literacy movement has brought a new focus to government information library instruction, be it in formalized classes, through individual or small-group consultation, or as a reference query. Replacing the old model of the librarian as a "living encyclopedia" who knows all and expects everyone to come to him/her for information is the new model of the librarian as a facilitator for information sharing. Here the librarian helps users learn how to recognize an information need, how to locate, evaluate, and use information, and how to develop their own critical thinking skills necessary to evaluate it.

Information literacy has moved to the forefront in education, especially as a curriculum requirement by higher education accreditation agencies. Integrating e-government information into the overall curriculum demonstrates its rich research potential and teaches essential public information. K–12 programs are also integrating information literacy with e-government information into their curriculum, and public libraries are realizing the need to pass on information literacy techniques to help their patrons access the rich e-government consumer and public services information available on the Web. In addition, many libraries are "mainstreaming" government information into general reference service. In response to growing demand, the librarians in these and all academic and public libraries need to increase awareness and use of online government information in information literacy initiatives.

In this environment, government information librarians no longer need to go to great lengths to illustrate the uniqueness of government information, nor are patrons constrained to rely on librarian expertise to meet their information needs. Library instruction, whether it be in an academic, public, school, or special library setting, offers the opportunity to use government information to illustrate principles of information literacy such as determining and differentiating between primary and secondary sources, developing critical thinking skills, determining bias, understanding issues of copyright and intellectual property, evaluating Internet sources, and understanding freeware databases versus restricted (or copyrighted) information. See Downie (2004) for an excellent discussion of integrating government information into the general information literacy framework.

Government information instructors can also provide added value to the electronic information available by evaluating electronic resources to determine whether they are indeed the best format to meet a particular information need. This holds true in any method of instruction in the use of government information, be it formalized library instruction, individual or small group consultation, or answering a reference question. In addition, because there is still much government information, especially older material, that is not digitized, it is important to remember that print resources still have much value in the research process.

INCORPORATING LITERACY COMPETENCY STANDARDS IN LIBRARY PROGRAMS USING GOVERNMENT INFORMATION

To integrate government information into other resources when meeting a particular information need, one must understand how this source will meet the need and why it is being chosen. For more formalized information literacy endeavors, defined learning outcomes (i.e., what the instructor wants the user to know and be able to do as a result of the interaction) should be included to serve as a guide in this process. The ACRL "Information Literacy Competency Standards for Higher Education," with its five standards and accompanying performance indicators, is an excellent source to consult. In addition, ACRL's "Objectives for Information Literacy Instruction: A Model Statement for Academic Libraries" (adopted January 2001) breaks down the standards and outcomes into smaller, measurable objectives to be used in instructional design.

Although less formalized information literacy instruction venues such as consultations and reference questions do not provide opportunities for formalized learning outcomes, there is still the need to be mindful of the "whys" and "whats" of a particular resource suggestion, whether its format is online or print. Much as a traditional reference interview should uncover the exact nature of the information need (consumer, research, etc.), so should the interview in the age of information literacy. Librarians providing government information should follow the same guidelines. Government information is an invaluable resource and has a solid place in a multitude of topics and disciplines. The more various user communities are exposed to what government information can offer in meeting their particular information needs, the more they can tap into these invaluable resources to meet other information needs.

Convincing librarian colleagues to use government information when they are not familiar with it can be a challenge. Keeping up with the explosion of available information is difficult. If librarians do not have an awareness of the rich research potential of government information, they cannot or will not integrate government information into their information literacy endeavors. Librarians who understand the importance of government information must pass this on to their colleagues through the professional literature as well as by offering workshops on how to find, evaluate, and use government information.

How can government information be incorporated into the framework of information literacy programs? As defined by the ACRL's "Information Literacy Competency Standards for Higher Education":

1. The information literate student determines the nature and extent of the information needed.

2. The information literate student accesses needed information effectively and efficiently.

3. The information literate student evaluates information and its sources critically and incorporates selected information into his or her knowledge base and value system.

4. The information literate student, individually or as a member of a group, uses information effectively to accomplish a specific purpose.

5. The information literate student understands many of the economic, legal, and social issues surrounding the use of information and accesses and uses information ethically and legally (ACRL 2000, 2–3).

Standard One pertains to knowing that information is needed. Understanding how and when information is created (the information cycle) and that different types of resources address different information needs are important aspects of this process. Government information is integral to this understanding. For example, government information is an invaluable source for consumer health information as well as IRS, FEMA, and Social Security forms and resources. Government information in the form of legislative materials provides access to laws and governing documents. A wide variety of statistical resources supplement subjects such as education, commerce, and crime. Information such as this, which was accessible via print volumes or loaded onto stand-alone computers in the past, is now available at the fingertips of anyone with Internet access. Because access to these resources also required librarian intervention in the past, the librarian was able to direct users to the best kind of information needed. Even with fingertip availability, the user is not always aware of what is needed or available, and in the current electronic environment there is a very real need for the government information librarian to provide instruction on how to approach sometimes complicated resources to obtain the best or most appropriate information.

Standard Two addresses accessing information efficiently and correctly. In this case the user must understand how to find different types of information using different methods and sources. An understanding of the differences between primary and secondary sources, popular and scholarly resources, and web and database searching is needed. Emphasis should be placed on appropriate specialized resources such as legal materials, congressional materials, maps, materials specific to certain disciplines such as soil surveys or environmental impact statements, or materials used for specific needs such as statistics (e.g., census, education, health, justice, or agriculture statistics). In an environment where much information is available via an online library catalog, it is important that users know which materials may not be included in the catalog or which may require librarian intervention to use. Librarians must make users aware of the kinds of government information that are available using both general purpose search engines (e.g., Google, Yahoo) and subject-specific search engines (e.g., USA.gov) as well as through library databases.

Standard Three deals with the ability to evaluate information critically. In an online environment, users especially need to evaluate a resource, asking such questions as these to determine whether it is appropriate:

- Is this a primary or secondary source?
- What is its authority?
- What is its purpose?
- What is its scope and coverage?
- It is accurate and reliable?
- Is it current?
- Is there bias?
- Is it relevant?
- It is useful?

Because government information often includes primary source material, it can be used in examples that compare primary and secondary sources. For example, the transcript of a certain senator testifying before a U.S. congressional committee (primary source) is more factual than a report of that testimony in a newspaper (secondary source), which may only summarize or even misquote it. The report of the recovery of New Orleans from Hurricane Katrina will have a different slant in New Orleans newspapers than in FEMA reports. Online information on the environment may have a different focus when presented by the U.S. Department of Interior compared to a logging company. In each of these cases, each organization has its own view of things, and each is correct in its own way, but each also has a viewpoint/bias that must be recognized. In this case bias is not necessarily a bad thing, and herein lies one of the values of government information. Librarians have successfully illustrated these information literacy principles using government documents examples in college classes on creative writing and technical writing (Drees et al. 2005; Hogenboom 2005).

Standard Four refers to the ability of users to organize information correctly and efficiently. By adding government information to the mix of resources, a user can easily combine primary and secondary resources, and information with different biases, to create a well-balanced perspective to answer his/her information needs.

Standard Five relates to the ethical and legal use of information. Issues of copyright and intellectual property as they relate to government information are important considerations for librarians. U.S. federal government information, produced at taxpayer expense, is made available with no restrictions to the American public, with some exceptions. Issues related to electronic copyright are still moving through the court systems, but the copyright-free example is still currently the rule. Librarians who use government information must keep abreast of how government information fits into the copyright mix. And, of course, users should also be made aware of additional copyright issues. Many government websites state that the material may be freely used but ask for attribution as a courtesy. State government information may still have copyright restrictions. In addition, much government information is repackaged by private publishers and may therefore fall under copyright restrictions, and government websites can link offsite to private or commercial websites, where copyright rules differ.

Authentication of e-information is also an issue. Although the GPO is currently working on e-signatures, it should be noted that, as of this writing, courts and law offices still do not recognize online versions of laws as legal documents, because of the ease with which online material can be tampered with.

Librarians should also understand and be able to explain basic intellectual property concerns related to patents, trademarks, and copyright, as granted and made available by the U.S. federal government, and should include this information in appropriate information literacy. It is also important that librarians include patents and trademarks as information sources when relevant to the information need (Drees et al. 2005). Patent and trademark depository libraries and librarians are good resources for learning how to integrate this information into library information literacy initiatives.[2]

There are also several practical, general ways to incorporate online government information into other library activities and services. For example, all of the major citation styles (e.g., Chicago, APA, MLA) now include rules for citing electronic sources, including e-government information; sample citations for government sites can be included in general citation instruction. Librarians can also make users aware of online government information by including it as resources in subject specific guides and other help materials they create. Highlighting various online government information resources and search engines in library publications and in interactions with internal and external user communities is another way to further "spread the word."

DELIVERING GOVERNMENT INFORMATION INSTRUCTION

How can a government information librarian best proceed to provide government information instruction in an information literacy environment? Formalized classes? Online course content? While answering a reference query? Following the tenets of outcomes-based education, the librarian must first determine the information need for each particular situation (e.g., consumer information, research paper, instruction on the research process itself, and others). The instructor must determine the level of ease with which each group can access online information. For example, a user may have limited Internet skills, have little information on how libraries are organized along the lines of online catalogs and database, or be a confirmed Google-only user. How much and what information is given depends on these factors. It is no use beginning with complex data if the group or individual has no understanding of basic government information or even of basic Internet searching.

Since individuals learn better when they are given only a small amount of new information at a time, it is better to begin small. Focusing on a particular aspect of government information (e.g., Medicare, Social Security, and IRS forms and resources; demographic, education, or employment statistics; business resources; biomedical articles) provides opportunities to demonstrate how the rich resources of subject-specific government information can meet a particular information need. This knowledge will open the door to further consideration of government information as potential sources to meet other information needs. In addition, overcoming the fear factor among users and creating empowerment are important aspects of the process that can be accomplished by demonstrating how this information can be obtained (e.g., using the search engine USA.gov, visiting government agency websites) in a more focused way so that users easily gain efficiency and effectiveness in their search. This is true for all manner of instruction.

The distance education movement and virtual reference offerings (e.g., chat, instant messaging, and e-mail) have created new opportunities to integrate online government information into instruction and reference interactions. Because all users are indeed global and may not have access to print resources, demonstrating the variety and richness of online government information becomes that much more valuable and showcases the incredible variety of research resources brought about by new technologies. The global aspect of distance learning should, however, also encourage librarians to be aware of jargon on websites. Distance learners may not be aware of terms such as "executive agency," and the instructor should pay close attention to and translate any jargon when explaining government websites and their arrangements and content. This attention to controlled vocabulary is also important with college students and particularly important in public library instruction, where many users are not Internet-savvy and will not understand certain terms related to the online environment or to government structure.

Teaching the user how to locate, evaluate, and use government information can also be accomplished through the creation of online tools such as guides and tutorials, which in turn can be embedded into online course content and library web pages. Librarians already share their guides and tools via a collaborative clearinghouse and handout exchange.[3]

Providing a greater understanding of the importance and richness of online government information can be even more daunting when instructing fellow librarians. "Seasoned" librarians may already have established online sources of information to which they turn. They may also feel the stress of the continual changes and additions brought by online information sources in general. One way to approach this problem is to determine the types of questions these librarians receive, whether in formalized instruction classes, consultations, or reference queries, and then demonstrate how online government information resources can efficiently and effectively provide the information needed for such questions. Another method is to find out how librarians search for information in their own particular subject area, be it online or in print, and then demonstrate how searching for online government information in a similar way can meet their needs efficiently and effectively, thus building on their own skills and making retention easier.

WHAT DOES THE FUTURE HOLD?

There will always be a need for qualified librarians to find government information to fulfill a need and to instruct others how to find it. Because government information has been online longer than many other materials, government information librarians have had the most experience navigating the complex environment of the Web. They are going to need this experience. As government (and all other) information moves even further toward a digital-only environment, government information librarians must pay attention to the next level of information literacy—the *knowledge* literacy environment. In this scenario, the next generation of users will be expected to integrate constantly changing information from multiple sources into their personal and business activities, exchange the information with others, and add their own personal or "tacit" knowledge to the mix, thereby creating new knowledge for others to integrate into their own knowledge bases. Controlling and manipulating this fluid type of information environment is known as *knowledge management* (see Bouthillier and Shearer 2002; Al-Hawamdeh 2003).

In the near future, much more information will be unpublished and beyond the scope of library catalogs and databases. Whereas currently librarians teach the Web as one of several sources available in the library, in the future the library will be only one of several auxiliary sources available to the information seeker, with the Web as a central focus of information. The emphasis will be on gathering and exchanging this information, and on adding personal or tacit knowledge to the mix. Instruction will focus on the structure and methods of web searching rather than on the structure of the information cycle, which uses static resources along a continuum of time. Information is static, but knowledge is fluid, and time on the Web is not a continuum; it is all *now* (Miller and Clements 2006). To future searchers, something will either be available on the Web or it will not be available anywhere.

How soon will this happen? In 2001 researchers were predicting the demise of the journal article as the key information source for undergraduates (Oppenheim and Smith 2001, 316). Research materials, once the exclusive domain of copyright-restrictive journals accessed through expensive and restrictive databases, are now often being made available as online freeware shortly after publication, or immediately at time of publication in the form of preprints or post-prints. Such nontraditional formats as speeches, testimony, newsletters, laws, technical reports, and consumer tips, which are now considered peripheral to the information cycle and are often not found in library catalogs or databases, will soon become the norm and gain in importance as different types of information for different purposes equalize their value with other traditional "research" materials such as books and journal articles (Miller and Clements 2006). Today there are already successful online web-centered information literacy classes that use the Web as a focus and the library as only an auxiliary source of information among many other resources. These classes make heavy use of government information (Brunvand and Pashkova-Balkenhol 2006). The future is now.

Why will government information librarians be the ideal choice to instruct in this new environment? Because government information has long existed in many of the nontraditional formats discussed, and government agencies have been leaders in adapting many of these formats into electronic form. Correspondingly, government information librarians have become leaders in accessing this type of electronic information.

How will the government information librarian best instruct in this climate? One of the facets of knowledge management, as discussed above, is adding tacit or personal knowledge to the information mix. Here is where government information librarians can shine, since they help users sort through the various search strategies on the Web and develop their own tacit knowledge base about online structures to serve them as they search the Web for new information. Librarians have a great deal of tacit knowledge about government information structure on the Web. They are able to navigate the Web, using government websites, search engines, and value-added search tools, many created by government information librarians. This tacit knowledge enables librarians to search quickly through the Web to find the right information for the right need.

They are also aware of other significant characteristics of electronic documents. For example, although government information is reliable, there are constant changes in the social and political context in which it is created, and it is not immune to manipulation. Several versions of individual documents are often available on the Web at the same time. Which is the official version? Librarians can teach how to look for authentication. Government information is also structured in a specific way. For example, it can be arranged by agency or branch of government, or subagencies, and some agencies fall under parent agencies. This fluid information can change with a new administration, an agency name change, or a new law. Discussion of PURLs can illustrate agency changes and explain why "disappearing information" may merely have migrated to a new website. Librarians can show students that other web information often parallels government information structures and advance their tacit knowledge of its structure. They can use different government search engines to show differing approaches to searching: by lexicon, by agency, by "most hits" Google method, and by showing differing results for each method.

Best methods for teaching about electronic information often suggest utilizing the knowledge-seeking behavior of the millennial, or born-digital generation, to teach the structure of the Internet. What kind of knowledge-seeking behavior is involved in knowledge management? With information literacy, librarians teach a certain type of knowledge-seeking behavior, based on the information cycle. The emphasis is on structure of information along a path from current news to journal articles, books, and reference sources, for the individual to use when seeking information for personal use or for research. But millennial students often work differently, often in groups. They demonstrate the pattern of knowledge exchange and collaboration, interacting through web pages, blogs, intranets, electronic discussion lists, and wikis (Notess 2004). Their "cycle" is the more complex "knowledge" cycle of the dynamics of collection, analysis, evaluation, organization, and sharing of information, which in turn creates new knowledge (Gandhi 2004, 373). For example, using this behavior, librarians can structure classes to give each member of the group a different agency and the same topic, so they can compare results. Each member of the group will develop tacit knowledge of their particular source and learn whether it can add to a certain topic the group is working on. Instructors can also direct group members to different sets of raw data so that users can learn how statistics differ between different sources and yet all be "correct." Users will thus develop tacit knowledge about problems with statistics and at the same time learn that government information is an excellent source of statistics. A great benefit of this type of instruction is that librarians will be passing on their tacit knowledge of web structure along with their tacit knowledge of online government information. Users will gain skills in web search techniques and at the same time become aware of the great resources available through digital government information. And, as librarians continue their study of government information on the Web, they will add to their own tacit knowledge of the complex world of the Web and continue to be leaders in information or knowledge instruction.

CONCLUSION

In this age of information explosion, the need for information literacy—that is, the knowledge that there is an information need and the ability to locate, evaluate, and use information efficiently, effectively, ethically, and legally—is vital. Having reliable, credible, high-quality relevant resources to turn to in order to meet the growing information needs of an informed population is also vital. Online government information is a rich source of reliable, credible, high-quality information. It can meet a host of information needs, be they current, scholarly publications on a medical issue; forms needed to apply for a passport; historical statistics on higher education; primary sources available from the Library of Congress's American Memory collection; the United Nations Security Council resolutions; or corn production figures for Iowa, and many others. It is the job of all librarians to raise awareness of the importance of government information and teach the user communities they serve how to locate, evaluate, and efficiently, effectively, legally, and ethically use government information. Through the study of information literacy, knowledge literacy, and modern instruction methods, librarians, including specialized government information librarians, will meet this task and become the information instructors of the future.

NOTES

1. Although many of the ideas explored in this chapter refer to e-government information, it is important to note that these ideas are often valid for all government information, regardless of format.

2. The U.S. Patent and Trademark Office posts a complete list of patent and trademark depository libraries at www.uspto.gov/web/offices/ac/ido/ptdl/.

3. The Education Committee of GODORT has created the Government Information Clearinghouse and Handout Exchange—www.ala.org/ala/godort/godortcommittees/godorteducation/clearinghouse/index.htm—to serve as a repository of such materials.

REFERENCES

ACRL Association of College and Research Libraries. 2000. "Information Literacy Competency Standards for Higher Education." Chicago: ACRL. www.ala.org/ala/acrl/acrlstandards/standards.pdf.

———. 2001. "Objectives for Information Literacy Instruction: A Model Statement for Academic Libraries." Chicago: ACRL. www.ala.org/ala/acrl/acrlstandards/objectivesinformation.cfm.

Al-Hawamdeh, Suliman. 2003. *Knowledge Management: Cultivating Knowledge Professionals.* Oxford: Chandos.

Bouthillier, France, and Kathleen Shearer. 2002. "Understanding Knowledge Management and Information Management: The Need for an Empirical Perspective." *Information Research* 8 (1), Paper 141. http://Informationr.net/ir/8-1/paper141.html.

Brunvand, Amy, and Tatiana Pashkova-Balkenhol. 2006. "Use of Government Information in Undergraduate Research." Paper presented at the Five-State Government Documents Conference, Boulder, CO, August 4.

Downie, Judith. 2004. "The Current Information Literacy Instruction Environment for Government Documents," pts. 1 and 2. *DttP: Documents to the People* 32 (2): 36–39; and 32 (4): 17, 20–22.

Drees, Kevin P., Kiem-Dung Ta, and Helen Peeler Clements. 2005. "Creating a Library Instruction Session for a Technical Writing Course Composed of Engineering and Non-Engineering Students." *Conference Proceedings*, 2409–2416. Chantilly, VA: American Society for Engineering Education

Gandhi, Smiti. 2004. "Knowledge Management and Reference Services." *Journal of Academic Librarianship* 30 (5): 368–381.

Hogenboom, Karen. 2005. "Going Beyond .gov: Using Government Information to Teach Evaluation of Sources." *Portal: Libraries and the Academy* 5 (4): 455–466.

Miller, Barbara, and Helen Peeler Clements. 2006. "Government Information as a Knowledge Management Resource for Library Instruction to the Millennial Generation." In *Brick and Click Libraries: Proceedings of an Academic Library Symposium*, ed. Frank Baudino and Connie Ury. Maryville, MO: Northwest Missouri State University.

Notess, Greg. 2004. "The Changing Information Cycle" (on the Net Column). *Online*, September–October, 40–42.

Oppenheim, Charles, and Richard Smith. 2001. "Student Citation Practices in an Information Science Department." *Education for Information* 19 (4): 299–323.

Chapter 12   Digital Preservation of Electronic Government Information

Projects and Practical Advice

M. Elizabeth Cowell

G overnment information in the United States is not preserved if it is housed only in a central location or maintained by a single federal, state, or local agency. Funding problems, catastrophe, and political shenanigans can all lead to the loss of valuable government information in this scenario. Single agencies may also choose to remove a digital document from public access. Understanding these risks to digital collections, it follows that the more collections that reside in a variety of physical and administrative locations, the better.

The FDLP is one case in point. Going strong since 1895, the FDLP has assured local, free access to government information via a network of more than 1,250 depository libraries. Tangible U.S. federal documents are secure because so many copies are distributed. Efforts to recall distributed publications from depository libraries result in public discussions that at times can reverse the recall. Content lost or damage to any one copy can be recovered through access to any of the thousands of other depository copies. Taking cues from the print world, any project with the goal of preserving digital government information needs to have this distributed model to be seen as a true preservation method (Cowell 2004). In this chapter we discuss current project proposals and ongoing programs designed to meet the daunting goal of preserving digital government information on the federal and state level in the United States. Our own goal is to encourage libraries big and small to jump into the game.

There is so much born-digital government material that falls into and out of the FDLP that multiple efforts are needed to collect and preserve it. Projects

M. Elizabeth Cowell received her MS in library and information science from the University of Illinois at Urbana-Champaign. She is U.S. government documents bibliographer at Stanford University. Her recent publications include "Preserving Electronic Government Information: What Role Does Policy Play?" (Advances in Librarianship, *2004) and, with coauthors Karrie Peterson and James Jacobs, "Government Documents at the Crossroads"* (American Libraries, *2001).*

addressed in this chapter include several Lots of Copies Keep Stuff Safe (LOCKSS) government information projects, including LOCKSS for state government with the Alaska State Library; the GPO LOCKSS Pilot Project; and the LOCKSS Fugitive Documents Network. Also covered are the Web-at-Risk project funded by the National Digital Information Infrastructure and Preservation Program of the Library of Congress, the OCLC Digital Archive product, the CyberCemetery and Congressional Research Service Reports projects at the University of North Texas; and the GPO's FDsys proposal. This may not be an exhaustive list, but it will give libraries an idea of some of the projects in process and be instructive about how libraries can evaluate and implement preservation programs for digital government information.

CRITERIA AND QUESTIONS FUNDAMENTAL FOR DIGITAL PROJECTS

To evaluate projects in terms of their preservation efficacy, I use six criteria (from Rosenthal et al. 2005):

Replication/Redundancy. More copies are safer, especially in separate physical and administrative locations.

Diversity. The system must support diversity among its components to avoid monoculture vulnerabilities; one glitch should not bring down the entire system. The system should allow for incremental replacement and avoid vendor lock-in.

Audit. Regular audits of the content must take place at intervals frequent enough to keep the probability of failure at acceptable levels and confirm that the data are preserved. Because the content is not likely to be accessed often, audit at ingest is not enough. There must be frequent audits among the replicas and a repair mechanism in place so that a damaged copy is repaired by the other replicas, not by an offline copy.

Migration. The system must support migration of media and format and move copies forward in time.

Economy. Cost-effective processes must be employed to give the system a greater chance of survival over time.

Transparency. The system must use open-source software that can undergo a wide review for vulnerabilities.

Discussion of preservation criteria is happening at many levels and places in the library world. Though not mirroring these criteria directly, a group of librarians and administrators who participated in a meeting at the Mellon Foundation offices to discuss electronic journal preservation in September 2005 agreed that issues of transparency, audit, and redundancy must be addressed in order to assure preservation of scholarly electronic journals (Waters 2005).

The following questions may already be answered by the digital preservations systems explored in this chapter. Will there be geographic diversity of collections?

Will there be a diversity of administrations holding the various collections to reduce the risk of error affecting many replicas? Will there be a diversity of funding in maintaining the various collections? If these criteria and answers to these questions are considered in the creation of a preservation system, continuing costs can be reduced to each institution. Many replicas spread throughout many administrative structures mean that we have to be less careful with each copy. In the end, the existence of many replicas will slow the process of failure down and give plenty of warning to enable repair. Using these criteria and finding answers to these questions, librarians will become empowered to evaluate digital projects as they arise and even consider starting digital projects in their own institutions.

LOTS OF COPIES KEEP STUFF SAFE (LOCKSS)

The LOCKSS program has a track record that can be analyzed. Three projects mentioned above—the Fugitive Documents Network, the GPO/LOCKSS Pilot or LOCKSS-DOCS, and LOCKSS for state government publications with the Alaska State Library—are part of the work of the LOCKSS Alliance. Although the initial focus of LOCKSS was electronic journal content, projects have grown to include other types of publications such as government information. According to the LOCKSS website (www.lockss.org):

> LOCKSS is open source software that provides librarians with an easy and inexpensive way to collect, store, preserve, and provide access to their own, local copy of authorized content they purchase. Running on standard desktop hardware and requiring almost no technical administration, LOCKSS converts a personal computer into a digital preservation appliance, creating low-cost, persistent, accessible copies of e-journal content as it is published. Since pages in these appliances are never flushed, the local community's access to that content is safeguarded. Accuracy and completeness of LOCKSS appliances is assured through a robust and secure, peer-to-peer polling and reputation system.

The LOCKSS software is freely available via the Sourceforge website (http://sourceforge.net/projects/lockss/), but membership in the Alliance includes an annual fee. Membership entitles libraries to participate in a wide variety of collection activities and to cache or "own" the content in their own libraries. "LOCKSS offers a community-based rather than a corporate approach. The LOCKSS Alliance is not a single not-for-profit entity, but a network of collaborators using an open source software model" (Seadle 2006, 76).

The GPO LOCKSS Pilot project, begun in May 2005, was a group of twenty-three Alliance members and the GPO working to "investigate using LOCKSS as a means to manage, disseminate and preserve access to Web-based Federal Government e-journals that are within the scope of the FDLP and the IES [International Exchange Service]" (GPO 2007a). The pilot included ten e-journals and went through a time line giving the team a month to capture each title and then a series of real-world scenarios. As of this writing, all of the e-journals have been cached by the participating libraries and two real-world scenarios have been completed. The first scenario involved rendering the depository content unavailable from the GPO servers and making sure the participating libraries could access the content from their caches. The second involved observing the repair of damaged content. The GPO concluded its final report and analysis on the GPO LOCKSS pilot in 2007 and reported that it is not adopting LOCKSS as a distribution technology for FDLP publications. The GPO associated high costs with using LOCKSS in its final report; in the my view, however, the bulk of the high costs are due to the fact that the GPO, for reasons unknown to the LOCKSS team, decided to harvest manually and republish all of the materials to be distributed in the pilot (GPO 2007b). The hope of the participating libraries and others in the depository community was that the project would be deemed a success and LOCKSS would be implemented in the production FDsys system as part of the GPO's preservation strategy. The GPO may still consider LOCKSS in the future but has not issued any further information since its pilot project final report.

The Alaska State Library is using LOCKSS as a tool for collecting and preserving Alaska state government publications (Alaska State Library 2005). Based on the shipping lists from the Alaska State Depository Program, URLs are crawled using the LOCKSS software and publications are distributed in caches around the state and country for preservations purposes. This model requires that participating libraries join the LOCKSS Alliance for support purposes, but it ensures that the libraries own the digital content they cache, mirroring the print depository program.

The Fugitive Documents Network, a project using LOCKSS technology, is in its nascent stages as a preservation solution for government information not distributed via depository programs. U.S. federal government information published by a government agency that is not included in the FDLP is called *fugitive*. For the purposes of this project, federal fugitive documents and potentially state, local, and international information that is not preserved in some way will be included. The test site for this project is the Federation of American Scientists (FAS) Project on Government Secrecy (www.fas.org/sgp/index.html), a site that contains many important digital government publications. For example, reports of the Congressional Research Service (CRS), though created with taxpayer support and addressing many important issues facing our nation, do not fall within the FDLP, but selected CRS reports related to national security and foreign policy are on the FAS site. All publications available on the FAS site are digital, though some may have print counterparts. Many are accessible only via this site, since they are made available to FAS staff via Freedom of Information Act requests, or "leaks." None of the documents on the site are considered classified. Currently eleven LOCKSS Alliance members have agreed to collect these materials. Once identified, the publications could very well be included in the FDLP if they fit the guidelines for inclusion in the program. On the completion of the test crawls, the group will solicit other fugitive titles to preserve.

Does LOCKSS meet the criteria and answer the questions asked above? Yes. Using the distributed framework, many libraries at many different institutions are caching these publications and provide access to their own local copies of the content. This ensures that the loss of one LOCKSS box will not bring down the entire system. LOCKSS software is freely available and open source, ensuring wide review. Many different caches ensure system diversity.

Using low-cost hardware makes the economy of the projects high. The system relies on a migration-upon-access strategy to move the format forward. This way, we can take advantage of the slow turnover of web protocols and migrate only those things that are used, which also enhances the economy of the project. Finally, the contents of each cache are constantly audited against each other to confirm that the data are preserved. If inaccuracies are detected, a constant polling process is initiated via the LOCKSS software to repair the broken/corrupted copy.

WEB-AT-RISK DIGITAL PRESERVATION PROJECT

Funded by the National Digital Information Infrastructure and Preservation Program of the Library of Congress (www.digitalpreservation.gov), the California's Digital Library's Web-at-Risk project plans "to develop a web archiving service that will be used by libraries to capture, curate and preserve collections of web-based government and political information" (CDL 2004). Working with partners nationwide, the Web-at-Risk is run out of the California Digital Library (www .cdlib.org/inside/projects/preservation/webatrisk/), the digital library arm of the University of California library system. This project is progressing on four paths: web archiving needs and usability assessment, partnership building for collaborative web archiving endeavors, experimentation and research into promising web archiving technologies and strategies, and the development of the Web Archiving Service (WAS).

Currently, the research team is working with curatorial partners to identify at-risk web content to be crawled and preserved. Initial crawls and an initial needs assessment have been completed. Releases in 2006 included analysis, display, and reporting tools. Future releases will be developed to improve end user access to the crawls and to help the curators evaluate their crawls.

Preservation features of the WAS have yet to be finalized in detail. From documentation available at the time of this writing, the experimental path is looking at strategies that include the preservation of "desiccated" or simplified formats of certain files. This can be seen as an approach to the migration criteria in that desiccating formats on ingest can remove the need for the migration of formats in the future though perhaps greatly increasing the cost of ingesting materials. Migration upon access would limit the cost to only those materials deemed useful by a user request.

The current storage layer is designed to be modular, which satisfies the criterion for diversity, as does the replication of stored data from site to site. The current storage software is the San Diego Supercomputer's Storage Resource Broker (SRB).

There are plans to test the SRB replication with data stored among project partners at New York University and the University of North Texas. It is not clear, however, how these replicated copies will be audited and maintained or if the participating libraries will actually "own" the content. Future releases in the project should give us more information about the preservation details.

OCLC DIGITAL ARCHIVE

From the GPO to state libraries around the country, OCLC has worked with information providers and libraries to meet the need to archive digital government information. Its Digital Archive (www.oclc.org/digitalarchive/) is a subscription-based service that allows libraries to select and archive web-based materials. Several state libraries currently subscribe to the service, which provides a web interface through which curators can harvest targeted websites.

According to the "OCLC Digital Archive Preservation Policy and Supporting Documentation" (OCLC 2005), the policy is based on two guiding documents, the Open Archival Information System (OAIS) Reference Model and the "Trusted Digital Repositories: Attributes and Responsibilities" document from the Research Libraries Group. As an outgrowth of the latter, Research Libraries Group has released "An Audit Checklist for the Certification of Trusted Digital Repositories" (RLG 2005) for comment. This checklist addresses some of our criteria in detail. For example, the checklist requires that repositories stipulate the number and location of copies of all digital objects and have mechanisms in place to detect data corruption or loss. Also included is a stipulation for processes for storage media migration. There is not an assumption of multiple copies, just requirements for attributes necessary if they exist.

In the most recent version of the OCLC preservation policy available at the time of this writing, a description of local and offsite backups leads one to believe that data can be lost for up to six weeks depending on the nature of the failure. There is no mention of an audit of these backups to ensure integrity. Fortunately, this document promises that OCLC's preservation policy will adapt as options for digital preservation change. Most notably, the 2006 announcement that OCLC will join the LOCKSS Alliance gives hope that the criteria will be met and that subscribers to the digital archive will have more assurance that access to their materials will be seamless in the event of a disruption.

UNIVERSITY OF NORTH TEXAS DIGITAL PRESERVATION PROJECTS

The Government Documents Department of the University of North Texas (UNT) holds several digital collections. Of note are the CyberCemetery (http://govinfo.library.unt.edu/default.htm) and the Congressional Research Service Reports Archive (http://digital.library.unt.edu/govdocs/crs/). The CyberCemetery is a partnership between UNT and the GPO to provide permanent public access to the websites and publications of defunct U.S. government agencies and commissions. Congressional Research Service reports are not immediately available to the public but must be requested and provided via a member of Congress. Both sites are maintained by the Digital Projects Unit of the UNT Libraries.

The UNT Libraries' Digital Projects Unit employs open-source software whenever possible. The system currently in use is the Keystone Digital Library System, created by IndexData, an open-source system customized for the Libraries' needs. The system acts as the public interface to the collections as well as allowing the creation and management of metadata. The system stores only web-presentable derivative images that are created upon ingest from the master files. The high-quality, rich digital masters are stored in another system that is currently being built. This system is considered the UNT Libraries' Digital Archive. The pieces that make up the Digital Archive are created using open-source tools and libraries.

When content is either reformatted or collected, the most open format possible is used as the container for the content in these projects. For web-harvested collections, there is no control over the type of content ingested, so it is accepted as it is received. This is the case for the CyberCemetery as well as other UNT web harvesting projects. At this time UNT has not conducted a full-format migration for any of the files being collected and archived.

The data in the Digital Archive, which is the preservation system, are replicated upon ingest to create two copies in the Archive. It is UNT's intent to increase this initial replication to three copies, with one being at a geographically disparate location from Denton.

The data in the Keystone system, which is the public access point, are replicated on a nightly schedule to a backup server that acts as a spare in case of problems with the main system. There are also weekly snapshots taken of the data on the Keystone system that are stored in a separate location.

The Keystone system and Digital Archive work together to ensure the integrity of the collections. When a file is ingested into the Keystone system, a hash is created for that file. This hash is used to verify that the file has not changed when it is ingested into the Digital Archive. UNT carries out an audit of the contents of the Digital Archive to ensure that the files have not changed in any way while in the Archive. The plan is to audit the Archive files annually.

UNT's Keystone system runs on standard enterprise-level servers for providing the public interface to the collections. The Archive is being built to allow UNT to take advantage of the constant increase in storage capacity of drives with the decrease of cost. The Archive does not need expensive enterprise-level storage because it is accessed on an infrequent schedule and speed is not an issue.

UNT is a leader in the preservation of digital U.S. government information. The preservation strategies it employs, though not aligning perfectly with the criteria mentioned in this chapter, are reviewed regularly by staff and reworked if necessary to reflect best practices in the preservation community. UNT's partnerships with larger institutions such as the GPO and the National Archives show a commitment to collect and provide public access to this important information for the long term, which is no small feat. Redundancy is considered important in these projects, but only UNT has administrative control of these copies. Distributing digital collections is an important step in relieving the pressure of permanent public access from one institution to many. As a partnership with the GPO, the CyberCemetery data most likely would transfer to the GPO if UNT could no longer carry out its preservation role. Multiple administrative bodies holding these collections would increase the likelihood of long-term preservation. More frequent audit and repair of data are ways to ensure that corrupted data are not perpetuated.

FDSYS

The GPO is working to create a new position for itself in the digital information reality. Publishing on paper is no longer viable as its mainstay, and encouraging agencies to comply with Title 44 and "publish" through the GPO is increasingly difficult in the web environment. Paper distribution to federal depository libraries diminishes in numbers every year, and even though GPO staff catalogs electronic items and assigns PURLS there is little confidence that these items will be available for long-term access. Enter FDsys, GPO's Federal Digital System. The GPO hopes that this system will answer permanent public access questions. What role will LOCKSS play? Will OCLC have a role? In conjunction with LOCKSS? All of these questions currently remain unanswered but may be addressed in the future by FDsys.

What we do know is that depository libraries want to play a role in the GPO's development of FDsys. With little or no coaxing, twenty-three depositories/members of the LOCKSS Alliance (some joined to participate in the pilot, some were already members) volunteered to be part of the GPO LOCKSS pilot to demonstrate how the FDLP can work in the digital environment. The GPO should not overlook the benefits of a distributed FDLP, as demonstrated by the value of the findings in the LOCKSS pilot project.

In response to a query about how the FDsys will or will not adhere to the digital preservation criteria used in this chapter, the GPO responded with a posting to the FDsys blog.[1] Although the headings of the response match the criteria, the responses do not necessarily address their nature. The system is scheduled for release in 2008, and the details of the preservation process were not available at the time of this writing. The GPO could only say in the blog what it "shall" do in the future development of FDsys. This being the case, how will LOCKSS or any other distributing technology be used to activate depository libraries in the electronic environment? Redundancy is addressed in terms of multiple copies, but the GPO makes no mention of geographically dispersed collections or collections cared for by administrations other than the GPO. Budget issues within the GPO could threaten the future of a large system such as FDsys. If Congress does not adequately fund the system, permanent public access to U.S. government information will be at risk.

CONCLUSION

Federal depository libraries have a vested interest in the outcome of digital preservation projects. Whether or not an institution is a depository or has a digital library program, the future of libraries is at stake. A library without collections is not a library. Third parties can be part of the solution only if they support this notion and distribute copies to be preserved at local institutions. If we completely outsource our collecting and preservation activities and act only to provide access to third-party entities, preservation is not assured, and our future as memory institutions that guard and preserve knowledge and make it accessible is at risk.

The specific digital preservation projects discussed in this chapter have increasingly blurred borders; participating in projects together as collaboration of institutions is vital in this environment. With its CyberCemetery, the University of North Texas collaborates with the California Digital Library, the GPO, and NARA. In its partnerships and new initiatives, the GPO collaborates with other government agencies, private enterprises, and libraries to preserve government information. Libraries and library networks are also collaborating in new and exciting directions for digital preservation including government information. It is heartening to see these organizations take advantage of the economies of scale offered in large collaborative projects to provide this vital service.

Libraries support democracy via our collections. Permanent public access to government information in all formats is one of the benchmarks of our democratic government; inadequate preservation of this material threatens democracy itself. If we do not encourage locally held and managed collections of government information, we are shirking our responsibilities as keepers of these important materials.

As these projects develop and new projects surface, libraries should have confidence in their abilities to contribute to them. Libraries should get involved in commenting on various projects as they proceed on the national, state, and local levels. The GPO provides a place for librarians to voice comments and concerns via the FDsys blog, and other projects accept comments from the library community as well. The more the library community is involved in evaluating and creating projects to preserve e-government information, the more likely the information will persist for use by future generations.

NOTE

1. To access the full text of this blog posting, search the GPO website, http://fdsys.blogspot.com, for the title "Digital Preservation in FDsys" or link specifically to the year and date.

REFERENCES

Alaska State Library. 2005. Monthly Shipping Lists. www.library.state.ak.us/asp/shippinglists/shippinglists.html.

CDL California Digital Library. 2004. *The Web at Risk: A Distributed Approach to Preserving Our Nation's Political Cultural Heritage*. www.digitalpreservation.gov/partners/project_cdl.pdf.

Cowell, M. Elizabeth. 2004. "Preserving Electronic Government Information: What Role Does Policy Play?" *Advances in Librarianship* 27:185–197.

GPO U.S. Government Printing Office. 2007a. GPO LOCKSS Pilot Project. www .access.gpo.gov/su_docs/fdlp/lockss/index.html.

———. 2007b. *GPO LOCKSS Pilot: Final Analysis, April 27, 2007*. www.access.gpo .gov/su_docs/fdlp/lockss/report.pdf.

OCLC. 2005. "OCLC Digital Archive Preservation Policy and Supporting Documentation." www.oclc.org/support/documentation/digitalarchive/preservation policy.pdf.

RLG Research Libraries Group. 2005. *An Audit Checklist for the Certification of Trusted Digital Repositories*. www.rlg.org/en/pdfs/rlgnara-repositorieschecklist.pdf.

Rosenthal, David S. H., Thomas Robertson, Tom Lipkis, Vicky Reich, and Seth Morabito. 2005. "Requirements for Digital Preservation Systems: A Bottom-Up Approach." *D-Lib Magazine* 11. www.dlib.org/dlib/november05/rosenthal/11rosenthal.html.

Seadle, Michael. 2006. "A Social Model for Archiving Digital Serials: LOCKSS." *Serials Review* 32:73–77.

Waters, Donald J. 2005. "Urgent Action Needed to Preserve Scholarly Electronic Journals." www.diglib.org/pubs/waters051015.htm.

Chapter 13   Managing Local Electronic Government Information in Libraries

Mary Martin

Traditionally, local government documents have been little understood and not widely available, representing what Bernard Fry termed a "domestic intelligence gap" for Americans (Hernon et al. 1978, vii). Despite the importance of local government and its publications, in libraries, municipal documents pose the greatest challenges for collection and access among government publications. The online environment is transforming the world of government information, and libraries, in turn, are changing how they acquire, manage, and archive that information. They are also changing how local e-government information is accessed and used, and, particularly, what is considered important enough to be disseminated and ultimately archived.

Although Wilson and Richey note that "online distribution of municipal documents remains haphazard, and long-term accessibility to important publications in an electronic format is still in question" (2005), libraries are in the process of reconsidering and developing their role in providing public access to local government information. In this chapter we identify how local governments, both city and county, are transitioning to e-government, what types of information they are making available electronically, and how libraries can manage and provide access to this information. We address the transformation of government information dissemination to electronic format and focus on some information and services that

Mary Martin is the librarian for business law and government information at the Libraries of the Claremont Colleges in Claremont, California, where she formerly served as head of government publications. She holds a BA from the University of California at Irvine and an MLIS from UCLA. She is active in GODORT and RUSA/BRASS (Business Reference and Services Section). Martin has written Local and Regional Government Information: How to Find It, How to Use It *(2005), as well as several book chapters and articles in the area of government publications. She teaches library school classes in several graduate library and information science programs. mary.martin@libraries.claremont.edu* are being made available online that do not fit within the traditional definition of "government documents."

DEFINING AND FINDING OFFICIAL LOCAL E-GOVERNMENT INFORMATION

In "Creating a Blueprint for E-Government," Patricia McGinnis (2002) notes that most governments are still in the early stages of providing information online. The sheer amount of information governments generate, update, and manage, often without the standardization and classification tools that make information easier to manage and share, is a significant obstacle. In the absence of established systems of managing electronic local government information (particularly in libraries), it is necessary to look at trends to see what is actually occurring in local e-government.

At present, local government entities are using their websites to convey information in specific areas, including providing access to basic information about services (hours, location), transactional processes, and government business. The information content is primarily about officials, groups, and services; local events; the promotion of tourism; business; transportation; recreation; and council agendas and minutes. Some local governments also offer online transactions, such as securing permits and paying small fees and fines, sometimes via commercial services. Governments are clearly becoming "cyber active" but are emphasizing information and services for business and other economic development activities rather than disseminating policy information to accompany policy decisions or delivering extensive public services (Stowers 1998). Finding online full-text municipal documents is still haphazard, although the situation is now beginning to change rapidly as more local governments are investing in infrastructure and technology for transitioning to e-government. Carmine Scavo states that

> local governments in the U.S. have been and remain very active in the development and use of Web sites to deliver services, promote local government activities, communicate with citizens, and so forth. However, while there is a great deal of activity, there could be more—local government use of Web sites has not yet attained the level that U.S. business, for example, makes of the Internet. (Scavo 2007, 299)

According to the Center for Digital Government's Digital Cities Survey, the fastest growing online service that cities are providing is applications for building permits, which increased from 34 to 51 percent in the survey year (2004/5).[1] The second-fastest growing segment is utility bill payment, which increased from 37 to 50 percent. Occupational license renewals submitted electronically were up 12 percent in the same year. Information on property assessment and tax information services were up from 19 to 27 percent. One additional upward trend is in the online submission of job applications; the number of cities responding to the survey that accept more than 25 percent of job applications online increased from 28 to 48 percent in the five years from 2001 to 2005.

In a few cases, cities and counties do provide electronic copies of important policy documents, such as general plans and environmental impact reports, but the practice of placing extensive full-text local government documents online is not yet widespread in the United States. For local governments, scanning and disseminating electronic copies of lengthy budget, planning, and similar documents for limited public consumption may be time consuming and costly, and even when online information is provided permanent public access to it may not be.

Although more local governments are investing in infrastructure, telecommunications, and technology for transitioning to e-government, they have discovered that commercial services can fulfill this need for them. For instance, dissemination of municipal codes (local laws) online is a current trend. Some city or county ordinances are being posted locally, but there are commercial services that specialize in formatting and creating electronic copies of these municipal codes, such as these:

- Municipal Code Corporation operates Municode.com (www.municode.com)
- American Legal Publishing offers a service to publish state and local codes (www.amlegal.com/index.shtml)
- LexisNexis Municipal Codes Web Library has a large collection of local government codes (http://municipalcodes.lexisnexis.com)
- Municipal Codes Online, hosted by the Seattle Public Library, provides links to city codes that have been digitized and put online (www.spl.org/default.asp?pageID=collection_municodes)

Local e-government information may be discovered by libraries and their users via direct access to the municipal websites, via commercial services with municipal codes, and via search engines, directories, indexes, and library web guides. Google is a general search engine that also provides an advanced engine, Google U.S. Government Search (www.google.com/ig/usgov), for searching all U.S. federal, state, and local government sites. Munisource (www.munisource.org) is a searchable online database that provides links to web pages of many local government entities as well as searches by name, country, specific resource, or topic; users may suggest new entries for the database. Another online directory, State and Local Government on the Net (www.statelocalgov.net), provides access to the websites of thousands of city and county governments and is searchable by topic and local government.

COLLECTION DEVELOPMENT

Finding municipal e-government documents and laws for users is just the beginning for libraries. The fundamental question for the library might be "why collect local government information at all?" The answer is because an informed citizenry is essential in a democracy and one of the foundations of this country. A comprehensive local government documents collection at the library can provide an essential link between the community and its government.

Levels of collection development are appropriate for different types of libraries, depending on staffing, finances, and the mission of the library. According to the final report of the 2006 "Public Libraries and the Internet Survey" conducted in Florida, public libraries are increasingly being called on to provide access to e-government services such as applying for government benefits and disaster relief.[2] This call has not, however, been matched by a corresponding increase in budget allocation for technology and expertise. The addition and expansion of a range of e-government services may stretch public library resources beyond their ability to keep pace with the demands of these services (Bertot 2006). Libraries facing these issues may find it more useful to create a simple framework of links, web guides, that anticipates user requests for local government information.

Libraries with the intention of establishing a comprehensive archive should follow public affairs, government, and technology literature to keep tabs on the direction of local e-government delivery of services and information. These sources often report on local government initiatives, many of which are descriptive of the process of creating e-government. Libraries facing these issues may find it most useful to seek out partnerships and collaborate with other libraries, library networks, and government agencies to archive and preserve electronic municipal documents.

The traditional method of handling local government print documents provides an excellent framework for developing an electronic documents collection at any level. Typical documents collected by libraries are budget, land use, ordinance and regulatory documents, financial information, annual reports, planning documents, statistical reports, surveys, and historical documents. In the print world, these documents were acquired, cataloged, and housed in the library. The collections in electronic format are disseminated electronically by government agencies and affiliates, accessed via the local library for public use, and, in some cases, archived electronically by libraries. As local government information proliferates on the Web, managing this information in libraries is challenging, but the task is made easier using electronic communication, government websites, search engines, and other new technologies. Libraries can move beyond providing their users simple online access to these collections and create a plan for providing access to local e-government information that meets the needs of their library community. For more detailed information on creating a collection development plan, see Martin (2005).

Local Collections

Collection development guidelines for electronic collections can be similar to those for a paper collection, with the caveat that what may have been formidable to collect in paper format (e.g., loose-leaf, updates) is more easily accessed online. There are few depository programs for local government documents, and most local government websites exist primarily to convey information or to provide online services. Any formal collection management of documents, whether in paper or online, is usually left to the attention of a librarian with the time to establish communication with local agencies to acquire information about the creation and distribution of documents.

Sheer numbers makes any kind of inventory or comprehensive identification and collection of local government documents impossible. At best, one can fall back on the traditional government documents librarian's method of tracking down government information of all kinds. That process is characterized by first ascertaining the likely provenance (government authorship) of documents that might contain the information and then searching the information available from that source. It helps to understand the nature of local government organization to know where to begin the search. Local news reporters can be good resources in a library's effort to build relationships within local government; they often have connections at city hall and with other local government entities.

Local government documents collections have traditionally been maintained by large academic libraries. Many smaller academic and public libraries have a more specific mission to meet user needs, with "government documents" or not, and need to scale their collection and the service to their user communities. For example, growing communities of Hispanic library users may require additional library services for finding and using online Spanish-language municipal government information. Regardless of level of collection development, all libraries can take the following collection development steps to identify necessary local e-government collections:

- Perform a user needs assessment.
- Identify the type of local governments within the library's community base.
- Identify local e-government dissemination policy and practices.
- Identify local community government needs and watch for important local issues and breaking news.
- Track and maintain typical local e-government questions asked in the library, preferably over a period of a year.
- Evaluate library services for local e-government information, including reference services, staffing issues, training, and library website information.
- Determine whether any additional library services are needed for local e-government information.
- Create a written collection development plan for e-government information.
- Review the collection development plan periodically to determine if needs or methods of delivering electronic documents have changed.

Some libraries collect electronic information by downloading and archiving copies of electronic documents. For local government information, however, classifying, archiving, and managing electronic copies of documents are particularly difficult, since larger libraries typically use cataloging services for their materials. Local government documents collections have traditionally been acquired and maintained by large academic libraries. They are usually cataloged with bibliographic utilities such as OCLC's WorldCat so that the cataloging can be shared with other libraries. This saves staff time for other libraries. Libraries are just beginning to catalog electronic documents using metadata and following cataloging standards for online websites. One additional way to pool resources is through digital library programs that partner with larger state libraries to provide cataloging for this material. The Seattle WAGILS program described below is an example of preserving, archiving, and cataloging digital local documents.

Web Guides

Whereas paper collections require cataloging and some sort of access via a card catalog, providing access to local e-government documents can be as easy as creating a government information web page listing links to local government entities and their documents. But local government entities, including municipal, county, and special district entities, can number in the tens of thousands. It would be useful for a library to develop a local government collection development plan that identifies its user communities and targets government sources useful to them. Here are some examples of library local government web guides, and others are described in the next section:

- California Local Government Information Website, by the Institute of Governmental Studies Library, University of California, Berkeley. http://igs.berkeley.edu/library/localweb.html

- Jacksonville Public Library. Recommended Websites: Local Government Resources. http://jpl.coj.net/res/sites/government.html

- Spokane Public Library Local Government Web page. "Spokane Government Resources" under http://new.spokanelibrary.org > Research > Find the Best . . .

- University of Michigan Documents Center. Local Governments and Policies. www.lib.umich.edu/govdocs/pslocal.html

Some libraries also download and archive copies of important electronic local government documents on library servers or may use a subscription service such as Archive-It (www.archive-it.org) for preserving local government websites and born-digital content. Copyright restrictions do not usually apply to government documents, including local government publications.[3] The first step is a user needs assessment. Once those needs are established and the relevant e-government resource links are identified, then creating a library web page that provides access is the next logical step. Some library web pages for local government information listed in the following section are good examples of how libraries are developing to meet user needs. Whether the library employs an internal webmaster or web team to create and edit the library website or contracts for services from an outside firm, the librarian should always be involved in the process and prepared to offer suggestions.

LOCAL E-GOVERNMENT IN CURRENT PRACTICE

The following selective survey of city and county websites illustrates the variety of ways local governments and their associated libraries are offering access to e-government information and services.

Mesa, Arizona

Residents of Mesa, Arizona, can access a variety of documents and services online, including the municipal codes and electronic utility bill payment. One helpful feature is an e-services link, which has links to several library services placed on the linking page, and a "one-call that's all" link to a city telephone directory. There are links to maps on redevelopment and planning and zoning. Links are also provided to e-court, online class registration, road construction information, various fee schedules, tracking a building permit code compliance case, tee-time reservations at the golf course, a citizen contact system, and a guide to opening and operating a small business. Links are available to other city website sections. One link is for several full-text government documents under "Capital Improvement Program 2007–2012" (www.cityofmesa.org/cip/CIP_Program_07-12.asx). Obviously these documents are of long-term interest to residents of the community. It presents an interesting opportunity for a library to determine if it has an interest in providing links to, cataloging, and archiving the documents.

Seattle, Washington

The City of Seattle website (www.seattle.gov) provides links to city services and information about the city council, including the city charter, municipal code, and recent legislative action. The website also includes maps of city parks that allow dogs off the leash (maps are considered government publications). In addition, certain activities can be accomplished online, such as paying for parking and traffic tickets, renewing and paying for business licenses, and making animal shelter donations. Though a large array of services are not yet offered, the information is useful.

The Seattle Public Library's website (www.spl.org) also links to local government information, city and county as well as federal and state government websites. The King County, Washington, website (www.kingcounty.gov) links to the Civil Rights Code sections on fair employment, fair housing, and fair contracting, as well as on how to file a complaint. The county website also has links to information services such as the King County Public Library. The relationship between the library and the local government is developed via electronic resources. The library's website (www.kcls.org) provides links to local government websites such as "City and Regional Resources," "City of Seattle," "King County," and "Other U.S. Cities." There is also a "King County Local Links" selection that provides access to an index page listing city links, codes, court decisions, and many other services.

Archiving government information is a task too often neglected. Washington State is working on a program to archive and manage state government documents that includes information for municipalities such as Seattle. The state has a virtual government documents website, Find-It! Washington (http://find-it.wa.gov), that includes e-government publications from Washington and the Pacific Northwest, including Alaska, Oregon, Idaho, and British Columbia. It includes selected books, pamphlets, and documents created by state and local government agencies. Some of the material was created by federal agencies. The website is an extension of WAGILS (Washington Government Information Locator Service), a program modeled on the federal government's GILS (Government Information Locator Service) program. This is one of the newest and most comprehensive programs to digitize, index (or catalog), and archive government information. It illustrates the movement of local and state governments toward preserving and archiving digital documents.

Jacksonville, Florida

Jacksonville, Florida, has a simply designed website (www.coj.net/default.htm). In addition to a search engine that searches lists of city offices and services, there is an e-government link that provides access to many local e-government services, including various inquiries, searching property records, mapping services, paying traffic and parking tickets online, bidding for government jobs, applying for jobs, voting, library services, and filing a variety of court documents. Although certain documents are readily available online, there seems to be no concerted plan to capture and archive municipal documents. This city, through its website, is doing quite well in expanding e-government services. Still, at the time of this writing, it was not actively identifying, downloading, and making local government documents accessible through its website.

Similar to the Seattle library, the Jacksonville Public Library (http://jpl.coj.net) has useful links to the local government websites and documents. Under "Recommended Websites," a Government Information page links to Local Government Resources. Some documents are available in full text electronically, but they seem to be located only at the city website. By selecting the "Community Access Partnership Network" link from a special pop-up box link on the Recommended Websites page, the user can access a page called Access Florida that provides links to state and federal assistance programs through the Florida Department of Children and Families. There are links to applications for food stamps, temporary cash assistance, Medicaid and Medicare, as well as assistance for Hurricane Katrina evacuees. The local government, although it does not maintain these websites, is providing a service by referring users to the proper resources.

Jackson, Wyoming

Another example of local government and library collaborating to provide citizen access to information is the simple but informative Jackson, Wyoming, website (www.ci.jackson.wy.us). In 2007 the first page of the website provided a prominent link to the government document "Pathways Master Plan." Now available via a website search or via links, this document is a planning/environmental impact report, a master plan that combines environmental sustainability with improvements in transportation routes. These types of documents are of great interest to residents of the community, and though they sometimes can be found at the library, often it is necessary to go to city hall to view a copy. Such local government studies are not unusual, but often they are not known to the public. Although there is no Jackson public city library, there is the Teton County Library. Searching its website (http://tclib.org), the user can find links to "Featured Collections" and "Government Documents." Provided on the home page is a description of the "Local Government Documents Collection," primarily in paper: "Local documents held by the Library are publications of Teton County, Wyoming and the Town of Jackson. The bulk of the documents provide information on finances, land use and planning, codes, the Jackson Hole airport and development master plans." There is an invitation to ask staff for further assistance. This is more information than many libraries provide about local government documents.

Sitka, Alaska

The official website of the City and Borough of Sitka (www.cityofsitka.com) has many links to city government information, including the city code, e-government services, and business information. The Doing Business with the City of Sitka/ Taxes web page provides a table that cross-references codes, licenses needed, forms to apply for license, and applicable taxes. There is a reciprocal link from the Sitka City Library to the official city page. This does not require any work on the part of the library, and it is evidence that the local government and library are working together to provide public access to government information. Another interesting link is the Sitka Library network, which links all public K–12 schools and the city library.

CONCLUSION

The examples in this chapter confirm that the transition of local government information from print to digital format is unique to each local government. They also confirm the findings of the Digital Cities Survey concerning which information and services are transitioning most quickly. Libraries providing access to local government information need to ask themselves how they can help serve their users. Library users will continue to demand access to local e-government information and services, and the reports on trends show that these are developing rapidly. Simple steps such as improving library web guides and creating collection development plans will improve library services for local e-government information at little cost. Finally, new technologies in harvesting and providing digital collections, along with library/government collaborations, promise a bright future for the access and delivery of municipal government information in the electronic environment.

NOTES

1. Center for Digital Government. Digital Cities Survey: Digital Cities Serving Americans New Digital Majority. Report of Major Findings from the 2005 Digital Cities Survey. www .centerdigitalgov.com/surveys.php?survey=counties. Downloads available.

2. See the range of reports available, including the 2006 report, from the Information Use Management and Policy Institute, College of Information, Florida State University's Public Libraries and the Internet website, www.ii.fsu.edu/plinternet_reports.cfm.

3. Government publications are defined by Title 44 of the U.S. Code as "informational matter which is published as an individual document at Government expense, or as required by law" (44 USC 1901). According to ALA's Key Principles of Government Information (www .ala.org/ala/washoff/woissues/governmentinfo/keyprins.cfm), property rights of government information reside with the people; therefore, copyright should not apply to information produced by government.

REFERENCES

Bertot, John Carlo, et al. 2006. "Drafted: I Want You to Deliver E-Government." *Library Journal* 131 (13): 34–37. Library Journal.com, August 15, 2006.

Hernon, Peter, et al., eds. 1978. *Municipal Government Reference Sources: Publications and Collections*. New York: Bowker.

Martin, Mary. 2005. *Local and Regional Government Information: How to Find It, How to Use It*. Westport, CT: Greenwood Press.

McGinnis, Patricia. 2002. "Creating a Blueprint for e-government." In *The World of e-Government*, ed. Gregory G. Curtin, Michael H. Sommer, and Veronika Vis-Sommer, 51–63. New York: Haworth Press.

Scavo, Carmine. 2007. "Development and Use of the World Wide Web by U.S. Local Governments." In *Digital Government Information*, vol. 1, 296–300. Hershey, PA: Idea Group Reference.

Stowers, Genie N. L. 1998. " State and Local Government Cyber-Budgeting." *Government Finance Review* 14 (1): 36–40.

Wilson, Yvonne, and Deborah Richey. 2005. "A Basic Primer on Collecting Local Government Publications." *DttP: Documents to the People* 33 (4): 9–11.

Chapter 14 State Government Information

Lori L. Smith

I n almost every state there is a library or similar entity required by law to acquire state publications and distribute them to a group of depository libraries for preservation and access by the public. In the print era these state libraries, and their equivalents, received physical copies of publications from state agencies, listed these publications in some sort of official bibliography, and distributed the copies to depository libraries around the state. Today, many state-published titles have ceased to be distributed in print and are made available only on the issuing agency's website. Online publications are cheap to produce, easy to update, and accessible to any person with the appropriate computer equipment and software. They are also easy to delete, prone to technical problems, and difficult for many people to find. If the agency decides to remove those publications from its site, all public access to those titles is lost. To resolve this problem, state libraries are now struggling to capture and preserve electronic publications for permanent public access and to provide tools to assist the public in locating state information that is published online.

State libraries, and other interested institutions, are taking a wide variety of approaches to address the issues of current and permanent access to electronic state publications. Many are seeking out electronic publications on the Web using a manual or automated process and capturing copies for permanent access. The Alaska State Library is using Web Spidering software and the LOCKSS system to harvest, compare, collect, and archive electronic documents. The Library of

Lori L. Smith received her BS from Ball State University and her MLS from Indiana University. She is head of the government documents department at Southeastern Louisiana University's Sims Memorial Library. She conceived, edited, and coauthored Tapping State Government Information Sources *(2004). Smith has been a member of GODORT for twenty years.*

The author acknowledges the assistance of the following librarians, who provided information for the case studies in this chapter: Bernadette Bartlett, Library of Michigan; Daniel Cornwall, Alaska State Library; Robert Dowd, New York State Library; and Annie Moots, Missouri State Library.

Michigan, among others, is finding documents manually and using OCLC's Digital Archive system to capture and preserve them. The Arizona State Library is spearheading an effort to create tools to be used in conjunction with OCLC's Digital Archive that will automate the process of capturing documents. Some states, such as Missouri, Iowa, and Oregon, have developed systems in which state agencies are required to notify the state library about the existence of online publications or to submit electronic copies. State libraries in New York and Wyoming are using the Hyperion module of SirsiDynix's ILS software to archive electronic documents. Other states are using similar modules in software from other ILS vendors. Many states, such as Texas and Georgia, have created databases of state documents to assist the public in finding them.

Other state libraries, however, are still exploring options and have not yet begun to preserve state publications that are born digital. In most states that are not actively involved in digital archiving, the state libraries are printing and cataloging, or at the very least cataloging, state publications that reside on the Web.

LOCKSS AND THE ALASKA STATE LIBRARY

The Alaska State Library began collecting born-digital state publications in 1998. At first, publications were located manually and printed. The print copy was cataloged and added to the library's noncirculating collection. Catalog records included a URL in the 856 field that led to the copy housed on the agency's server. In 2002 the library began using Teleport Pro Web Spider software to locate and harvest online publications. In 2004 the library switched to the Capturing Electronic Publications (CEP) software created by the University of Illinois at Urbana-Champaign in conjunction with three other institutions.

Beginning in July 2005 the library began storing electronic copies of state publications on its own server. A print copy was still made and kept, but the URL in the catalog record was changed to point to the copy on the library's server.

Staff of the library became familiar with the LOCKSS system by participating in a trial of the software performed by the GPO. The coordinator of the Alaska Depository Program determined that LOCKSS would also be useful for archiving electronic state publications (for details on LOCKSS, see chapter 12).

In December 2005 a software plug-in was written so that the LOCKSS system could collect publications included on the Alaska State Documents shipping lists. Since January 2006, Alaska documents have been made available through LOCKSS. As of May 2006 the following institutions had cached copies of Alaska documents on their local servers: Alaska State Library, Georgetown University, Northeastern University, Rice University, Stanford University, University of California at Berkeley, University of Connecticut, University of Illinois, University of Maryland, University of Michigan, University of Notre Dame, University of Pittsburgh, University of Utah, University of Wisconsin-Madison, and Vanderbilt University. None of those institutions is an Alaska state depository and no formal depository agreements have been signed. As of this writing, none of the Alaska state depositories other than the state library had joined the LOCKSS Alliance. (OCLC, creator of the Digital Archive system described below, joined the LOCKSS Alliance in June 2006.)

In February 2006 the state library began adding Open WorldCat links to its monthly shipping lists of Alaska documents. These links allow the browser to connect to the bibliographic record for a specific title in the WorldCat database and check to see which libraries in the country are listed as holding copies. One example of an electronic publication that has been archived by the Alaska State Library is the *Annual Report of the Alaska Oil and Gas Conservation Commission*.[1] That page of the library's website also includes a "See what other libraries, if any, hold physical copies of this title" link that leads to the record for that title in WorldCat.

OCLC DIGITAL ARCHIVE AND THE LIBRARY OF MICHIGAN

The Library of Michigan (LM) first began investigating methods to preserve electronic publications in 1997. In conjunction with the State Archives of Michigan and the State Records Center, LM researched options and did a survey of state agencies to determine how they were managing information. Although the process resulted in a list of criteria for an archive of electronic documents, no system was found that would meet all the criteria.[2] Eventually LM became involved in OCLC's pilot project of a system to capture and archive electronic documents. This pilot system became the Digital Archive, which went live in 2002.

The Digital Archive's Web Harvester software allows the user to do item-by-item archiving of electronic documents by creating a Digital Archive record using OCLC's Connexion cataloging service, harvesting the document with Web Harvester, and ingesting the document into the Digital Archive. Archived documents are stored on OCLC's servers. The document can then be accessed via Connexion, FirstSearch, LM's online catalog, ANSWER (http://35.9.2.51/search~S37), and Michigan's statewide catalog, MeLCat (http://elibrary.mel.org/search/).

One state document that has been archived by LM is the *Annual Report of the Department of Corrections*.[3] The fact that OCLC is responsible for storing the data is one of the major selling points of the system. As its website indicates,

> OCLC is actively developing processes for full preservation of digital assets to ensure complete renderability, regardless of technology changes. This preservation system will likely involve a combination of migration and emulation. But here's the bottom line: OCLC is working to figure this stuff out so you don't have to—which means you can preserve something almost as precious as your digital assets: Your peace of mind. (OCLC 2007)

Between October 2002 and spring 2006, LM archived more than six hundred electronic documents. These documents were selected for archiving on the basis of the same criteria used to select print titles to include in the depository program. In

LM's online catalog, records for electronic titles include links to both the agency-hosted version and the archived version. In the annual checklists created by LM, archived documents are listed separately from print depository titles in a section headed "Electronic Titles."

LM staff members spend approximately 35 hours per week finding and archiving electronic documents. The Michigan documents outreach coordinator estimates that at least two full-time equivalent employees would be needed to do a thorough job of finding and harvesting electronic documents manually.

Although a lack of resources has prevented LM from archiving a larger number of publications, a more automated service being created by the Arizona State Library in conjunction with OCLC, the Web Archives Workbench (see below), may assist LM in the future to archive more publications and websites with its existing resources. Based on its positive experiences with OCLC and the Digital Archive, in 2006 LM switched the focus of its depository program from print to electronic. Now documents will be collected and distributed to depositories in print only if they are not available online.[4]

Other libraries that use the Digital Archive include the Connecticut State Library, the New Mexico State Library, the State Library of Ohio, and the Wisconsin Reference and Loan Library.

ECHO DEPOSITORY PROJECT AND THE ARIZONA STATE LIBRARY AND ARCHIVES

Richard Pearce-Moses (director of digital government information, Arizona State Library, Archives and Public Records) and Joanne Kaczmarek (archivist for electronic records, University of Illinois at Urbana-Champaign) outlined a new approach to collecting and preserving web-based documents in an article published in the Spring 2005 issue of *DttP: Documents to the People* (Pearce-Moses and Kaczmarek 2005). This approach, the Arizona Model, begins with the observation that electronic documents might be managed more efficiently if materials published on a website were viewed as a hierarchy of series and subseries, like those in an archival collection, rather than as individual publications. To collect and manage digital documents according to the Arizona Model, the archival principles of respect for provenance and respect for original order must be followed. This keeps documents in context and aids in their later interpretation.

To apply the Arizona Model, the following steps would be used:

1. Identify websites that contain state publications that are appropriate for the state library to acquire. Web Spider software can be used to follow all the links from a "seed" list of sites and to create a list of linked domains. Staff can then analyze the list to select those domains that are associated with an agency that is "in-scope." Organizational charts and other tools can be used to ensure that no agencies are missed.

2. Build a taxonomy that shows the hierarchical relationship of agencies, divisions, and so on and relates each to its domain address.

3. Review each domain to find series and subseries of publications that are "in-scope" and should be acquired. An understanding of the directory structure of the site is necessary to determine series and subseries, so site analysis software may be needed to view the structure of the site.

4. Assign descriptive metadata from a controlled vocabulary to each series and subseries.

5. Acquire documents via an automated process based on the information gathered in the previous steps. When each document is downloaded, a package of information containing all files needed to reconstruct the document is created.

6. Load the packages into the digital repository system for preservation and public access.

In 2004 a group of institutions including the Arizona State Library, the University of Illinois at Urbana-Champaign, and OCLC obtained a grant from the Library of Congress to test the Arizona Model and develop the software tools necessary to implement the model. This grant led to the ECHO DEPository Project (Exploring Collaborations to Harness Objects in a Digital Environment for Preservation). The project has four core activities: develop methods to use the Arizona Model to select electronic materials for preservation according to archival principles; develop software tools to select and preserve electronic materials; test and evaluate the existing open-source digital repository systems; and determine what problems may be encountered in preserving digital resources for an extended period of time.[5]

The major software package being developed and tested in conjunction with the project is OCLC's Web Archives Workbench (WAW).[6] The WAW will have four components: the Discovery Tool, the Properties Tool, the Analysis Tool, and the Packaging Tool. Used together with OCLC's Digital Archive repository software, these tools will use the Arizona Model to locate, harvest, assign metadata to, and preserve electronic documents with a minimum amount of intervention from humans. After the initial setup, the process will be highly automated. In August 2006, OCLC acquired Digital Media Management, the company that produces the digital archiving software CONTENTdm. This will allow OCLC to integrate CONTENTdm more thoroughly into its line of products and provide additional experienced staff to assist OCLC in developing the WAW.

STATE AGENCIES SUBMIT DOCUMENTS: MISSOURI STATE

Missouri's depository library program was created in 1977. Beginning in that year, print copies of state publications were distributed to forty-one depository libraries. When digital documents became prevalent they were, for a time, printed, cataloged, and added to the state library's collection. In 2004, with the passage of House Bill 1347, the depository library program was replaced by the State Publications Access Program, intended to preserve and provide access to both digital and print publications.[7]

The new law required every state agency to determine the format in which its publications would be issued and to submit to the state library an electronic copy "of each publication created by the agency in a manner consistent with the state's enterprise architecture." For titles issued in print, agencies must still send five print copies to the state library: one for the Missouri State Library, one for the Missouri State Archives, one for the Library of Congress, and two for the State Historical Society of Missouri. As of July 2006, about 95 percent of state publications were still being produced in print. Agencies were also required by the new law to designate a liaison to the program and notify the secretary of state about that person's identity each year.

On the state library's website (www.sos.mo.gov/library/) there is a place for agency liaisons to submit electronic publications via FTP. An alternate method allows the agency liaison to submit the URL of each publication along with the publication date and an indication of the formats in which the publication was issued. Each liaison is given a user ID and password in order to submit publications.

An FAQ page on the state library's site outlines the types of publications that should be submitted and provides a list of acceptable digital formats. After the electronic documents are submitted, they are stored temporarily on the library's FTP server and then transferred to OCLC's Digital Archive system. The documents are made available via links in the state library's online catalog (http://arthur.missouri .edu/search~S6), in the state's consortium catalog, MOBIUS (http://mobius.missouri .edu/search/), and in the WorldCat database.

Though the law now requires agencies to submit their documents to the state library, there is no enforcement mechanism in place to motivate them to do so. As of July 2006, according to a state reference services librarian, only eight to ten of the roughly sixty agency designees were conscientious about submitting electronic copies of their publications. In most cases she found it difficult to contact the designees who were not being cooperative, and she often found it easier to upload documents from agency websites herself rather than get the designees to do it. If a document was not available online, that was when it was most difficult for the library to obtain an electronic copy. Though an agency-initiated system of submissions sounds good in theory, the lack of an effective method of enforcement means that this approach to collecting and archiving digital documents can involve an extra level of frustration for the librarians involved.[8]

SIRSIDYNIX HYPERION AND THE NEW YORK STATE LIBRARY

Although the New York State Library has been collecting state publications since 1818 and distributing documents in a modern depository system since 1989, the New York State Document Depository Program was not legally established until 1993. From 1989 to 1994 documents were distributed to depositories on microfiche or in print. Beginning with publications issued in 1995, print documents are being scanned, saved as PDF images on the library's server via SirsiDynix's Hyperion Digital Media Archive software, and made available via links in the library's online catalog, Excelsior (http://nysl.nysed.gov), as well as in OCLC's WorldCat database. Most titles, especially large publications that are unwieldy as electronic files, are still being distributed to depositories in print. Publications that are available in a digital format on agency websites are being manually harvested, printed for the state library's collection as needed, and ingested into Hyperion. Digital documents are selected for archiving based on the same criteria used for including paper titles in the depository program.

In July 2006, the senior librarian in the documents section estimated that 30 staff hours per week were being spent on scanning documents and 10 hours per week were being spent downloading digital documents.

Hyperion supports a large number of file formats, but the library most often archives documents as PDF files. Hyperion has a graphical user interface for staff to use in managing files and performing administrative functions, and it has a web browser interface for the public to use in accessing the files. Since Hyperion works in conjunction with SirsiDynix's Unicorn ILS, access is restricted according to the same security rules that govern access to bibliographic records. The system administrator is allowed to perform more functions than staff, and staff members are allowed more privileges than patrons. Files stored on the Hyperion server are backed up locally by the library's system administrator.

When a new file is added to Hyperion, metadata, including the item's title, author, file size, scan resolution, and so on can be created. These data are indexed and searchable by patrons. Files are also organized into a hierarchical structure that can be browsed by the user (http://purl.org/net/nysl/nysdocs/nyspubs/). Finally, each harvested file is routed through a full-text processor so that the complete text of the document is keyword searchable. Digital documents that were created by scanning the print editions are not keyword searchable.

New York State Library patrons can find digital documents in Excelsior by doing a normal search of the entire catalog or by clicking the "Digital Collections" button. In the Search Digital Collections section, patrons have the option to search by content or resource type or to browse New York state government publications by branch of government and then by agency. Eventually a specific title can be clicked to view the full text in a new window. Software that blocks pop-ups must be disabled to view the document. If the patron finds a record for a digital document in the course of a normal search, clicking the link in the record opens the appropriate spot in the browse hierarchy. Again, a specific title may be clicked and pop-up blocker software must be disabled.[9]

DATABASES OF STATE PUBLICATIONS

Though many state libraries, and similar agencies that coordinate depository library programs, make state publications accessible via links in their online catalogs, some have also created separate databases of state publications. Following are links to some of these databases:

Georgia Government Publications Database: www.libs.uga.edu/govdocs/ collections/georgia/gapubs.html

Iowa Publications Online: http://publications.iowa.gov

Kentucky E-Archives: Electronic Records Archive: www.e-archives.ky.gov

KSPACe: Kansas State Publications Archival Collection: www.kspace.org

Nebraska State Government Publications Online: www.nlc.state.ne.us/docs/ pilot/pilot.html

New Jersey Government Publications on the Web: www.njstatelib.org/ NJ_Information/links/index.php

SoDakLIVE: Land of Infinite Variety Electronically (provides access to South Dakota documents not available elsewhere in an electronic format): http:// home.sodaklive.com/e-docs.htm

TRAIL: Texas Records and Information Locator: www.tsl.state.tx.us/trail/

THINGS TO CONSIDER WHEN PLANNING AN ELECTRONIC ARCHIVE

- Does current legislation support your mandate to archive digital publications? If not, consider spearheading the passage of new legislation that will. It will help you convince all stakeholders in the process about the importance of preserving digital publications. If agencies will be required to perform specific functions, it may be necessary to include some sort of enforcement mechanism in the law to encourage all parties to participate fully in the program. If your process will be more automated, keep in mind that your digital archive will need stable funding in order to guarantee permanent access.

- Is there another agency that you can cooperate with on the archiving of state publications? A state library and state archives working together may be able to accomplish more than either agency working alone.

- You will need to determine which types of publications and which file formats to collect and archive. You may wish to create a formal collection development policy for electronic documents. Keep in mind that users of the archive need the appropriate software on their computers to view each format available. Archiving fewer formats reduces the complexity of access for the user.

- Although the PDF format has become common for creating electronic documents, keep in mind that large PDF files can take a long time to load and may even crash a computer. If you have the power to do so, save large documents as multiple small PDF files rather than one large file.

- Assign metadata elements to your archived publications to assist the public in finding them with search engines and to note the hardware and software environment in which the publication was created. You will need to determine which data elements are required for each document.[10] On the other hand, state agencies may be concerned about members of the public finding outdated editions of their publications in your archive rather than the current editions presented on their own sites. So, you may want to use the robots.txt protocol, as the Alaska State Library does, to prevent search engines from indexing your archived publications.

- Even if you use Web Spider software to capture electronic documents, reviewing and cataloging the harvested documents take a considerable amount of staff time. A full-time person may need to be dedicated to those duties.

- If the system you use allows you to name the files in the archive, templates should be established for naming certain types of files. For example, the Alaska State Library has templates for annual reports, multipart documents, and serials.[11]

- Digital media decay faster than print and microform. Over time, your files must be refreshed by being saved to newer versions of the same medium or migrated to newer media. Software needed to view the digital documents must be refreshed or migrated as well.

- Your state may place copyright restrictions on its publications or websites. It may be necessary to make special arrangements to ensure that your archive does not violate copyright laws. You may want to create a statement of the copyright status and appropriate usage of materials in your digital archive.[12]

- How can the public be assured that online documents are truly official and have not been tampered with since their publication? Many online documents are updated frequently, so how often should a copy be captured and archived? Though no one seems to have found a good solution yet, authentication and version control are ongoing problems with digital documents. Those involved in creating a digital archive should be aware of these problems and remain alert for potential solutions.

- Take time to consider how digital preservation will be integrated into the overall goals of your institution. This will serve as the foundation on which you can build more detailed policies and procedures.

SOFTWARE VENDORS AND DIGITAL ARCHIVING INFORMATION RESOURCES

Archive-It: www.archive-it.org

Capturing Electronic Publications, Graduate School of Library and Information Science, University of Illinois at Urbana-Champaign: www.isrl.uiuc.edu/pep/#CEP

Center for Technology in Government, University at Albany–Library of Congress Collaboration for Preservation of State Government Digital Information, Publications and Results: www.ctg.albany.edu/projects/pubs?proj=lc&sub=pubs

CONTENTdm, DiMeMa, Inc: www.dimema.com

Digital Archive, OCLC: www.oclc.org/digitalarchive/

Digital Preservation in State Government, Best Practices Exchange 2006, March 27–28, 2006, Wilmington, NC: http://statelibrary.dcr.state.nc.us/digidocs/bestpractices/

DSpace Federation, Massachusetts Institute of Technology Libraries and Hewlett-Packard Labs: www.dspace.org

ECHO DEPository Project, University of Illinois at Urbana-Champaign; OCLC; and Library of Congress: www.ndiipp.uiuc.edu/index.php

Fedora, Cornell University Information Science and University of Virginia Library: www.fedora-commons.org

Greenstone, New Zealand Digital Library Project: www.greenstone.org

Interwoven: www.interwoven.com/index.jsp

Lots of Copies Keep Stuff Safe (LOCKSS), LOCKSS Alliance: www.lockss.org

Nevada State Library Survey Results (surveys how other state libraries handle digital publications): http://dmla.clan.lib.nv.us/docs/nsla/stpubs/usstateinfo.htm

Robots.txt Protocol: www.robotstxt.org

SirsiDynix, Hyperion Digital Media Archive: www.sirsidynix.com/Solutions/Products/digitalarchive.php

Teleport Pro, Tennyson Maxwell Information Systems, Inc. (Tenmax): www.tenmax.com

CONCLUSION

All around the country, state government agencies are working in partnership with the Library of Congress, library software vendors, and other organizations to find effective and efficient ways to acquire, organize, preserve, and deliver electronic state documents. Some systems being tested show great promise but, until a definitive system has proved its worth over time and been widely adopted, state publications will continue to slip through the cracks. Titles that are born digital will "die" without having been captured and preserved for permanent public access. They will simply disappear.

Therefore, individual depository libraries in each state may wish to begin, or continue to, print hard copies of those digital publications that will be of lasting value to their collections. Depositories with sufficient resources may want to create their own digital archiving system to supplement whatever system is being created at the state level.

Eventually, a set of standards and technological tools will do for electronic documents what acid-free paper did for print publications: allow libraries to collect information resources in a format that remains vibrant and useful for generations to come.

NOTES

1. See this report on the state library's website at http://library.state.ak.us/asp/edocs/annual/ ocm36039785/index.html. For more information about the Alaska State publications program, see http://library.state.ak.us/asp/asp.html.

2. At the request of the State Archives and Records Center, LM itself uses the terms "preserve" and "digital preservation system" rather than "archive" or "digital archive."

3. See this report in the Digital Archive at http://digitalarchive.oclc.org/request?id%3Doclcnu m%3A50015449.

4. For more information about the Michigan Documents Depository Program, see www .michigan.gov/hal/0,1607,7-160-17449_18637_18651---,00.html.

5. For more information about the ECHO DEPository Project, see www.ndiipp.uiuc.edu/index .php. For more information about the program at the Library of Congress that provided the grant to fund this project, see the Digital Preservation page at www.digitalpreservation.gov/ index.html.

6. See http://webarchives.oclc.org/WAW/Acknowledgements.doc.

7. For the Missouri State Publications Access Program legislation, see www.house.mo.gov/ billtracking/bills041/bills/hb1347.htm. The law went into effect on August 28, 2004.

8. For more information about Missouri's State Publications Access Program, see www.sos .mo.gov/library/reference/statepubs/about/.

9. For more information about the New York State Document Depository Program, see www .nysl.nysed.gov/statedoc.htm. For more information about Hyperion, see www.sirsidynix .com/Solutions/Products/digitalarchive.php.

10. The Texas State Library issued regulations that require state agencies to insert specific metadata elements into the web pages they create to aid in automated harvesting and preservation of state publications. For more information, see the state library's manuals and guides for agency liaisons at www.tsl.state.tx.us/statepubs/liaisonmanual.html.

11. The templates used by the Alaska State Library are formatted as follows: Annual Reports, www.library.state.ak.us/asp/edocs/annual/OCLCnumber/index.html; Multipart Titles, www.library.state.ak.us/asp/edocs/2006/multi/OCLCnumber/index.html; and Serials www .library.state.ak.us/asp/edocs/per/OCLCnumber/index.html.

12. Nebraska has a policy useful as a sample: www.nlc.state.ne.us/docs/rights.html.

REFERENCES

OCLC Online Computer Center. 2007. "Our Commitment." www.oclc.org/digital archive/about/commitment/default.htm.

Pearce-Moses, Richard, and Joanne Kaczmarek. 2005. "An Arizona Model for Preservation and Access of Web Documents." *DttP: Documents to the People* 33 (1): 17–24.

Chapter 15   Managing Electronic International Government Information

Issues and Practices

Catherine Morse

There are many long-standing challenges for managing international government organization (IGO) material in libraries, such as acquisitions, bibliographic control, and promoting access. In the electronic environment, different strategies are required to manage these ongoing challenges. Librarians have always been concerned with the information policies of IGOs, but now they must also advocate effective policies covering the dissemination and preservation of digital information. The working environment of the documents librarian may have changed, but the role of the librarian remains the same: to organize, preserve, and promote access to information.

In this chapter we cover managing electronic information produced by IGOs, but not by national governments. IGOs are organizations made up of member states that have signed a treaty or charter. These organizations do not allow individual persons to become members. IGOs are formal organizations; often the founding treaty or charter outlines the scope and structure of the organization.

IGOs are created with a specific scope or set of goals. They can have a geographic focus or a subject focus. A geographic focus can be either global (e.g., the United Nations) or regional (e.g., the European Union). Examples of subject-based IGOs include the Organisation for Economic Co-operation and Development (OECD) and the Organization of the Petroleum Exporting Countries (OPEC).

Catherine Morse is a subject specialist for economics, international documents, law, and public policy at the Harlan Hatcher Graduate Library of the University of Michigan. She teaches a course in government information at the University of Michigan's School of Information and is an active member of GODORT.

IGO INFORMATION BASICS

It is important that librarians who manage electronic information for a particular IGO take the time to learn about it. Understanding the work and structure of an organization is a great asset to the librarian in locating and managing information produced by that organization. A well-designed IGO website reflects the structure of the organization. The bodies within the organization may have their own web pages that describe their work and how they fit into the organization as a whole. Navigating an IGO website is a good way to get to know that organization's structure, mission, activities, and products.

IGOs produce information, documents, and publications, issued from a variety of contexts within its work, including reports, working papers, meeting records, resolutions, periodicals, statistical resources, press releases, and conference materials. This material is produced for different audiences, including members of the organization, the public, scholars, students, and policy makers. Often the charter of the IGO requires the production of documents that record the work of the organization. The subject matter of IGO information varies depending on the work of the organization.

IGO information output can often be divided into two broad categories: documents and publications. This is an important distinction that affects the way the IGO disseminates the information electronically and also has a major impact on library collection development, management, and reference. In addition, IGOs produce websites and online resources such as databases, which are an excellent source of information but may not fit into the categories of documents and publications.

IGO *documents* are generally issued to record the operation of the organization, such as the meeting records of the UN Security Council. Documents are created for internal use, although they may be made public. IGOs that emphasize transparency try to make their documents publicly available, sometimes even online. Other IGOs may consider their documents to be internal records and not meant for public consumption.

In print, documents are often softbound, monochrome, stapled together or a single sheet of paper. They usually have the IGO masthead and a visible document classification number. Often documents are later compiled into sets available for purchase in electronic, microfiche, or other format. Many IGOs have moved to issuing their documents online, in part, and requiring log-in for access to restricted documents. The information policy of an IGO governs access to such documents and informs the IGO's decision to maintain the documents online, including documents that are later revised. The electronic version may not be a dependable archival copy for libraries, which often rely on purchasing documents sets for their collection.

Even an IGO that restricts its internal documents may want to inform the public of its work. IGO *publications* generally fulfill an organizational mission to gather, analyze, interpret, and disseminate information related to its specific area. Publications are created specifically for external consumption—to inform policy makers, scholars, and the general public about the overall goals and work of the organization. For many IGOs publishing is a priority, and the publications may be purchased electronically via online databases and resources or in CD, DVD, or printed formats. Publications may or may not be available for free on the IGO website; many are produced to be sold. Publications can take the form of yearbooks, reports, statistics, conference proceedings, and periodicals. IGOs may post electronic versions of older publications, once replaced, and reserve the newer publications for distribution through their sales program or electronic resources.

IGO publications often look like books that come from commercial publishers, often bound with glossy colorful covers. Publishing priorities and funding for publications vary greatly among IGOs and are related to each IGO's mission. A major difference between an IGO and a traditional publisher is that the former often does not have the resources of a traditional publisher to market its publications; it all depends on the IGO's funding source and financial base. IGOs with many member nations from industrialized countries often do have excellent publications departments.

Many IGO publications, such as those from the UN, World Bank, and OECD, are under copyright, but even publications under copyright may still be available for free online. The International Organization for Migration and the Asian Development Bank (ADB) are two IGOs that make many of their copyrighted publications available for free on their websites. Freely available copyrighted publications create a challenge for librarians. There is no guarantee that those publications will be available on the website when they are needed. Does the library have a policy for cataloging freely available resources on the Web? Does it have the infrastructure to allow the librarian to download publications and save them to a server? Would this violate copyright or is it covered under "fair use"? Does the library have the resources to support the librarian printing out and binding electronic publications to be put on the shelves? As an alternative, does the library have the funding to purchase access to electronic databases that include the publications? Is the funding likely to continue, or would the library possibly lose access in the future? Online content is often dynamic. Would printing out specific electronic documents make the information less usable, less authentic? Do these downloaded documents have long-time research value to a library's collection?

Electronic IGO publications can, then, complicate the collection development work of the librarian. Although it may seem that freely available online publications would make a librarian's job easier, in fact the librarian must now devote additional time to the acquisition and preservation of these materials, two job functions that in the print world might be handled elsewhere in the library.

Many vendors bundle online IGO publications and make them available for purchase or subscription. Examples of online libraries of IGO publications include SourceOECD, the World Bank e-Library, and MyiLibrary. SourceOECD provides all formally published OECD information plus the working papers and makes statistics available in searchable databases with output in PDF or exportable data tables. The World Bank e-Library contains current and recent titles: 1,600 World Bank publications and more than 2,400 Policy Research Working Papers. MyiLibrary makes publications from several different private publishers and IGOs (e.g., UN, World Health Organization, and World Bank) available on one platform.

IGO INFORMATION POLICIES

The information policy of an organization is an expression of all the decisions that affect each phase of the information life cycle. Hernon et al. (2002, 9) define the different components of the information cycle:

1. Creation, collection, and gathering;

2. Production, processing, and publication;

3. Transmission, including distribution and dissemination;

4. Retrieval and use; and

5. Retention or disposal, including storage and archival management.

Librarians must understand the IGO's role in each phase so that they can adjust their own collection management strategy accordingly. If the IGO considers mounting a document on its website to be the primary method of information transmission, then the library must decide how to manage this information. Will the librarian need to check the website periodically for new online publications to add to the catalog? Or would library users be better served if the library prints, binds, and catalogs a tangible copy to add to the library's collection? Or perhaps the librarian can download the document to a library server to preserve an electronic copy, as permitted by copyright policy, which varies widely among IGOs.

Librarians cannot resolve these challenges alone; they should work within their institution or librarian association to encourage IGOs to plan each step of the information life cycle carefully. The International Documents Task Force of GODORT is a vocal advocate for users of IGO information. It has written letters to the UN urging permanent access to resources such as the UN High Commissioner of Human Rights Treaty Database and calling for publications of the Economic and Social Commission for Asia and the Pacific to be included in the UN depository program.

The UN is a complex organization made up of numerous bodies and specialized agencies. Information policy decisions are made by a few different groups: the Joint Inspection Unit; the Committee on Information within the General Assembly; and the Department of Public Information, which includes the Dag Hammarskjöld Library and United Nations Publications. Agencies within the UN such as the UN Environment Programme or UN Educational, Scientific and Cultural Organization (UNESCO) can also establish their own policies regarding document and publication dissemination.

Similar to most organizations, IGOs may restrict certain types of information, such as policy documents, meeting minutes, project reports, and project evaluations, often at the behest of member states. Many IGOs have information policies that outline what will be restricted and what will be made available to the public. Some IGOs such as the UN or UNESCO make meeting minutes of many of their committees immediately available; others like the World Trade Organization (WTO) automatically restrict meeting minutes for a period of time.[1] The WTO information policy also describes the derestriction process and how previously restricted information can be reevaluated. The information policy may also distinguish between the types of information the organization will make available on its website and the types of information it will publish in print or distribute through a depository program.

Many IGOs have been criticized for lack of transparency. In response, some, including the UN, World Bank, IMF, and OECD, have revised their information disclosure policies. As part of the policy revisions, these IGOs developed access policies for their archived documents that included two major developments: the default classification for most information will be public, and restricted items will be automatically derestricted after a specified amount of time has elapsed (Eckman 2005, 23).

The IMF is moving toward greater transparency by disclosing more information about its policies and operations, publishing more reports, and making more information available online. The IMF also established an office (the IEO) in 2001 to provide independent evaluations of its work. IEO reports are available on the IMF website.[2]

The World Bank revised its information policy in 2001 and 2005 to increase transparency and openness about its projects and operations. The new revisions allow for greater access to board minutes; the Country Assistance Strategies, a policy paper series that includes analysis and recommendations for programs; and the operational policy and strategy papers, which outline each program's policies and strategies for poverty reduction (World Bank 2006).

OECD information policy, revised in 1997, is based on the "belief that information should be considered unclassified until an active decision is taken to classify it, and that in many instances the need to maintain a security classification is time-limited."[3] It categorizes information intended for member states as either "unclassified"; "for official use," communicated only for official purposes; or "confidential" information that would harm the interest of the OECD or a member state if disclosed.

OECD internal information can be downgraded from "for official use" or "confidential" on the basis of a proposal by a member country or the secretary-general. Information classified as "confidential" is automatically downgraded to "for official use" three years after distribution unless the secretary-general decides otherwise or a member country objects. Similarly, information classified as "for official use" is automatically declassified three years after the distribution date unless the secretary-general decides otherwise or a member country objects. An important clarification in the policy states that just because a document has been declassified does not require that it be disseminated in any way.

DEPOSITORY LIBRARIES

Traditional dissemination of IGO information was through member countries and depository library programs. Depository libraries have officially contracted with IGOs to provide housing support for the collections and receive documents and sales publications. In the electronic environment, traditional roles and usefulness of depository libraries are being challenged. Originally, many IGOs organized depository library programs to help with information dissemination outside and within their member nations.

Some depository systems, like the UN program, allow new member libraries to join. Others, like the World Health Organization, limit the program to one depository library per country. Depository programs vary widely in requirements and responsibilities for the contracting institutions, but a depository agreement consistently implies a formal relationship between an IGO and a library. For some, like the IMF, it means that a library in a developing country receives IMF publications free of charge.[4] In other systems, like the World Tourism Organization, the programs offer depository libraries a discount on purchased publications.

The UN depository library program is the largest IGO depository library program. The Dag Hammarskjöld Library manages more than four hundred UN depository libraries worldwide. Libraries must pay to join or renew their depository status each year; libraries from developed countries pay more than those from developing countries. The number and types of materials included in the deposit can change.

The UN depository program includes unrestricted UN documents as well as many, though not all, sale publications. No electronic resources are included in the UN depository program. Libraries receive print copies of the *Monthly Bulletin of Statistics* on deposit but do not automatically have access to the online version. The Dag Hammarskjöld Library provides comprehensive written instructions for managing a UN depository library collection. Since the depository program does not include electronic information, the guide is strictly for managing a print collection, although the guide itself is available online.[5] This is a common problem with depository program instructions and requirements; they are frequently not updated to include electronic information management issues.

The UN has indicated that it is moving toward an electronic-only policy for distribution of its documents. Although electronic access will undoubtedly make UN documents available to more users than a print-based depository program, there are valid concerns about the long-term preservation of the documents.

IGOs in general do not seem inclined to re-create the depository model for the electronic world whereby depository libraries receive special access to online resources. For example, the UN Official Document System (ODS), an online full-text repository for documents, was first introduced as a password-protected database available only to subscribers or to UN depository libraries that opted to substitute ODS access for print copies of documents. As part of an effort to achieve greater transparency, the UN decided that starting in 2005 ODS would become freely available to everyone with Internet access.[6] There is no longer "special access" for UN depository libraries. Electronic IGO information is either available by subscription, available at no fee on the IGO website, or restricted. This creates an interesting situation for depository libraries. Is there value in remaining in the depository program if the documents are freely available on the website? Do IGO websites provide archival research material that may be reliably accessed by the library in the future?

BORN-DIGITAL DOCUMENTS

IGOs have begun creating digital information that does not exist in any tangible format. This born-digital material comes with a new set of challenges for librarians. IGOs such as the Joint United Nations Programme on HIV/AIDS or the International Organization for Migration make some of their publications available only as free online PDFs, with no print counterpart. Dynamic IGO web pages and IGO-created databases raise similar concerns. This content does not translate easily to print. Libraries must determine if and how to provide access to such information. Should a link to the online content be included in the catalog? Could this content be printed, bound, and placed on the shelf? Could an electronic copy be saved on a library server, or would that violate copyright? Could the information be acquired via subscription from the IGO or a vendor? In many ways, it is more difficult and time consuming to deal with freely available born-digital publications than it is to manage tangible documents. If the library has not established policies or support for this challenge, it could leave the documents librarian spending more time in an acquisitions role. On the other hand, many librarians are not comfortable leaving these valuable resources unarchived and unprotected.

GODORT's International Documents Task Force recently surveyed IGOs to gather information about their plans to archive electronic information (Church 2004). The findings illustrate why it is important for libraries that provide access and services for IGO information to bring IGO information policy into their plans for managing these materials. An overwhelming majority of IGOs that responded to the survey do not make their documents and publications available comprehensively on the Internet. Not even half of the IGOs that responded intend to archive permanently the material they do mount on the Internet.

The survey also demonstrated that for many organizations the responsibility for archiving is left up to individual offices within the organization. The fact that IGOs do not have a coherent organization-wide electronic preservation policy is of great concern to librarians, information users, and the general public. With a lack of policy on access and preservation, information becomes vulnerable. Rather than one central department taking responsibility for archiving all electronic information, individual units are deciding how long and in what format to keep information on their websites. Ultimately, this situation affects the collection development decisions of libraries and could affect decisions and consortial agreements to digitize and provide access to both historical and current IGO information electronically.

COLLECTION DEVELOPMENT

In the print era, libraries developed international documents collections by establishing depository status, ordering through IGO catalogs, and contacting individual IGOs to request documents. Now libraries depend more heavily on vendors to create large online libraries (Morrison 2002). These may be issued by either the IGO or commercial sources such as aggregator databases, but it is important to remember that content is not necessarily comprehensive, historical, or archived via these electronic databases.

The best collection development policy for a library in the digital age is uniquely geared to its users' needs. Many IGOs offer their products in different formats. For libraries, different formats may work best for different purposes. Statistics are popular when they are available electronically and especially if they can be downloaded into spreadsheet-compatible software. They are not as easy to use when they are available as PDFs. Many researchers may not appreciate having to read four hundred pages of text online; they often prefer longer books and reports in print format. Ideally, a local needs assessment would illustrate patron preferences for different types of material.

It is important to compare the differences between online, CD, and print publications. Are footnotes, references, and methodologies included in electronic versions? If so, are they as easy to use as in the print counterpart? For popular databases it may make sense to subscribe to the print and online versions, so that patrons can consult both at the same time. Subscription and purchase contracts for electronic information should be checked carefully. Limitations in access and content may suggest that alternative formats for the material should be ordered as a substitute or supplement to the electronic information.

Even if the product has the same cover and title in different formats, it may not contain the same information or have the same functionality. Occasionally data are available in one format that are not available in others. Do not assume that once the online version is available the older paper volumes can be weeded. Check content closely before discarding older print volumes; often online products contain only information from recent years.

Many libraries purchase IGO print publications from a vendor such as Bernan or Renouf. Vendors can help simplify the acquisition of IGO materials by fulfilling standing orders for print publications. Standing orders make collection development easier by ensuring that the library is sent one copy of all publications, or of all publications that match certain criteria.

Sometimes valuable information is available only on CD. This may be the case for the near future, especially for IGOs that lack full funding to support online electronic information and products. CDs allow for the functionality of digital resources without the expense of an online database subscription. Statistical materials available on CD often allow users to export tables into other applications. When considering the purchase of a single CD, consider how many patrons will want to use it. Is a stand-alone CD sufficient, or should the library invest in the usually more expensive networked version? Another important factor is the amount of staff time it takes to maintain networked CDs. Online databases are more reliable than local library CD networks. Online access usually costs quite a bit more than a networked CD, but reliability and less staff maintenance time can be worth a lot to a library.

At many libraries a group or committee of librarians must evaluate an online resource to approve a library's decision to purchase or subscribe. Once the trial access has been established, the librarians involved evaluate the resource on the basis of their needs. There are many things to consider when purchasing access to one of these online collections. Is there a one-time fee, or are there yearly costs? What other pricing options are there; is the library a member of a consortium for which there is or could be negotiated a consortial price? Does the library get to keep any electronic files or would the information disappear if the online resource disappeared? Is access granted via a password or IP authorization? Will any branch campuses be included in the license? Does the license allow nonaffiliated members of the public to access the resource in the library? Is there a limit to the number of simultaneous users? Are there restrictions on the number of pages a user can view per minute? Are there printing restrictions?

Purchasing a subscription to an online library such as SourceOECD, the World Bank e-Library, or MyiLibrary is more complicated than buying printed publications. Usually the publishers or vendors do not advertise the subscription price on the Web, as is done for print materials. Instead, the librarian contacts the vendor or perhaps fills out an online form indicating interest in more information. The price for large online packages depends on many factors including the nonprofit status of the institution, the country of the institution, and the number of full-time enrolled students. There may be discounts available depending on depository library status or the library's consortia membership. It is imperative to understand the importance of the information to users when considering purchasing an online electronic resource.

It is also important to remember that subscriptions to online resources are recurring costs. When libraries subscribe to online resources, they are paying for access rather than ownership. If the library has to cancel a print subscription, at least it keeps the volumes previously purchased; if the library cannot afford continuing a subscription database, it loses access to everything.

Sometimes libraries that subscribe to an information product in one format may get a discount on another. The amount of use and the way patrons use the material should determine if more than one format is needed. Also, the library may have the option of subscribing to the product in package options offered for a variety of products, and sometimes this may be negotiable.

MANAGEMENT OF ELECTRONIC IGO INFORMATION IN LIBRARIES

Once the library purchases or subscribes to IGO electronic information, the international documents librarian has the challenge of integrating these resources in various formats into the collection. This raises some important questions. What web guides are needed to help patrons get started? Are there any library web pages that should be updated to alert patrons to the new resource? How does the library organize its online resources? Is there a separate database for federated searching of electronic resources in addition to the library catalog? If the library subscribes to a big online library such as the World Bank e-Library, are there enough resources to analyze individual titles? If the library is receiving print copies along with a subscription for the online version, do the catalog records include links to the online versions? Should the library purchase any catalog records for some of the material to be loaded into the library's catalog?

Even if the information is available at no fee online, there is still a cost involved in cataloging the website. Many libraries are hesitant to catalog what is freely available on the Internet and have restrictions on what to include in the local catalog. In addition, selected IGO journals may be available in full text electronically for non-IGO aggregator resources. For example, the *UN Chronicle* is available for free online as well as in several commercial aggregators. It is important for the international documents collection manager to find a way to promote access to useful websites in a way that is sustainable for the library. Online guides and links from the library's website may be a viable alternative if cataloging freely available websites, online serials, or databases is not an option.

MASS DIGITIZATION PROGRAMS FOR IGO MATERIALS

Since the dawn of the Web, libraries have identified specific collections to be digitized. IGO materials have often been digitized in isolated projects with a finite scope. Examples of such projects include the GATT Digital Library done by Stanford University; the League of Nations Statistical and Disarmament Documents digitized by Northwestern University; the League of Nations Photo Archive digitized by Indiana University; and the Eighteen Nation Committee on Disarmament Documents digitized by the University of Michigan.

Mass digitization programs such as the Google Books Library Project, the Open Content Alliance Archive, or the EU Digital Libraries Initiative are different because they have a much larger scope. The Google Books Library Project and the Open Content Alliance Archive are digitizing the print collections of major research libraries. The EU Digital Libraries Initiative proposes to digitize a great deal of the content in the EU member states' national libraries.[7] These mass digitization programs are bound by copyright laws, but the noncopyrighted materials in these libraries, which include sizable international documents collections, will become accessible around the world via the Internet.

CASE STUDY: DAG HAMMARSKJÖLD LIBRARY, UNITED NATIONS

The Dag Hammarskjöld Library (DHL; www.un.org/Depts/dhl/) is housed at the UN headquarters in New York. The library's primary mission is to support the information needs of the secretariat, delegations to the UN, and other UN groups. As a part of its mandate, DHL must collect a copy in every language in which a document is officially issued. To help inform the public about the work of the UN, DHL has created research tools that are available from its website.

The freely available DHL online catalog, called the United Nations Bibliographic Information System (UNBISnet; http://unbisnet.un.org), is an important online research tool. UNBISnet contains catalog records for UN documents and publications as well as non-UN-produced materials in the DHL collection. The catalog links to full-text documents and publications when available. UNBISnet also includes a database of UN voting records and an index of speeches.

UNBISnet records are retrospective back to 1979, and earlier for selected documents. DHL has plans to digitize the older card catalogs and add the records to the catalog. When the retrospective conversion project is complete, UNBISnet will reflect the entire holdings of the library.[8]

UN documents are individually cataloged in UNBISnet. DHL does not use Library of Congress Subject Headings to describe the subject matter of documents; instead, it maintains its own thesaurus specific to UN documents. All General Assembly, Economic and Social Council, and Security Council resolutions, as well as additional documents, are cataloged in UNBISnet with links to the full text from the ODS.[9]

ODS is an online repository of UN documents. UN agencies like DHL can create links to documents contained in ODS. This allows DHL to include links in its catalog to the full-text documents in ODS. ODS includes documents going back to 1993, with UN Security Council documents available back to 1975. Current documents, including all UN resolutions, are uploaded regularly to ODS. Also, ODS contains documents in all six official UN languages: Arabic, Chinese, English, French, Russian, and Spanish.

DHL also maintains the United Nations Info Quest (UN-I-QUE; http://lib-unique.un.org/lib/unique.nsf) database as a ready reference tool for frequently asked questions. UN-I-QUE is designed to find documents of a recurring nature, retrospective back to 1946. Although a useful tool, this database does not provide as much bibliographic information as UNBISnet, nor does it link to full texts in ODS. It is designed as a quick tool to help librarians and other information seekers locate UN document symbols that can be used to find more in-depth information.

DHL has created several additional tools to help the public access UN information. The United Nations Documentation Research Guide (www.un.org/Depts/dhl/resguide/) is an invaluable resource for UN research. DHL reference librarians maintain a useful blog called *UN Pulse*, meant to alert readers to recently released UN documents and publications.[10] It is updated regularly, especially when UN reports are in the news.

DHL has adapted to the new electronic information environment in order to fulfill its mission. Its focus has shifted from preserving a print collection in a brick-and-mortar repository to making UN information available online and sharing it with patrons all over the world. To demonstrate its new mission, the library will change its name to the Dag Hammarskjöld Library and Knowledge Sharing Centre. After the retrospective digitization and cataloging of its collection, the print collection will be moved to a storage facility.

CASE STUDY: HARLAN HATCHER LIBRARY, UNIVERSITY OF MICHIGAN

The Harlan Hatcher Library is a depository library for the UN, Food and Agriculture Organization of the United Nations (FAO), and ADB. The FAO and ADB depository collections are composed mostly of publications also available for sale. These publications are included in Mirlyn, the library catalog, and added to the collection much like books purchased from private publishers. The library's UN collection includes both documents and publications. The publications are cataloged in Mirlyn and the documents are shelved and accessed in the Government Documents Center. Selected series within the print documents, for example, *Multilateral Treaties Deposited with the Secretary-General,* are included in the catalog. Documents are organized by the UN document symbol. The *Official Records* are separated from the masthead documents and bound.

United Nations databases that are freely available such as ODS are included in the catalog; however, the contents of ODS, the records for individual documents, are not analyzed. Freely available online publications such as the *Human Development Report* are included in the catalog.

Subscription-based IGO databases such as the UN Comtrade are cataloged in Mirlyn as well as in SearchTools, a separate database of online resources. Online libraries such as SourceOECD and the World Bank e-Library are cataloged as databases and their contents are analyzed. The Hatcher Library also collects print copies of OECD and World Bank publications. These items are cataloged in Mirlyn, and links are added to the online content available in the subscription packages.

IGO information is also managed through the Hatcher Library's Documents Center website (www.lib.umich.edu/govdocs/intl.html), which includes a list of links to selected IGO homepages. Subject-based web guides such as "Statistical Resources on the Web" (www.lib.umich.edu/govdocs/stats.html) integrate IGO information with information from the U.S. federal government and other sources.

The Hatcher Graduate Library is involved with digitization programs that include IGO information. The bound collections in the Hatcher Graduate Library will be digitized as part of the University of Michigan's partnership in the Google Book Search Library Project. At the present time, only the bound UN *Official Records* will be included in this project; however, exploration of digitization options for the unbound UN materials continues. Links to the full text of items that are not under copyright will be available through the Google Book Search interface as well as through Mirlyn.

RECOMMENDED WEBSITES TO ACCESS IGO INFORMATION

Asian Development Bank, Publications—ADB.org. www.adb.org/Publications/default.asp

Indiana University, League of Nations Photo Archive. www.indiana.edu/~league/index.htm

IOM, International Organization for Migration—Publications. www.iom.int/jahia/page8.html

MyiLibrary Ltd., MyiLibrary. www.myilibrary.com

Northwestern University, League of Nations Statistical and Disarmament Documents. www.library.northwestern.edu/govinfo/collections/league/

Organisation for Economic Co-operation and Development, SourceOECD .http://new.sourceoecd.org

Stanford–World Trade Organization/GATT Digital Library: 1947–1994. http://gatt.stanford.edu/page/home

United Nations, Official Document System. http://documents.un.org

United Nations Educational, Scientific and Cultural Organization, UNESDOC. http://unesdoc.unesco.org/ulis/

University of Michigan Digital Library, Eighteen-Nation Committee on Disarmament. www.hti.umich.edu/e/endc/

World Bank Group, Documents and Reports, www-wds.worldbank.org; and World Bank e-Library, www.worldbank.org/elibrary/

World Trade Organization, Documents Online. http://docsonline.wto.org

CONCLUSION

The international documents environment is changing dramatically, and online information offers the possibility of increased exposure to a wider audience of users. However, libraries face additional challenges in managing a dynamic online collection: in making subscription decisions for electronic resources; in providing web guides and access via cataloging for electronic resources; in following IGO information policy and making appropriate adjustments to library management of IGO electronic resources; in partnering or providing access to digitized materials; and in providing permanent access to IGO electronic information. It is also a vital concern to libraries and their users that IGOs are not properly preserving and providing permanent public access to their electronic information. The challenge of preservation requires libraries to work with IGOs to develop strategies for the goal of online permanent public access.

NOTES

1. World Trade Organization, "Procedures for the Circulation and Derestriction of WTO Documents" WT/L/452 (16 May 2002).
2. IMF, "Independent Evaluation Office (IEO) of the IMF—Papers Related to the IEO," www.imf.org/External/NP/ieo/pap.asp.
3. Quotations and following discussion of OECD policy from OECD (1997).
4. See IMF, "Integrating IMF Communications Operations: Responsibilities of the External Relations Department (EXR)," www.imf.org/external/np/exr/docs/2005/020805a.pdf.
5. UN Secretariat, Instructions for Depository Libraries Receiving United Nations Material, ST/LIB/13/Rev.5 (March 5, 1995).
6. UN Joint Inspection Unit, "From the Optical Disk System to the Official Documents System (ODS): Status of Implementation and Evaluation," JIU/REP/2003/3, www.unjiu.org/en/reports.htm.
7. Google Book Search Library Project, http://books.google.com/googlebooks/library.html; Open Content Alliance, www.opencontentalliance.org/index.html; European Union, "Commission Unveils Plans for European Digital Libraries," Press Release IP/05/1202 (September 30, 2005), http://europa.eu/rapid/pressReleasesAction.do?reference=IP/05/1202.
8. UN General Assembly, Twenty-eighth Session, Report of the Secretary-General, *Modernization and Integrated Management of United Nations Libraries: Update on New Strategic Directions*, A/AC.198/2006/2 (February 9, 2006).
9. UN, *United Nations Bibliographic Information System Thesaurus*, http://lib-thesaurus.un.org/LIB/DHLUNBISThesaurus.nsf.
10. UN, *UN Pulse: A Service/Blog of the United Nations Library—Connecting to UN Information*, http://unhq-appspub-01.un.org/lib/dhlrefweblog.nsf.

REFERENCES

Church, Jim. 2004. "Archiving International Government Information on the Internet: Report from a Survey by the GODORT International Documents Task Force." *DttP: Documents to the People* 30 (1): 37.

Eckman, Chuck. 2005. "Information Classification and Access Policies at Selected IGOs." *DttP: Documents to the People* 33 (2): 23–25.

Hernon, Peter, Harold C. Relyea, Robert E. Dugan, and Joan F. Cheverie. 2002. *United States Government Information: Policies and Sources*. Westport, CT: Libraries Unlimited.

Morrison, Andrea. 2002. "International and Foreign Government Publications: Collection Development Issues." *DttP: Documents to the People* 30 (2): 22.

OECD Organisation for Economic Co-operation and Development. 1997. Council Resolutions on the Classification and Declassification of Information. August. http://appli1.oecd.org/olis/1997doc.nsf/linkto/C(97)64-FINAL.

World Bank. 2006. "World Bank Disclosure Policy: Additional Issues: Follow-Up Consolidated Report (Revised)." www-wds.worldbank.org/external/default/WDSContentServer/IW3P/IB/2005/03/16/000112742_20050316141535/Rendered/PDF/261200v60R200310112110.pdf.

Chapter 16 Foreign Countries' Electronic Government Information

Jian Anna Xiong and Jing Liu

Acquiring and managing foreign government information, defined in this chapter as government information other than U.S. government information (and excluding IGO information), is a challenging area of librarianship because of the wide range of government information and the number of foreign countries with their own government structures and publishing systems. Global e-government development makes more and more foreign government information available online. It brings opportunities and challenges to librarians. It raises many new discussions among librarians about how to search, access, and acquire foreign nations' government documents, how to improve this work, and how to share it (e.g., Sherayko and Smith 1993; Lee 1997; Smith 1998; Morrison 2002). Other topics being discussed include bridging the digital divide through e-governance (e.g., Mutula 2005), implications of e-government on public libraries (e.g., Berryman 2004), and e-government web promotion strategies (e.g., Chang 2004).

In this chapter we address global e-government development—its rapid growth, benefits, and challenges to users. We also discuss developing library web guides as a common, basic solution to meet the challenges. Some libraries that foresee the trends in e-government and potential value of foreign information have already developed web guides to online foreign government information resources. To help more libraries, especially those new to this subject, develop their own web guides and handle the increasing number of online foreign government informa-

Jian Anna Xiong is assistant professor and government information librarian at Southern Illinois University Carbondale. She is active in research, reference, and instruction services. Xiong is now serving on the GODORT Cataloging Committee and Chinese American Librarians Association Midwest Chapter Public Relations Committee. axiong@lib.siu.edu

Jing Liu is the Chinese studies librarian at the University of British Columbia. She has an extensive record in publishing and presenting research and is now actively pursuing international cooperation in information services. jing.liu@ubc.ca

tion resources more effectively, we recommend four basic guidelines and provide selected resources. We also cover topics such as using official web portals and commercial sources for searching and accessing online foreign government information, copyright and fair use, and evaluating online government resources.

GLOBAL E-GOVERNMENT: GROWTH, BENEFITS, AND CHALLENGES

Regardless of the level of development or political structure, governments at many levels have sought to take advantage of the Internet to provide government information and services electronically. As of this writing, the newest *UN e-Government Survey 2008* was just made available online. It states that the real value of e-government is not in the technology but in its application of processes of transformation. It focuses on the importance of knowledge management as a tool for countries to move from e-government to connected government. Concerning e-participation in e-government, the report states that 189 countries were online in 2008 compared to 179 in 2005 (UN 2008, xi–xii, 14). About half of the countries had some form of integrated portals or "one-stop-shopping" windows compared to 35 percent in 2004 (UN 2005, 77). The information and services published on government websites are also increasing. According to a 2004 UN global e-government survey, 85–92 percent of all countries had websites on which they were providing some or all of their databases, laws, policies, and other documents (UN 2004). Generally, one can find some or all of the following information on government websites:

- Official national government gateways/portals designed to access all government agencies' and departments' websites, leading to all government information and public services. These are important resources for libraries and users.
- Directory information, including organizational charts and functions of government branches and agencies.
- Executive agency reports and publications, including annual reports.
- Government news and announcements, including official gazettes and important meeting activities.
- Laws, rules, and regulations issued by national, provincial, and local governments.
- Trade, commerce, and business information.
- Social service information and communications with citizens, including press releases and mail exchanges, such as a mayor's e-mail box. Citizens can input opinions online on some projects or report officials' corrupt behavior.
- Travel and visitor information.
- Scientific information and standards.
- Interactive forms for citizen and public use.
- Statistics.

Concerning future development of e-government information and services, a leading consulting company in measuring e-government performance stated that governments are evolving "from their first tentative steps publishing information online to developing sophisticated interactive and transactional capacities across a broad range of services" (Accenture 2005, 2). In this environment, a new concept, *t-government*, is emerging in Europe. A study by Booz Allen Hamilton (2005) commissioned by the U.K. Cabinet Office provides details about the new idea of worldwide best practice in e-government.

The global trend of providing government information and services online brings many benefits to the public. E-government information is easier than ever to search and access. It is searchable online 24/7, continually updated, and current. For the most part, it may be viewed at no cost and often has few copyright restrictions, as set by each government's laws. Most of this information is freely viewable and immediately downloadable from the Internet. For libraries, there are no shipping fees such as for paper and other tangible products and few acquisition costs to add e-government information to the collection, although costs of web maintenance, metadata, and cataloging may apply. There is no need to wait for materials; access is as immediate as the networks allow.

At the same time, global e-government also brings many challenges for searching and accessing information. For example, the number of government websites is increasing daily. Along with these individual government websites, a variety of web portals and web guides are generated by government and nongovernment, public and private sources—and the number of such portals and guides is also increasing. As a result, users have more and more information channels and portals to examine and stay current with.

Take the People's Republic of China (PRC) as an example. There were 27,143 Chinese websites registered under domain .gov.cn in October 2006 compared to thirty-four in October 1997.[1] Some of these 27,143 websites are individual government agency sites, such as http://english.mofcom.gov.cn, the Ministry of Commerce. Some are joint government project websites, such as www3.chinaport.gov .cn/en/china-eport1.html, for China E-Port, an important national data-exchange platform currently involving twelve ministries and administrations. Still others are government portals such as www.gov.cn, the official web portal of the Central People's Government of the People's Republic of China.

Chinese government websites are not all found in the .gov.cn domain. Others are registered under domains such as .com, .org, .net, which are typically used by private companies and independent organizations. Reading "About Us" information on these websites or studying a country's government structure can usually help verify the nature of the website owner. For example, www.xinhuanet.com/english/ is the website for *Xin Hua News Online*. Although ".com" usually indicates a private company's website, the owner of *Xin Hua News Online*, Xin Hua News Agency, is a government institution directly under the PRC State Council.

The authorized government portal site to China is www.china.org.cn. It is generated by the China Internet Information Center (CIIC) and published under the auspices of the China International Publishing Group and the State Council Information Office in Beijing. The China Internet Network Information Center (CNNIC), the state network information center of China, is available at www .cnnic.net. CNNIC was founded as a nonprofit organization in 1997, but it is not independent; it takes orders from the Ministry of Information Industry for the conduct of daily business, and the Computer Network Information Center of Chinese Academy of Sciences has responsibility for the administration of CNNIC.

In addition to the Chinese government websites, there are many online government resources, including data centers, portals, databases, and web guides, registered under various domain names other than .gov.cn for searching and accessing Chinese government information. They are established by non-Chinese governments or public or private resources. For example, China Data Online (http://141.211.142.26/index.asp) is provided by the All China Marketing Research Company. All China is authorized by the National Bureau of Statistics, PRC, to disseminate nonconfidential data collected by the Bureau. Portals to the World: Links to Electronic Resources around the World (www.loc.gov/rr/international/portals.html) was created and is maintained by the U.S. Library of Congress. It does not directly disseminate Chinese government information, but it offers selective links to Chinese official government websites. Still another example is OffStats: Official Statistics on the Web (www.library.auckland.ac.nz/subjects/stats/offstats/), a free library database established by Rainer Wolcke, developed and expanded by Anne Wilson at the University of Auckland Library. This database is searchable by country, region, or topic. It does not directly disseminate government information, but it includes selective links to official statistical websites that provide statistics by and about individual countries.

The evaluation of foreign government websites and resources is another challenge. Since online resources are abundant and the levels of information technology infrastructure of countries differ greatly, the content, scope, and quality of these resources vary considerably. It is necessary, though time consuming, to evaluate each of them and record findings. Since many of these online resources are constantly being updated, regular reevaluation is also necessary, and again time consuming.

Still another challenge for libraries is how to handle disappearing online government documents and websites. Governments have the authority to set up a website or take it down at any time without notice to the users, according to each country's legal restrictions and requirements. Governments have the authority to publish any government information, news, publications, and databases on the government websites for the public to access, and also the authority to remove it without notice. Such changes can take place at any time. It is, then, challenging to keep track of emerging and disappearing online government information resources. There is a need for national information policy to address this problem. There are archiving efforts in place as governments digitally preserve significant websites (see below).

Libraries also need to know when and what new government information is published and when historical documents are declassified, digitized, and published online. These questions challenge everyone, from novice users to veteran information specialists. A librarian who sees the value of capturing and developing web guides to government information resources must decide whether to link to this information and maintain it in a library web guide, purchase it from a government or private source, or add or purchase bibliographic records for the library catalog. Combinations of these options also should be considered.

LIBRARY WEB GUIDES: A BASIC SOLUTION

To increase efficiency in searching, accessing, and managing foreign online government information resources, developing a web guide is a common, basic solution for libraries. Searching in Google on "web guide, foreign government, library, site: .edu" is one way users may find existing library web guides. Many libraries, though, still do not have their own web guides to emerging e-government information resources outside the United States. For libraries considering developing their own web guide, we recommend four basic guidelines, discussed in detail in the next four sections of this chapter:

- The library must have a consistent policy that supports the curriculum of the institution, or the mission of the library, before generating a web guide.
- Librarians must be able to evaluate online government information resources.
- Librarians must have some knowledge of the copyright and intellectual property regulations of online government information resources.
- Librarians must have knowledge of searching and accessing online government information.

LIBRARY POLICY

To set up a consistent library policy for a library web guide, libraries might think about the following questions as they relate to the library or departmental mission in best serving users:

- What countries or geographic areas should be covered by the web guide?
- Should the web guide include only English online resources or also resources in other languages?
- What subject areas should be covered by the web guide?
- What levels should the web guide focus on: national, state/provincial, local?
- What types of material should be included: specific online government publications, websites, portals, databases, quasigovernmental resources, other related resources?

- What type of list or guide should be created: a simple web guide that lists and links the resources on the library website, something more complex, or should the library link to an existing web guide?

- What type of archiving is needed for the guide? Should some of the information be archived in print, or saved to a tangible electronic medium or to a digital archive? How likely are problems such as an unavailable website?

- Should annotation, abstracts, or evaluations of each online resource be provided?

- Should the guide or web page be cataloged? If yes, should be it cataloged locally in the online library catalog or contributed to OCLC's WorldCat (www.worldcat.org), one large network of library content and services, and shared more widely?

- How much maintenance will the guide demand, and can the library sustain it?

- Could the guide be replaced by a commercial electronic resource? With what benefits and drawbacks? With what costs? How do the creation and maintenance of the guide relate to the library's collection development policy?

Some libraries already have a well-established collection of foreign government information in other formats, such as paper, microfilm, or CD. Some government information continues to be available in these formats, although some online titles have ceased in tangible format. Some resources are available electronically via an aggregator as well as directly from the government online. Librarians face increasing workloads with the transition to e-government information from print formats. As government portals and commercial vendors enhance their ability to provide stable access to their online content, librarians are choosing to discontinue the print format and eliminating duplicated print subscriptions. Library collection development policies need to be revised and reviewed constantly in relation to these concerns and in relation to the development of web guides.

The extra cost of purchasing equipment for accessing online information resources, the effort of capturing, evaluating, and preserving online government information resources, along with the uneven developmental status of foreign websites might encourage libraries to maintain the status quo, choosing not to pursue foreign e-government information resources aggressively. Other factors are the changing availability of vendor-supplied resources and their changing costs and obscure copyright and ownership issues. Why should libraries rely on a resource priced beyond their means, or on one not available because of consortia decisions that affect the pricing structure for the individual library?

EVALUATING ONLINE GOVERNMENT INFORMATION RESOURCES

The resources included in a web guide must be selected through proper evaluation. There are many good sources for evaluating Internet resources in general.

Hope N. Tillman, director of libraries, Babson College, Massachusetts, provides some inspiring generic criteria and key indicators that can be specifically applied to online government information resources (Tillman 2003):

Authority. Is the resource created and maintained directly by a government entity? If not, does it have government authorization? The content of a nongovernment resource collecting and disseminating government information without government authorization needs more careful assessment for authenticity. (For more on the issue of authenticity, see Jacobs 2005.)

Language. Not all foreign government web portals, websites, databases, or publications are available in English. Sometimes only the home page of a government website is in English. Although the full texts of some online foreign government publications are translated into English, it is common that only the abstract of a publication is available in English. In our experience, many American users seeking foreign government information are interested only in English resources, but there are also many users interested in the original languages. It is wise to indicate language information in the web guide so that users need not click each of them to find out.

Fee. Is the resource free of charge? If not, does the government have plans to provide the same content free of charge in the near future? As a librarian, this online resource needs to be further evaluated to make the final decision. Morrison (2002) and Eckman (2001) provide many suggestions to help librarians make balanced, careful decisions. If the online resource is free, does it require free subscription or registration? In our experience, many users expect to be able to access only free online information resources that do not require any additional registration or subscription. Including fee information in the library web guide can help users filter unwanted resources without spending time and effort in further exploration.

Content coverage. On most websites, "About Us" and "Site Map" can help users get quickly familiarized with the full scope of special features of the site in order to confirm whether the entire site meets their needs.

Currency. How frequently is the online resource updated? When was it last updated and what was updated?

Stability of information. Will the resource stay online?

Active links. Are the links operational? Are there links to other sources? Are the links kept current?

Contact. Are there telephone numbers, e-mail addresses, contact person's name, phone, fax number, or mailing address? If time and energy allow, we recommend testing the contact service, at least the free e-mail service. It can be helpful to know if the responses are prompt or the answers satisfying.

Usability. Is the content well organized online? Is the site easy to navigate? If it is a website or database, test its search function. How is the speed of connection? Are there any special software/hardware/multimedia requirements?

COPYRIGHT AND FAIR USE

Ownership of foreign government information via commercial sources is hard to identify, so licensing for access to these sources can be complex. Copyright protection responsibilities and access limits need to be clarified before the library starts an online subscription. On one hand, more and more government information is entering the public domain, being accessible with few limits; on the other hand, there is no international agreement on how to share and handle foreign government information or safeguard access limits. Some commercial vendors may not be the legitimate owners of the foreign government's information source; they may process the raw data without the government's permission. Ownership disputes may arise as the developing countries' copyright laws mature. Library subscribers risk losing their access if they happen to select this kind of vendor, which is why some libraries are reluctant or cautious to reach licensing agreements with foreign commercial vendors.

SEARCHING AND ACCESSING E-GOVERNMENT INFORMATION

To search and access foreign online government information effectively, librarians should develop knowledge of foreign governments' administrative structures, publication practices, and information policy, or they should understand where and how to find this information. We conducted a survey in early 2006 among U.S. government information librarians, East Asian studies librarians, and Chinese American librarians through various librarian electronic discussion lists including GOVDOC-L, Intl-Doc, CALA-L, and Eastlib.[2] These discussion lists were chosen because their subscribers likely have working or personal experience with Chinese online government information, a status confirmed by survey. The unpublished survey results show that many respondents are aware of developing Chinese e-government, but that most respondents undervalue the existing Chinese government websites and available online government information services. In the survey, most respondents stated that they had little familiarity with Chinese e-government information resources—a major barrier to effective searches of Chinese government information online as well as to collection development.

Increasing librarians' awareness of national e-government information and services can help librarians generate high-quality web guides and also help them improve their reference, instruction, and web services. Awareness in the following areas will help:

Online developmental status of government websites, web portals, web guides, databases, and networks for the countries of interest: What is currently available? Which websites are under development? Which are new? Which are official or authorized by government agencies to disseminate government information? What is the level of authorization of private companies?

Current news and major political events: This basis of government publications librarianship is even more important in the digital age. For example, being aware of meetings such as the Korean Peninsula Six-Party Talks will help librarians search news for the specific meeting dates and thereby catch specific speeches, landmark agreements, or reports.[3]

Web guides generated by other libraries: Librarians must take advantage of the Internet to build up a network of online collections and guides, related professional organizations such as GODORT's International Documents Task Force website, subject librarians' discussion lists such as Eastlib; and professional journals such as *DttP: Documents to the People* or *Government Information Quarterly*.

In the remainder of this section we review a variety of resources valuable for searching and accessing foreign e-government information.

Books and Journals

Information seekers can consult English-language reference books and journals that discuss foreign government information, especially electronic information, to identify foreign government publications. These titles may be consulted for guidance prior to searching foreign government websites. They provide a wealth of information about a government's structure, publishing policy, related history, and significant publications. Below is a selected list of recommended, essential titles to start with:

Journal of Government Information (now merged with *Government Information Quarterly*), which for years provided a good acquisition guide in its notable documents issue on foreign government information. For example, one can find articles such as "China's Statistical System and Resources" (Xue 2004), an excellent resource about Chinese statistical publications and many essential Chinese government statistical resources, with a section devoted to web resources.

DttP: Documents to the People. In this journal one can find articles such as "International and Foreign Government Publications: Collection Development Issues" (Morrison 2002), which addresses many important issues and provides practical suggestions and other important resources.

Government Information on the Internet (Notess 2000) covers international and foreign government information on the Internet in chapter 10. It provides links to the main executive and legislative foreign government websites as well as brief descriptions of the main content and language of the selected websites. A total of 250 websites for international government organizations and foreign governments are listed in the directory. This is an important resource that should be maintained and updated. One weakness is that it does not always indicate where government websites fail to link within the same or different administrative levels. More essential individual government websites and nongovernment websites authorized to disseminate official government information should also be included.

Directory of Government Document Collections and Librarians (Tulis and Barkley 2003)

Acquisition of Government Information Resources and Other Foreign Documents (Sherayko and Smith 1993)

An Annotated Guide to Current National Bibliographies (Bell 1998)

Guide to Official Publications of Foreign Countries (Jover 1997)

Official Web Portals

Official web portals of foreign governments contain the most comprehensive information on government resources and services. They usually serve not only government agencies themselves but also individual citizens, businesses, and foreign individual and institutional users. Therefore, they are the most important and reliable e-government information sources for libraries as well.

Many new and complex government portals are being developed around the world. Asian governments have made great progress. For example, Singapore provides a gateway to all government services to its citizens, including payments and online transactions, and other countries use portals for information dissemination. Officially launched on January 1, 2006, the People's Republic of China's central government web portal, in traditional and simplified Chinese-language versions, provides information about government affairs, online services for citizens, enterprises and foreigners, interactive communication between governments and citizens, and other practical functions (www.gov.cn). An English version provides commercial and travel information for non-Chinese speakers. According to Alexa (a professional web information service provider), the traffic ranking of this portal at the beginning of a trial launch hit 3,803 over the three trial months among more than 12 million websites. It ranked second among major national government websites, next only to the Canadian government website.[4] Although the PRC government's portal is not capable of offering one-stop and seamless services to its citizens yet, it can be used as an information gateway for country studies or as a search engine for the latest central and local government information.

Users of official government portals should be aware that a country may have more than one official government web portal. This may make it more difficult to find government information and services. Australia is one example. In an Accenture (2004) study, Australia had nineteen government customer-focused portals and two government-entire online entry points. The study suggested merging the two online entry points, pointing out that they might be the reason Australians complained of difficulty finding the correct website and chose not to use the Internet more frequently for government services.

Web Guides

For specific country information, a search engine may be used to find the national portal or web guide to government information, e.g., National Government in the Yahoo! Directory (http://dir.yahoo.com/Government/Countries/). All sites included in the guide are evaluated by Yahoo editors and organized into subject-based categories and subcategories. As of this writing, 148 countries are listed in this directory. On each country's page one can find general information about the country's capital, population, location, and news. Active links to more comprehensive information about the government, people, geography, and so forth are provided.

Portals to the World: Links to Electronic Resources from around the World (www.loc.gov/rr/international/portals.html), maintained by the Library of Congress, provides links to electronic resources from around the world and includes more than just foreign government information. The information resources are organized first by country, then by subject, and offer brief annotations. Additionally, national libraries may be good starting places to find a country's web guide or portal.

Another helpful place to start is a country's foreign embassy. For example, all Chinese embassy websites can be accessed through active links at the PRC Ministry of Foreign Affairs (www.fmprc.gov.cn/eng/wjb/zwjg/2490/default.htm). Each foreign embassy's website provides government information in the native language of its location on policies and activities, speeches, about China, travel in China, and so forth.

Related professional organization websites usually provide useful links. For example, the website of the ALA's Government Documents Round Table, International Documents Task Force (IDTF) includes useful links to lists of foreign national governments, general guides, and guides to information from specific foreign countries or regions (www.ala.org/ala/godort/taskforces/internationaldocuments/links.htm).

Check the web guides published by other libraries and see what is already done either by linking from a professional organization or searching guides to foreign online government information resources. One popular example is International Documents Collection—Foreign Governments (www.library.northwestern.edu/govinfo/resource/internat/foreign.html), compiled by Northwestern University Library, which provides links to a list of foreign national governments, including national ministry websites for foreign affairs, state, statistics, and finance. The list is organized by country name, without annotation. Many U.S. libraries that collect or provide information about foreign government information link to this resource instead of creating a new one. Another example is Foreign Government Resources on the Web (www.lib.umich.edu/govdocs/frames/forfr.html), compiled by the University of Michigan Library, Documents Center. This online resource is more than a simple list of official foreign government websites. It is categorized both geographically and by information type and includes brief annotations. Another advantage of this resource is that both the information about each country and that issued by each country's government are on the same page. Such "about" and "by" information is often sought by the users at the same time. This website also provides links to news sources, search engines, and translation tools.

There are numerous area and regional guides maintained by academic and other institutions that organize online foreign government information. Government and Law in Latin America (http://lanic.utexas.edu/subject/government/), compiled by the Latin American Network Information Center, provides government-related information grouped by government, human rights, military, political science, and law and justice, as well as transparency and corruption. The guide is available in English, Spanish, and Portuguese.

Specific country studies web guides can be helpful. For example, Chinese Studies Internet Resources (www.library.ucla.edu/eastasian/china.htm#BUS), compiled by the East Asian Library, University of California, Los Angeles, provides links to Chinese government websites mixed with other nongovernment information and arranged by subject.

Subject guides such as Statistical Sources, Foreign Countries (www.libraries .rutgers.edu/rul/rr_gateway/gov_info/gov_info_intl.shtml#foreign2), compiled by Rutgers University Library, provides links to important statistical resources about and by foreign governments. Other examples are Foreign Law: Legal Research Resources on the Internet (www.lib.uchicago.edu/~llou/foreignlaw.html), by Leonette Louis-Jacques from the University of Chicago, and Finding Chinese Law on the Internet, by Joan Liu (www.nyulawglobal.org/globalex/China.htm), from the Hauser Global Law School Program.

Online Reports

Many survey and study reports on e-government available online provide updated information about the performance, progress, and status of national e-government. For example, Accenture conducts annual surveys on e-government leadership and has published reports such as *Leadership in Customer Service: New Expectations and New Experiences* (Accenture 2005) and *eGovernment Leadership: High Performance, Maximum Value* (Accenture 2004).

The UN conducted global e-government readiness surveys beginning in 2002, and most recently in 2008. Data from the reports can be accessed via the United Nations' UN E-Government Knowledge Base (www.unpan.org/egovkb/), which also links to the annual UN e-government readiness reports, which began in 2004 and included information from the surveys. The annual *Global E-Government Readiness Reports* (www.unpan.org/egovkb/global_reports/index.htm) summarize survey results and provide updated information about the progress and status of e-government in 191 UN member states, with comprehensive analysis and discussion of the issues. They also rank readiness and participation of countries' e-government. According to the 2008 report that ranks the top thirty-five countries in each category, the top ten countries in terms of e-government readiness were Sweden, Denmark, Norway, the United States, the Netherlands, the Republic of Korea, Canada, Australia, France, and the United Kingdom, and the top ten countries in e-government participation were the United States, the Republic of Korea, Denmark, France, Australia, New Zealand, Mexico, Estonia, Sweden, and Singapore (UN

2008, 20, 58). These top-ranked countries are industrialized and advanced technologically. They have better-developed online government websites, networks, and databases, better online customer services, and better online resource sharing among internal government agencies. It is easier for librarians to search and find digital government information about these top-ranked countries.

Online Media Resources and Resource Guides

Government and nongovernment news sources are excellent for tracking new online government publications, announcements, opinions, and activities. Many news media resource guides at different levels of government are also published online. Some are completely free to read and search, and some have online searchable archives. Some require registration, and access and services may vary between free and fee. Some foreign media resources are available in both the original language and English.

Access World News (AWN) and World News Connection (WNC) are two frequently used commercial resources for searching and accessing foreign news. AWN (www.newsbank.com/libraries/product.cfm?product=24) is a comprehensive, searchable web-based resource of full-text newspapers globally. It covers all levels—local, state, regional, national, and international—and offers translation of much international news from the vernacular into English. WNC (http://wnc.dialog .com) is a valuable research tool for monitoring non-U.S. media sources. Its material is provided to the National Technical Information Service by the Foreign Broadcast Information Service. International news items are added daily.

Other useful online world media guides provide basic browsing and searching features for free. Examples are Mondo Times (www.mondotimes.com/index.html), AllYouCanRead.com (www.allyoucanread.com), and ABYZ News Links (www .abyznewslinks.com). These web guides are more than just lists of newspapers, radios, and magazines. They include media not only at the national level but also by region, state/province, and even city. They include brief annotations of the news being covered, viewpoints of the sources, and readers' ranking of the content. They are well maintained and usually provide a place for users to report broken links. If the news is available in different languages, separate links are provided. For a review of these three online websites, see Xiong (2006).

Online Archives

It is noteworthy that projects for archiving web information are beginning to emerge, although "archives of material published on the Internet are still in their infancy" (IIPC 2006, 1). Libraries are participating in many of these projects.

The International Internet Preservation Consortium (IIPC; www.netpreserve .org), launched in July 2003, is a promising example of international collaboration for preserving Internet content. The consortium is led by the National Library of France, with the national libraries of Australia, Canada, Denmark, Finland, Iceland,

Italy, Norway, Sweden, the United Kingdom, and the U.S. Library of Congress and Internet Archive participating. The consortium website provides additional information about its goals, mission, working groups, and major objectives as well as press releases, reports, forums and workshops organized by the consortium, and tools developed by the consortium for downloading archived digital documents.

Another project is Archive-It, created by Internet Archive "to build an 'Internet library,' with the purpose of offering permanent access for researchers, historians, and scholars to historical collections that exist in digital format" (www.archive-it .org/public/about-us/). Archive-It has been storing and providing access to archived web pages since 1996. Internet Archive also works closely with several national libraries and archives around the world, such as the U.S. Library of Congress, the U.S. National Archives, the British National Archives, the National Library of Australia, and Bibliothèque nationale de France, to create web collections focused on an event, topic, or selections from a web domain. The site may contain data, reports, statistical yearbooks, press releases, methodological guides, or other information of continuing interest to social scientists and historians. Seventy-five sites in roman alphabets from Sub-Saharan Africa, Central Eurasia, East Asia, Latin America, the Near East, Russia and Eastern Europe, and South Asia are included.[5]

It is important that librarians discuss, study, and participate in these web archiving efforts as much as possible. These projects may be especially helpful in extending access to the online government documents of those countries with less-developed e-government.

Commercial Sources

Although a wealth of foreign government information is publicly available via official web portals, it is important to remember that not all is for free. State or private companies recognize the commercial value of the once-monopolized government information in many countries. Some information companies have started to gather free government information from a variety of sources, or purchase raw data from the government agencies, and repack it into value-added online databases that are sold for profit. For example, Factiva (www.factiva.com), a Dow Jones project, provides global content, including Reuters newswires. In addition to financial news, Factiva offers a single point of access with multiple language interfaces and multilingual content covering nearly 9,000 sources, allowing users to conduct in-depth research on foreign country affairs. Online China Data Service (http://141.211.142.26/) is an example of a private company providing a specific foreign country's statistical data. It offers Chinese national, provincial, county, and city statistics, including census, industrial, and economic data, mapping statistics, and so forth.

Some traditional academic library online content providers, such as LexisNexis and Cambridge Scientific Abstracts, also provide foreign government information. LexisNexis publishes *Current National Statistical Compendiums* on microfiche and publishes country information and statistics in a variety of online databases.[6] Cambridge Scientific Abstracts publishes Public Affairs Information Service (PAIS)

International, a database containing references to journal articles, books, government documents, statistical directories, gray literature, research reports, conference reports, publications of international agencies, microfiche, online information, and more. It includes publications from more than 120 countries. In addition to English, some of the indexed materials are published in French, German, Italian, Portuguese, and Spanish.[7]

Because of different information policies and standards, some information in the public domain in the West may not be freely available in some developing countries. For example, to meet strong market demand, WTO documents were translated into Chinese and published for profit by private companies, which caused controversy and doubt concerning the Chinese government's ability to distribute the information efficiently to the public.

On the other hand, some government information agencies had been transformed to become commercial digital content providers. Wanfang Data (www .wanfangdata.com), for instance, has been a task force of the Institute of Scientific and Technological Information of China since the 1950s. It is now focusing on digitizing and providing access to patents, national and industrial standards, and government policies and regulations. It even provides information in English on Chinese business, military, defense, and science and technology to individual researchers and libraries in Europe and North America. Because of its close partnership with several ministries in China and its own collection and technology, Wanfang Data is playing an important role in providing commercialized Chinese government information to Western users.

CONCLUSION

Countries publish current online government information for the public, including many free and immediately accessible resources that are of interest to library users. This information brings opportunities as well as challenges to librarians. It will be a long time before foreign government materials are even mostly digital, especially for developing countries, but it is clear that governments are moving forward with e-government development around the world though regional differences vary greatly (UN 2008, xiii). Although it requires extra work for librarians to create or improve a useful library web guide—searching, evaluating, and adding foreign online government information resources to the guide; updating it regularly; and using it properly—the result is valuable to the library and its users. This work may be in addition to the work required to develop and manage physical collections of foreign government information and to the work required to evaluate commercial resources that include foreign government information. Many librarians today have increased job responsibilities, and foreign government information resources are often undervalued in their libraries. It may be hard to find funding and other assistance to develop this area. There may be difficulties in developing and maintaining a library web guide for online foreign government information resources.

Still, no matter how challenging, the global trend of e-government development in countries manifests in much more government information available online and *only* online. The need to search and access online foreign government information is increasing daily. Librarians must be well prepared to embrace global e-government, the new "connected government," and meet these challenges.

NOTES

1. China Internet Network Information Center, "Domain Names Registered under '.cn,'" 2006, www.cnnic.net.cn/html/Dir/2003/12/13/2020.htm.

2. GOVDOC-L is a moderated electronic discussion list dedicated to government information issues and the FDLP (http://govdoc-l.org). Intl-Doc is a moderated list dedicated to publication policies of intergovernmental organizations; foreign national government publications are discussed as well. The home page for the list is available at www.ala.org/ala/godort/taskforces/internationaldocuments/intldoc.htm. CALA-L is an electronic discussion list as well as a communication channel for the Chinese American Librarians Association. Its home page is available at www.cala-web.org. Eastlib is a moderated discussion list for East Asian Librarians in North America (http://wason.library.cornell.edu/CEAL/Eastlibinstructions.htm).

3. As example: Xin Hua News Agency, "Six-Party Talks Achieve Breakthrough," http://news.xinhuanet.com/english/2005-09/20/content_3514438.htm. In the news, this is mentioned that a landmark agreement on resolving the nuclear standoff on the Korean Peninsula was announced September 19, 2005, in Beijing.

4. "Govt Website Ranks 744th around World." January 3, 2006, www.china-embassy.org/eng/xw/t229240.htm.

5. One can see what is so far available in the Archive on national government statistics at www.archive-it.org/collections/national_government_statistical_websites.

6. Information about the scope, availability, and countries covered in the collection can be found at LexisNexis, "Current National Statistical Compendiums on Microfiche," www.lexisnexis.com/academic/3cis/cisi/CurrentNationalStatisticalCompendiums.asp.

7. CSA Illumina, "PAIS International," www.csa.com/factsheets/pais-set-c.php.

REFERENCES

Accenture. 2004. *eGovernment Leadership: High Performance, Maximum Value.* www.accenture.com/NR/rdonlyres/D7206199-C3D4-4CB4-A7D8-846C9428 7890/0/gove_egov_value.pdf.

———. 2005. *Leadership in Customer Service: New Expectations, New Experiences.* www.accenture.com/NR/rdonlyres/F45CE4C8-9330-4450-BB4A-AF4E265C88D4/0/leadership_cust.pdf.

Bell, Barbara L. 1998. *An Annotated Guide to Current National Bibliographies.* 2nd rev. ed. Munich: K. G. Saur.

Berryman, Jennifer. 2004. "e-Government: Issues and Implications for Public Libraries." *Australian Library Journal* 53 (4): 349–359.

Booz Allen Hamilton. 2005. "Beyond 'e-Government: The World's Most Successful Technology-enabled Transformation.'" www.boozallen.com/media/file/151607.pdf.

Chang, Yuuh-Shihng. 2004. "The e-Government Web Promotion Strategies Based upon the Technological Supporting and Information Requirements." *Journal of Information, Communication and Library Science* 10 (June): 51–64.

Eckman, Chuck. 2001. "International Information Update. Acquiring International Documents: Challenges, Strategies, Sources." *Journal of Government Information* 28 (2): 179–183.

GODORT. 1997. *Directory of Foreign Document Collections and Librarians.* 7th ed. Bethesda, MD: Congressional Information Service.

IIPC International Internet Preservation Consortium Access Working Group. 2006. "Use Cases for Access to Internet Archives." www.netpreserve.org/publications/iipc-r-003.pdf.

Jacobs, James A. 2005. "Authenticity." November 3. http://freegovinfo.info/authenticity.

Jover, Susan. 1997. *Guide to Official Publications of Foreign Countries.* 2nd ed. [Bethesda, MD]: CIS.

Lee, Catherine W. 1997. "The Impact of Electronic Globalization on Foreign Document Collections in the United States." *Journal of Government Information* 24 (3): 203–212.

Morrison, Andrea. 2002. "International and Foreign Government Publications: Collection Development Issues." *DttP: Documents to the People* 30 (2): 96–98.

Mutula, Stephen M. 2005. "Bridging the Digital Divide through e-Governance." *Electronic Library* 23 (5): 591–602.

Notess, Greg R. 2000. *Government Information on the Internet.* 3rd ed. Lanham, MD: Bernan.

Sherayko, Carolyn C., and Diane H. Smith. 1993. "Acquisition of Government Information Resources." In *Management of Government Information Resources in Libraries,* ed. Diane H. Smith, 38–39. Englewood, CO: Libraries Unlimited.

Smith, Karen F. 1998. "Foreign and International Documents." In *Tapping the Government Grapevine: The User-Friendly Guide to U.S. Government Information Sources,* ed. Judith Schiek Robinson. Phoenix, AZ: Oryx Press.

Tillman, Hope N. 2003. "Evaluating Quality on the Net." www.hopetillman.com/findqual.html#my.

Tulis, Susan E., and Daniel C. Barkley. 2003. *Directory of Government Document Collections and Librarians.* 8th ed. Bethesda, MD: LexisNexis.

UN United Nations. 2005. *UN Global E-Government Readiness Report 2005.* http://unpan1.un.org/intradoc/groups/public/documents/un/unpan021888.pdf

———. 2007. UN E-Government Readiness Knowledge Base. www.unpan.org/egovkb/.

————. 2008. *UN e-Government Survey 2008: From E-Government to Connected Governance* (ST/ESA/PAD/SER.E/112). http://unpan1.un.org/intradoc/groups/public/documents/UN/UNPAN028607.pdf.

Xiong, Jian Anna. 2006. "Online Asia and Pacific Rim Newspaper Resources: Mondo Times, AllYouCanRead.com, and ABYZ News Links." *Charleston Advisor* 7 (3): 5–11.

Xue, Susan. 2004. "China's Statistical System and Resources." *Journal of Government Information* 30 (1): 87–109.

Index

Note: Page numbers followed by *f* indicate figures.

in information literacy instruction, 156
and reference services, 139
print resources. *See* tangible resources
prison libraries, outreach by, 57
privatization of government information, 6
processing
of batch-loaded records, 129–131
and web technology, 17–18
Program for Cooperative Cataloging
(PCC), 87
programs in libraries, 142
provenance and Arizona Model, 187
public access to information. *See* access to
information
public libraries
and cost of e-government services, 177
outreach opportunities, 49–50, 55
See also libraries
publications
changing meaning of, 17
vs. documents in IGOs, 196–197
publishing and web technologies, 17–19
PURL (persistent uniform resource locator)
program
in cataloging records, 47, 55
in information literacy instruction, 160
in MARC records, 106–107, 108*f*
overview, 25, 89–90
updating of URLs, 90

Q

quasi-governmental organizations and
digitization projects, 80

R

RDA (Resource Description and Access),
109, 115–118, 121
RDA/ONIX framework, 117
recalls of products, 145
record loading in bibliographic control,
127–129
redundancy as preservation criterion, 11, 165
reference interview, 154
reference services, 136–151
changes in, 51–53
IGO information, 204
integration of documents into, 137, 153
local government information, 177–178

promotion of, 140–142
ready reference resources, 142–149
spatial information, 36–37
staff training, 139–140
reformatting, 15
refreshing of data, 192. *See also* migration
of data
*Registry of U.S. Government Publication
Digitization Projects*, 79
Regulations.gov, 143
Rehabilitation Act of 1998, 50
related items in MARC records, 102–103,
104–105
reliability of content
and independent verification, 11
and nonlibrary organizations, 75
and social and political context, 160
remote electronic resources, physical
description of, 99–100, 101*f*
remote hosting model
and fee-based services, 81–82
and preservation, 73–74
replication as preservation criterion, 165–166
reproducibility of web-based government
information, 20
Research Libraries Group, 169
Resource Description and Access (RDA),
109, 115–118, 121
rural communities as underserved
population, 48–49
RUSA (ALA Reference and User Services
Association), 139

S

SACO (Subject Authority Cooperative), 87
school libraries
outreach opportunities, 49–50, 57–58
See also children; curriculum support;
information literacy
science fair topics, 64
Science.gov, 143
SDTS (spatial data transfer standard)
format, 40
search engines and portals
in fee-based services, 81
for foreign governments, 218, 219
for ready reference, 142–143
and spatial information, 37